MW01115565

The Zen of
FULBRIGHT

This publication is not affiliated with the Fulbright Program, the United States Department of State, or the Institute of International Education. The views and opinions expressed within this book are just that—opinions—and do not constitute any kind of legal or professional services. Those interested in the Fulbright Program should consult other competent professionals before adopting any of the suggestions in this book.

The opinions in this guide do not represent the official views of the Fulbright Program.

© 2014 Thomas Burns
All rights reserved

Don Davis Press
Los Angeles, California
info@fulbrightguide.org

Layout design by Heather Watson

Library of Congress Cataloging-in-Publication Data
Burns, Thomas
    The Zen of Fulbright: The unofficial guide to making the most of your U.S. Fulbright Scholarship / Thomas Burns

ISBN-13: 978-0991547203
ISBN-10: 0991547209

10 9 8 7 6 5 4 3 2 1

The Zen of
FULBRIGHT

The unofficial guide to making the
most of your U.S. Fulbright Scholarship

Thomas Burns

DON DAVIS PRESS

2014

To the Fulbright Scholars of tomorrow.
To the dreamers and doers who inspire us all.

Contents

Managing your Fulbright work
Fulbright ambassadorship
Reporting to Fulbright
Grant extensions
How to say goodbye

Why is returning home so difficult?
What if I'm not ready to leave my host country?
What will happen to my Fulbright work after I return home?
How can I stay connected to the Fulbright community?
Your career after Fulbright
Giving back to Fulbright
Paying your Fulbright forward

Sample application essays

Preface

In 2009 I received a Fulbright Scholarship to spend ten months producing a collection of photographs in Armenia, Azerbaijan, and Georgia. My research goal was to explore how the legacy of post-Soviet transition in the South Caucasus manifested in our most basic medium of expression—the human form—nearly twenty years after the dissolution of the USSR. I applied to the Fulbright Program seeking an opportunity to grow as an artist, serve my country, and deepen my relationship with a part of the world that fascinates me. Though I anticipated a rewarding experience, I never expected just how transformative that year would be. As with many program alumni, my Fulbright experience overseas has proven to be one of the most important years of my life.

After returning home I hungered for contact with peers and colleagues who could relate to the intensity and excitement of the Fulbright experience. A familiar theme surfaced often in conversations with fellow alumni: While we were all deeply honored to be chosen for the Fulbright Program, many of us wish we had better understood going into the grant just how much potential the fellowship holds. Most of us were so focused beforehand on our research or teaching assignment that we couldn't see the bigger picture of what was possible to achieve as a Fulbright Scholar.

An idea began to take shape: How can program alumni help future Fulbrighters take advantage of the incredible opportunities the Fulbright Program provides? How can we help the next generation of grantees *start* their Fulbright grants with the lessons we learned during our time overseas?

This book is the result of contributions from program alumni eager to pay forward their Fulbright experiences. It is our hope that the stories and advice within will empower future Fulbright Scholars to dream bigger and reach even farther than those before them.

Los Angeles, California

A word of thanks

Writing this guide was a deeply collaborative effort. I owe
a tremendous debt of gratitude to the dozens of Fulbright
Scholars who agreed to be interviewed, who contributed to
the project's research, and who took the time to write down
and submit their own Fulbright stories. Added to these key
contributions were hundreds of informal conversations with
Fulbrighters, Fulbright Program administrators, university
fellowship advisers, and international education specialists who
helped distill the massive amount of raw data into a cohesive
manuscript. Without these contributions this guide never
would have achieved the diversity of experiences that it was
always intended to present.

Many thanks as well to editors Ed Zahniser and Joy
Drohan for their attention to detail, and to Allyson Martinez
for sharing her expertise in navigating the field of international
education.

I owe a special note of thanks to Heather Watson,
whose tireless encouragement helped push this project through
its doldrums and into existence. Without her, this guide never
would have reached completion.

Introduction

In the long course of history, having people who understand your thought is much greater security than another submarine.

U.S. Senator J. William Fulbright

For most of us, the biggest obstacle standing between where we are today and what we want to achieve is fear. There are logistical hurdles to overcome, of course—too little time, too little money, too little experience—but underneath them lies our fear of the unknown, and fear of failure. Often the more ambitious our goals are, the more paralyzing this fear can be.

To apply for a Fulbright Scholarship is a daunting task. Strangely, actually being selected for such a prestigious program can be even scarier. What if I arrive in my host country and find out my language skills aren't good enough to complete my project? What if I don't live up to everyone's expectations? *What if I fail?* All of these fears can be managed and overcome, and this guide helps show you how.

The Fulbright Program attracts an extremely driven, socially conscious cohort of applicants eager to represent their country, broaden their horizons, hone their leadership skills, and grow as experts in their fields. Fulbright Scholarships empower these grantees to move beyond the walls of their laboratories, classrooms, and artist studios to apply their ideas in a practical, international context. The program encourages you to reach out and explore how your training and goals can contribute to larger discourses on democracy and international exchange. Few opportunities can deliver this scale of professional growth and transformation in such a short period of time, and this potential makes the Fulbright Program a powerful engine of intellectual pursuit and social change.

A quick tour of the Fulbright Program

On a personal level, Fulbright is about self-discovery. If you only have one point of reference for your understanding of your academic field, it's not going to be very rich and it's not going to be very accurate. Fulbright is a way of getting a better sense of what Russian history is, or what intercultural psychology is. It's an opportunity to see something from a different perspective so that you have a three-dimensional view of your subject, and not one based only on your undergraduate experience.

On a national level, I think the Fulbright Program is a great way for the United States to enrich its academics by having the international community engage with individuals in the American educational community very early in their careers.

Lilith Dornhuber deBellesiles
Research Fulbright to Germany
Philosophy

There's a whole other world that I didn't know existed before my Fulbright that I now know is out there and so much deeper in so many ways. Ultimately, getting the kind of cultural and historical understanding of a place that Fulbright provided made me understand myself as an American that much more. That's probably the biggest reason to do a Fulbright: To understand your own culture and where you come from by diving deeply into the culture of another place.

Mike Seely
Research Fulbright to Poland
Filmmaking

Most people have heard of the Fulbright Program by reputation, but few understand how large and diverse it really is. Created in 1946 through legislation put forward by U.S. Senator J. William Fulbright, the program was designed to promote mutual understanding between the people of the United States and the people of other countries. It has grown to be the U.S. government's flagship international exchange program, giving over 300,000 Americans and foreign citizens opportunities for overseas study, teaching, and research. It is widely considered one of the world's most prestigious fellowship programs.

The Fulbright Program pursues its mission by providing financial support, non-financial resources, and community to accomplished students, artists, scholars, and professionals who demonstrate exceptional potential for leadership. Though the funding it provides is called variously a scholarship, fellowship, or research stipend, Fulbright is, at its core, a grant program. Each year it awards thousands of grants to American and foreign citizens for study, teaching, and research overseas. These grants and their administrative support are funded primarily through an annual appropriation from the U.S. Congress. Additional support comes from foreign governments and host institutions overseas.

The Fulbright Program is run by the U.S. Department of State's Bureau of Educational and Cultural Affairs. Most American Fulbrighters don't interact with the State Department directly but with Fulbright's partner organizations that administer the grants, and with Fulbright Commissions and U.S. Embassy staff overseas. A vast network of Fulbright Program Advisers at colleges and universities across the United States also facilitates the application process. One of the program's largest partners, the Institute of International Education (IIE), is the main point of contact for those who want to apply to the Fulbright U.S. Student Program, the most popular Fulbright program for American college graduates and young professionals.

Though the term "Fulbright Scholar" is used to describe all Fulbright grantees, many different grant programs exist within Fulbright. This guide focuses on two of the largest programs for young American citizens: Fulbright's traditional study/research grant and the Fulbright English Teaching Assistant (ETA) Program. Beyond these grants, the Fulbright Program offers many other opportunities for research, study,

The Fulbright Program at a glance

- Sponsored by the U.S. Department of State's Bureau of Educational and Cultural Affairs

- Designed to increase mutual understanding between the people of the United States and the people of other countries

- Thousands of grants awarded annually to scholars and professionals in a wide range of fields and career levels

- Provides participants—chosen for their academic merit and leadership potential—with the opportunity for study, teaching, research, and professional development overseas

- Active in more than 150 countries worldwide

- Since its inception the program has provided grant funding to more than 300,000 participants

- Many Fulbright alumni go on to serve in leadership positions in government, academia, business, the arts, science, media, and other professional fields

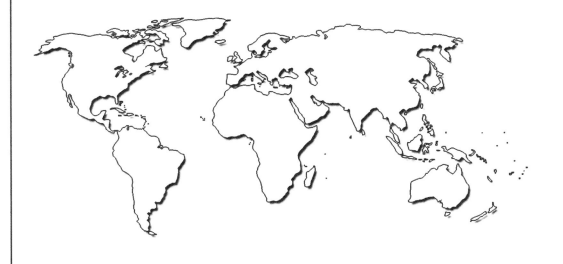

What really matters is the cultural experience you have with people in your host country. The Fulbright Program administrators were dead-on when they told us this at the orientation in Washington, D.C., but I kind of shoved it off to the side. "Oh yeah, cultural interaction. Sure, I can see that, but it's not really the main point." I really didn't believe them. Six months into the grant I realized that the cultural aspect of the experience is really the essence of Fulbright, and that the project and the research are just a means to get to that end.

Matt Wesley
Research Fulbright to Nicaragua
Public Health

I definitely agree with the bigger role and purpose of being a Fulbrighter: the person-to-person diplomacy. Serving as an ambassador of U.S. culture and talking about that with people in the country you visit, and learning from them, fulfills the purpose of the program in the vision of Senator Fulbright.

Natalia Ksiezyk
ETA Fulbright to Argentina

and teaching overseas for candidates at all levels of professional development in a wide range of fields.

Fulbright's mission: international exchange

On an official level, the Fulbright Program is one of the U.S. government's most effective engines of cultural, or "soft," diplomacy. Much like the Peace Corps and other exchange initiatives of the Department of State, the Fulbright Program is built on the premise that unofficial interaction across cultural lines leads to greater understanding between peoples and, by extension, stronger relationships between the United States and other countries. One element that makes the Fulbright Program so effective on a global scale is its idea of *mutual* exchange. The program not only sends accomplished Americans overseas but every year also invites thousands of Fulbright Scholars from other countries to study and teach in the United States. International partnership lies at the core of the Fulbright mission.

Fulbright's goal to promote cross-cultural interaction and mutual understanding is clear enough on paper, but what does it mean for grantees in the field? The program's guiding philosophy of community engagement lies at the heart of its role as an international leadership program. Fulbrighters serve overseas as unofficial cultural ambassadors. How they engage their host countries—from classroom work, to public speaking engagements, to interactions with the neighborhood grocer—can shape how individuals, families, and even entire generations of the local population view the United States. This mission places Fulbrighters in a position of immense responsibility.

Describing the Fulbright Program in terms of cultural diplomacy is useful, but it doesn't do justice to the program's true impact, which goes far beyond diplomatic interests. Promoting mutual understanding isn't just good for world politics; it's good for progress and innovation on a larger human scale. Ideas stagnate in vacuum and flourish with input. The intellectual investments Fulbright affords in research, education, and social innovation yield results that increase exponentially over time. The more advanced our ideas, the greater the potential for our relationships to grow and expand. The more our relationships grow and expand, the more opportunities there are for our ideas to advance. Remember—breakthroughs happen most often at the intersection of disciplines. A Fulbright Scholarship can be a powerful tool for making these connections happen.

Treat your Fulbright grant as a once-in-a-lifetime experience. There's never going to be another time in your life, even if you get another fellowship, when you're going to be so well looked-after by the Fulbright Commission, have an immediate group of intelligent, engaged, interesting colleagues, and have the freedom to do what you want academically. It's unique.

Lilith Dornhuber deBellesiles
Research Fulbright to Germany
Philosophy

The Fulbright family

The Fulbright Program is grassroots peace-building at its best, but for grantees it also often serves as a global leadership development program. The achievements of program alumni speak for themselves: The Fulbright community includes Nobel Prize winners, MacArthur Foundation Fellows, Pulitzer Prize winners, judges, members of the U.S. Congress, diplomats, and foreign heads of state. Fulbright alone isn't responsible for these alumni's accomplishments, of course, but few dispute its role in their success.

Many Fulbrighters don't realize how expansive the alumni community is. Over 300,000 of the world's smartest, most accomplished, and most civic-minded citizens have been awarded Fulbright grants since the program started. Most alumni remain fiercely loyal to the Fulbright community's commitment to international education and exchange. They often seek out contact and collaboration with their Fulbright colleagues. The Fulbright experience is a powerful unifying force.

Yes, the Fulbright is great to put on my CV and it might get me a conversation with somebody down the road professionally, but what I really take away from it is the community. It sounds corny, but it's true. Those relationships that I would not have had without the Fulbright are lasting relationships. People who are just interested in résumé-building through Fulbright should understand that there's so much more that you can get out of it. Lifelong relationships and friendships and people that you care about. I tried to live every day of my Fulbright knowing that this was a rare opportunity.

Winston Scott
Research Fulbright to Guatemala
Anthropology

How can this guide help you?

This guide is designed to help American Fulbright applicants and grantees make the most of the incredible opportunities the Fulbright Program offers. The program and its partners do an excellent job managing one of the world's largest, most successful, and most diverse academic exchange programs. Fulbright alumni speak of the incredible support the program offers grantees to help them achieve even their most ambitious goals. Learning how to make the most of this opportunity, however, requires the guidance of those who have walked a similar path.

This guide serves as an unofficial handbook on what the Fulbright experience is like on the ground. It is written by the people who know this experience best: Fulbrighters themselves. Their stories and advice show you what worked, what you might do differently, and what you can learn from their victories and defeats. These stories are powerful lessons about how to make the most of the resources Fulbright provides. The opportunities are there, but you must seize them.

This guide isn't designed just to help you craft a winning Fulbright application. It's designed to help you create a well-rounded, productive, and rewarding Fulbright experience. This

The grant has been most beneficial to me in the community of people I met. At the Fulbright regional conference that I went to, I met people who I'm going to be friends with and work with my entire life. For me it's really about the community of Fulbrighters.

Rose Cromwell
Research Fulbright to Panama
Photography

experience begins with the application process and continues throughout your time overseas and far beyond the end of the grant. This guide lets you overhear countless conversations with Fulbright alumni whose grant experiences span the gamut from the mediocre ("I really could have done more.") to the transformative ("I was self-actualized."). Success is what happens when preparation meets opportunity. This guide gives you the tools to create such a meeting.

These pages will not give you "the secret" to getting a Fulbright grant. There isn't one. There is preparation, diligence, and a willingness to dream big and venture outside your comfort zone. If your end goal is to be awarded a Fulbright grant, you are missing the point. A Fulbright fellowship is an opportunity for future achievement, not a reward for past accomplishments or mere padding for your résumé.

This guide walks you through the phases of the Fulbright experience, from the application process, to working overseas, to returning home, and to life as a Fulbright alumnus. Much of this advice is common sense, but in the chaos of application deadlines and daily life overseas even the best of us can lose sight of what needs to be done and how to do it. If you are considering applying to the Fulbright U.S. Student Program, this book will help you

- develop a stronger Fulbright project idea.
- build a community of supporters around your Fulbright work.
- prepare for your time overseas.
- create an application that does justice to you and your ideas.
- identify the powerful resources available to you as a Fulbrighter.
- hone your leadership skills.
- formulate realistic goals for your Fulbright experience.
- anticipate the challenges of overseas fieldwork.

Fulbrighters are an inspiring bunch. Studying them and the program that has given them such rich opportunities gives you a window onto the kind of innovation, ambition, and social consciousness that ultimately fuels all positive social change. If you want to explore these accomplishments, this guide lays out some of the countless steps, missteps, and battles undertaken to get there. The philosophy of this guide is that with enough passion, preparation, and guidance, you can share in the Fulbright experience.

If you look at the history of the United States, a lot of the folks that came up with really great ideas or great art or great literature, they left where they came from and went out and experienced the world and then came back. And that was often the inspiration for the things they did. With Fulbright it feels like you're no longer making blind decisions. You see the spectrum of possibility, the way other people live. You can reassess. Going abroad and living in a place that does things differently, or thinks about things differently, will help you figure things out. We need more money for Fulbright. We need more people to be having these experiences.

Blake Scott
Research Fulbright to Panama
History

Fulbright has changed my outlook on the odds of being employed, what it means to be employable, and what I want out of it. Not just in terms of a career, but in terms of how satisfying it's going to be in my lifetime.

Nic Wondra
Research Fulbright to Georgia
Political Science

How to use this guide

There is a lot of independence and flexibility with Fulbright that is not necessarily there with other research grants. It's an opportunity to go and live in another country and to do a research project that you created. There's really no limit to what can be done if you can craft a strong research proposal.

The fact that Fulbright requires grantees to have some proficiency in the host country's language really encourages you to interact with other people and improve your understanding of another culture. Staying in another country for an extended period of time allows you the opportunity to really get to know that place, to get to know those people.

Something else that makes Fulbright distinctive is that it's funded by the U.S. State Department. You have an official connection with the U.S. Embassy in your host country because you are a Fulbrighter. Many other research programs funded by the U.S. government don't offer that same relationship.

On top of all this, as a Fulbrighter you become part of a very extensive network of people who have also had that experience, which is very unique.

Tiffany Joseph
Research Fulbright to Brazil
Sociology

This guide is designed to complement—not replace—the wealth of information that the Fulbright Program and its partners give you. It will not tell you everything you need to know about applying for a Fulbright Scholarship. Before reading this book, begin with Fulbright's own literature: Nobody knows the details of the program better than they do.

What this unofficial guide *does* give you are hundreds of Fulbright stories and tips from around the globe. Together these paint a picture of what is possible for you to achieve. You won't find country-specific recommendations like where to go for the tea in Istanbul or how to find an apartment in Moscow, but you will learn how to do this kind of research yourself. This guide gives you insights from dozens of formal interviews and countless informal conversations with American Fulbright alumni, university Fulbright advisers, and international exchange experts. The Fulbright alumni we interviewed were selected to cover a wide range of academic fields and host countries visited.

If you are a Fulbright applicant, this guide should make up only part of your research about the program. Fulbright and its partners manage searchable online databases of past grantees, organized by type of grant, host country, and field of specialty. Most of these alumni will be happy to chat about their experience, and you shouldn't underestimate the value of this resource. The more information you have, the stronger your application and your overseas experience will be.

This guide presents a broad spectrum of experiences and opinions about the Fulbright Program, but it is not affiliated with the program in any official way. The stories and opinions within are candid and sometimes contradictory, but their value lies in their diversity. No two Fulbright experiences are the same, but many lessons Fulbrighters learn during their grants can be applied across the spectrum.

If you are interested in one of the two most popular Fulbright grant programs for young American citizens—the traditional Fulbright study/research grant and the English Teaching Assistant (ETA) Program—this guide is for you. Those interested in Fulbright's many other programs, including grants for visiting scholars to study or teach in the United States, should consult the Fulbright website for more details. Fulbright's programs are simply too diverse to cover in one guide.

The Fulbright Program

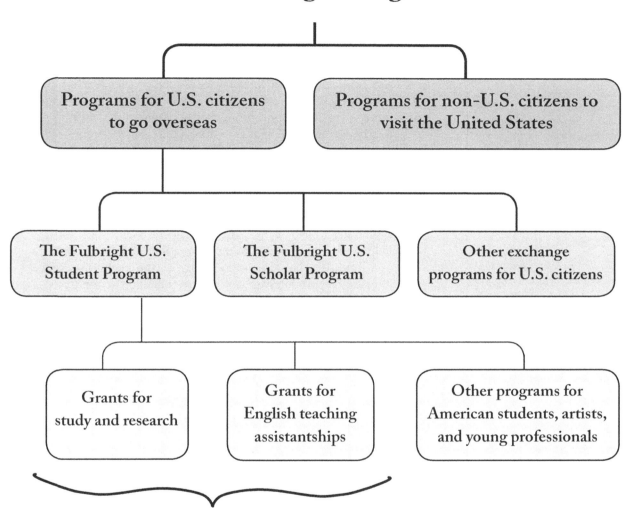

Programs for U.S. citizens to go overseas

Programs for non-U.S. citizens to visit the United States

The Fulbright U.S. Student Program

The Fulbright U.S. Scholar Program

Other exchange programs for U.S. citizens

Grants for study and research

Grants for English teaching assistantships

Other programs for American students, artists, and young professionals

This guide focuses on these two grants for U.S. citizens!

Going to Turkey helped me decide what kind of architect I was going to be. After my Fulbright I knew I was not the architect that was going to work 100 hours a week on someone else's big skyscraper building. I want to be the architect that structures my own projects and teaches on the side. I want to be a multi-disciplinary designer that deals with the context and the neighborhood, and works on projects geared towards people. The Fulbright totally changed my perspective on how I practice as an architect.

Shadi Khadivi
Research Fulbright to Turkey
Architecture

I feel like the kind of people that Fulbright accepts are those that want to do their part to make the world a better place.

Maya deVries
Research Fulbright to Panama
Biology

Being selected for a Fulbright Scholarship—even just applying for one—is a big deal. If you're nervous, that's normal. A wise uncle once said, "If you aren't nervous, you're not reaching far enough. But if you're scared, I mean really terrified, then you might be reaching too far." If you are scared, this book will help you deal with your fear by showing you how to manage the tasks ahead. If you are one of the few who aren't nervous at all, chances are you're not reaching far enough. This guide will show you ways to reach farther.

The most rewarding Fulbright experiences don't happen by accident. They result from tireless preparation, fearless initiative, and a willingness to dream big and venture into the unknown. It is up to you to seize the opportunities that the Fulbright Program offers. This guide will help you do just that.

The following pages are full of advice and insight that can improve your Fulbright experience. But at the end of the day, making the most of your Fulbright isn't about finding the right place to live or the right language teacher—these only help manage the smaller bumps along the road. Successful Fulbrighting is built on a philosophy, an approach to seeking out positive, productive relationships that elicit action from ideas and inspire us and those around us to use these ideas to make the world a better place.

Let's get started.

Fulbright shows you how you want to walk through the world in relation to your work and your personal life. You begin to realize that your work is your life—work isn't just compartmentalized. And if you can see work as every aspect, every interaction, every conversation you have, you're going to learn a lot more. I think that's what the Fulbright tries to teach you: That you can learn in so many different realms.

Blake Scott
Research Fulbright to Panama
History

Chapter 1

The Big Picture

Never doubt that a small group of thoughtful, committed citizens can change the world; indeed, it's the only thing that ever has.

Margaret Mead

A Fulbright Scholarship can be an immensely powerful tool for achievement, but making the most of its opportunities requires preparation, focus, and discipline from the grantee. The more you know about how Fulbright can help you accomplish your goals, the more transformative your Fulbright experience will be. A Fulbright Scholarship is a means to an end, a tool that when used well gives you the time, resources, and community to develop your ideas and translate them into action. The more compatible your goals and methods are with Fulbright's mission, the more successful your Fulbright experience, and your Fulbright application, will be.

The most productive Fulbright Scholars don't sit back and wait for their Fulbright experience to unfold; they charge ahead to leverage the program's potential. These grantees accomplish so much not because they hold the title of Fulbright Scholar, but because they have the courage to pursue their vision, take initiative, marshal support, forge alliances, and persevere through countless discouraging challenges. The Fulbright Program wants you to succeed, but ultimately you must make that happen.

While a Fulbright Scholarship can be a life-changing experience, it is important to remember that it is not the only option available to pursue your goals. Nor is it the only way to serve your country, build your career, or help solve the world's problems. Couldn't someone with the right background and motivation pursue an overseas project without Fulbright? Absolutely. And if you choose not to apply, or aren't selected to the program, that's exactly what you should do. Pushing ahead with an overseas project you believe in despite the status of your Fulbright application is, ironically, a very Fulbright thing to do.

What's the difference between Fulbright's "Student" and "Scholar" programs?

The Fulbright is an adult grant and you have to treat it that way. No one's checking up on you and this leads to a more productive time there. The experience would have been completely different if every week I had to check in with someone. We had to do a final report online, but as individuals we didn't have to turn in a paper or any final product. I really feel like it's all up to you. Once you get the grant, they leave it up to you to use your time as you please and make the decisions that you think are appropriate.

Lauren Hermele
Research Fulbright to Romania
Photography

In the broad sense, all Fulbright Scholarship recipients are Fulbright Scholars. But on an administrative level there are differences between the many programs Fulbright offers. These differences relate mostly to the duration of the grant, the type of activity it supports, and the professional level of the grantee. Fulbright's two largest programs for American citizens are the Fulbright U.S. Student Program and the Fulbright U.S. Scholar Program. This guide focuses on the former.

Fulbright's U.S. Student Program provides grant funding for graduating college seniors, graduate students, young professionals, and artists to study, teach, or conduct research overseas. Calling it a "student" program can be a bit confusing because most Fulbright Student grant recipients are not students while overseas on their grants. Many are not even students when they apply.

The Fulbright U.S. Scholar Program is geared toward older applicants—college and university faculty and experienced professionals. If you have already received a PhD, you are no longer eligible for Fulbright's U.S. Student Program and should explore the opportunities available through the U.S. Scholar Program.

What kind of support does a Fulbright Scholarship provide?

For the right candidate, a Fulbright grant helps vision, hard work, and community consciousness coalesce around a single project, teaching assignment, or course of study. By providing support with relatively few grant requirements, the Fulbright Program creates opportunities for you to design and manage your own research project, develop a body of work, and build relationships with international peers and colleagues. Grantees have a real opportunity to achieve working fluency in a foreign language, become an area expert, and demonstrate their ability to work independently in an unfamiliar environment. They pursue these goals while representing the United States internationally in a professional but unofficial manner. Together, these opportunities constitute a chance to develop your leadership skills in a powerful way.

More importantly, by situating the projects and studies it funds within a broader mission of promoting exchange and mutual understanding, the Fulbright Program invites grantees to participate in a much larger narrative of progress and democracy. This not only helps infuse the Fulbrighter's work with civic-minded purpose (even projects that aren't explicitly civic-minded) but dramatically expands its potential impact. A Fulbright English teaching assistant in Oman, for example, could propose new learning initiatives at the school, contribute to a national conference on education reform, meet with local Fulbright alumni in her field, organize American cultural events, raise outside funding for extracurricular projects, or even meet with local government officials to discuss education policy. Couldn't a non-Fulbright English teacher take this same initiative? Of course, but Fulbright support can make this kind of achievement easier, more influential, and more likely to lead to bigger things.

When you have a job in the United States, or if you're in a graduate or undergraduate program, there are deadlines that come up. Every couple days, every week, every couple months, every semester. And you're going to have a very material product from that period: You got a grade, or you wrote a paper, or whatever you did. And in order to do that you have to stay within some sort of standards of boundaries.

The Fulbright Program says, "I think you're a smart person and you've got some good ideas. Here's money for a year. Learn everything you can in that year and let's see what you'll become of it. At the same time, represent your country and have some sort of exchange." The boundaries of what you're allowed to learn are fairly limitless. They're up to you.

Blake Scott
Research Fulbright to Panama
History

What a Fulbright Scholarship provides the grantee

_____ **Autonomy**

U.S. Fulbrighters, particularly independent researchers, enjoy a remarkable amount of freedom in their work. There is no obligation to submit a completed project at the grant's end. Fulbrighters are free to take risks, fail, and alter the course of their research projects as they see fit. This freedom is the rarest of gifts in the professional world.

_____ **Financial support**

Fulbright covers basic living, research, and travel costs. This financial freedom allows Fulbrighters to focus on their work.

_____ **A safety net**

The health and safety of Fulbright grantees is looked after by the U.S. Department of State through U.S. embassies and Fulbright Commissions abroad. Fulbrighters often work in remote places, and it's nice to know that the U.S. government has your back.

_____ **Professional credibility**

The Fulbright name conveys prestige and its reputation opens doors. This access dramatically raises the ceiling on what grantees can achieve if they dream big.

_____ **Access to the Fulbright community**

Your Fulbright community includes not only other American grantees in your host country, but tens of thousands of Fulbright alumni from all corners of the globe. These are accomplished academics and professionals, often at the top of their fields, who are deeply committed to the Fulbright cause. This community is Fulbright's biggest asset, and it holds tremendous potential to transform your Fulbright experience.

_____ **Opportunities for service and ambassadorship**

Those who know the Fulbright Program very often look to its grantees for leadership, and this expectation can provide incredible opportunities to bring positive change to the world. It is not uncommon for Fulbrighters to be invited to lecture or teach while overseas, but it is up to the grantee to seize these opportunities when they present themselves.

_____ **Opportunity for language immersion**

Fulbrighters in countries where English is not widespread have a rare opportunity to gain working fluency in a foreign language. In some cases Fulbright will even subsidize a grantee's language study through the **Critical Language Enhancement Award**. But fluency does not happen on its own, even in an immersion environment. It takes hard work and a willingness to resist spending time with other English-speakers.

A word about Fulbright health coverage

In the past the U.S. Department of State has provided American Fulbright grantees with supplemental health and accident insurance designed to augment whatever existing health insurance policy the grantee already has. This coverage is helpful if you experience a major medical event that requires evacuation, but past Fulbright health plans have not been designed to offer full healthcare coverage. They may not cover visits to the doctor for preventative care or for dependents who accompany you overseas. They also might not cover you when you are traveling outside your host country.

Making sure you have access to adequate healthcare is important. Take the time to investigate Fulbright's latest healthcare plan. Paying monthly premiums for outside health insurance can be a serious financial burden when living on a Fulbright stipend.

Bringing family overseas

Fulbrighters are permitted to bring family with them on their grants. In some cases Fulbright offers a small monthly "spousal supplement" for accompanying family members but typically will not pay for their travel to the host country. Fulbrighters are certainly permitted, however, to use their travel allowance—usually a set payment amount—as they see fit. Program rules don't prohibit family members from seeking work in your host country, but the Fulbright Program does not typically provide assistance in making these arrangements.

Much of the value of a Fulbright grant is in the freedom it provides. Being able to really dive into creative projects knowing that I could experiment and fail and it didn't matter. With creative experimentation there's always the risk of failure, and when you're in the professional world, people don't hire you to experiment creatively. With the Fulbright I felt that I could try something weirder than usual and not worry about the client and not worry if it was going to succeed or not.

I didn't realize beforehand that the Fulbright would be so open. I thought there would be more strings attached to the grant. Once I was in Poland and doing it I saw that I could take the project in any direction I wanted. In a lot of ways there was a lot more freedom than when I was in graduate school, where there are classes and deadlines. With Fulbright, all the people, all the contacts, all the shoots—everything was my own schedule.

Mike Seely
Research Fulbright to Poland
Filmmaking

With Fulbright there aren't the strictures of bureaucracy and institutional rules. And that's really great, because it allows you to work. You can work with people you wouldn't normally have access to. The Fulbright allows you to do more.

Joshua Noonan
Research Fulbright to Georgia
    and Azerbaijan
Political Science

The monthly stipend

You won't get rich from your Fulbright grant, but most Fulbrighters agree that whatever the program may lack in remuneration it more than makes up for in opportunities far more valuable than cash. But even Fulbrighters must make ends meet and, depending on your destination, life overseas can be expensive. Regardless of how you choose to handle your personal finances, applying your ideas in a practical, real-world context often requires capital. Back home idealism alone sometimes seems sufficient to change the world, but when we take our ideas into the field we begin to understand that action often requires resources beyond good intentions and intellectual moxie.

Fulbright pays grantees a monthly stipend, sometimes separated into housing and cost of living allowances. The stipend is intended to cover basic costs associated with your Fulbright work and living overseas. It is not designed to cover the cost of extra obligations like mortgages, credit card debt, travel, or additional materials and equipment (cameras, computers, etc.). Nor is it meant to cover additional health insurance or student loan payments.

Most Fulbrighters receive a one-time travel allowance to cover transportation to and from their host country, and often a small one-time book allowance for research and teaching materials. Fulbrighters who bring spouses may also receive a small monthly supplement. Some countries arrange homestays for English-teaching Fulbrighters that cover room and board in addition to the stipend, but research grantees and most ETA applicants can expect to pay for their own living arrangements.

Feelings about the Fulbright stipend vary greatly among grantees. Most find the amount adequate to live comfortably, travel, and pursue their Fulbright work as long as they budget responsibly. Fulbrighters with low project expenses who live in developing countries or outside major cities may even be able to save a bit each month. Grantees who come to Fulbright from the professional world, however, may find the transition to the Fulbright income level a bit jarring. The Fulbright stipend is not intended to compete with professional salaries in the United States. The best way to prepare for this is to conduct an honest assessment of what your expenses will be while overseas and budget accordingly.

The Fulbright stipend didn't quite cover my costs. I probably spent a thousand dollars extra. It really depends on where you're going. Toronto isn't necessarily cheap, and I was living right in the city, which is where most Fulbrighters were living. No one chose to live in the suburbs. And I think that's smart, because we're there for such a short period of time. We got to know the city really well.

I was lucky in the sense that I didn't have to put much money into my actual research, but I had some friends that had to put some extra into their research from their funds and who really didn't feel like Fulbright covered it all. I had one friend who was able to do a Fulbright in conjunction with his PhD and he was also receiving funding from the University of Toronto, and I think that was probably a smart move on his part.

Laila Plamondon
Research Fulbright to Canada
Psychology

I thought it was easy to live quite comfortably on the Fulbright stipend. For housing allowance we were allotted 600 euros [in 2009] to cover rent and utilities. This could go a very, very long way in some parts of the country. If you were in the capital city, it didn't go quite that far, but it was still plenty of money. Then there was also the monthly stipend, roughly $350 a month. All the Fulbrighters my year in Romania had their money broken up like that. It was sort of annoying.

Some Fulbrighters were traveling a lot out of the country, and they would complain about not having enough money. If you're coming here to travel to other places, you shouldn't just rely on Fulbright money to do that.

Hannah Halder
ETA Fulbright to Romania

The money Fulbright gave us was enough. It could have been more, of course, but we were in lucky circumstances. We were renting an apartment owned by my wife's family, so we were paying very low rent. We met a couple of Fulbrighters in Lodz who were paying these crazy expensive apartment prices. And being in Lodz was a benefit, as opposed to Krakow or Warsaw where the prices were definitely higher. Overall the stipend was enough for us, but without the cheaper apartment it would have been a little tight.

Mike Seely
Research Fulbright to Poland
Filmmaking

The stipend was so small it was difficult to get out and engage the country in a meaningful manner. I had to stay home to save money. Look at what you're going to be doing for your project. Know what resources you have going in. I had to spend my own funds on translation and travel. I tried to work with the Fulbright Commission, but they couldn't change anything.

Courtney Doggart
Research Fulbright to Turkey
International Relations

I made more on my Fulbright than I'm making now at Berkeley as a PhD student. The stipend was very good. For me it was definitely sufficient to help meet my goals. I traveled a lot, and I could do that on the Fulbright stipend. I could pay for language lessons, and she charged twenty dollars per lesson for two hours. It wouldn't have been enough if I was flying all over Central America, but I wasn't doing that.

Maya deVries
Research Fulbright to Panama
Biology

What will the Fulbright program expect from you?

Unlike many grant programs, Fulbright does not require that grantees submit work at the end of the grant period. The program's main interest is to promote mutual understanding and the exchange of ideas. In many ways it is more interested in the relationships you form than the work you accomplish. The program does have expectations of its grantees, however, and it selects candidates largely for their potential to meet these expectations:

1. **Serious commitment to engage the host country**

   Fulbright is a social fellowship. It gives grantees tools to develop their ideas in a practical, international context that encourages collaboration, partnership, and exchange, both professionally and outside of work. Whether in the office or the library, or over a beer at the local pub, this exchange is the essence of the Fulbright Program.

   If you travel every weekend to visit American friends or spend hours every night chatting online with family back home, you are not getting the most out of your Fulbright experience. Homesickness is normal, but the more you can let go of the old and familiar and embrace the new and uncertain, the more rewarding your Fulbright will be.

2. **Responsible ambassadorship**

   Far more people than you realize will watch how you interact with their country. When you help a student with an assignment outside of class or smile at the neighborhood florist on your way to work, people notice. These seemingly insignificant moments can shape local perceptions of Americans in important ways. As a Fulbrighter you will have tremendous power to affect how entire communities in your host country, and the children and grandchildren of those communities, view the United States. The Fulbright Program takes this responsibility seriously and expects grantees will as well. You don't have to get up every morning asking how you can be a better ambassador—just be aware of your responsibility and be yourself.

3. **Commitment to productivity**

   Whether you teach English in Estonia, research bird migration in Oman, or study Yeates at Oxford, your Fulbright work will almost certainly evolve from what you proposed in your application. Most Fulbright projects do. Many projects undergo serious transformation, and a few research Fulbrighters each year end up changing their research topic entirely. Fulbright recognizes that this is part of the Fulbright experience and will

While I was on my Fulbright I always had the sense, "I don't know if I'm doing exactly what I said I was going to do, or what they think I'm going to do, or what they're hoping I'm going to achieve." But I knew that I could only do my project the way that it was leading me. It was only in coming back and reconnecting with the folks at IIE [Institute of International Education] that I learned how that really is what they expect the experience to be.

That is not to say that you can wander and drift through your year and come back with a few good stories. I think that as long as you're immersed in your project, you constantly question what it is you're there to do, and you're reformulating your questions, then that achieves the goal of Fulbright. That carries out that mission of cultural exchange. A lot of times it's not about the answers, but about figuring out what the questions are that you're really trying to explore.

Deanna Fei
Research Fulbright to China
Creative Writing

work with you to make these changes. What's important is that you stay productive and keep the program updated with developments. It's OK to alter the course of your Fulbright work. It is *not* OK to give up and to treat the rest of your grant as a vacation. Fulbright expects that you are committed to creating a productive experience.

4. **Lasting commitment to the Fulbright mission**

   Most Fulbright alumni are eager to embrace the Fulbright mission as a lifelong endeavor. This is what makes the Fulbright Scholarship such a powerful engine of diplomacy. As a Fulbright grantee it's important to remember that sharing your overseas experience with friends, family, and colleagues back home is no less important to your role as an cultural ambassador than representing the United States in your host country.

   The Fulbright experience doesn't have to end when your grant is over. There are lots of ways to stay involved with the Fulbright alumni community and to support the Fulbright mission through career decisions and leadership opportunities.

When it comes down to it, I think what Fulbright really wants is people representing the United States in a positive, professional, and educational way. There's the Peace Corps, and they're also representing the U.S., and they're doing great things. But the Fulbright Program is different. It's a very meaningful role to take on when you are in a country where even educated English-speaking people haven't met many Americans. It happened to me all the time where people I met said, "You're the first American I've met." It's shocking to hear that. You really want to do the best you can to break down some of the stereotypes about Americans, or try to give them a more accurate picture of what America is. I always felt like I was on. I didn't want to misrepresent or do anything that would disappoint them.

And sometimes they were disappointed. When they think that everyone in America has these rich fantastic lives, and you tell them that there is also a lot of poverty and a lot of issues, you can see in their eyes that they do get disappointed. But it's important that they know that.

Ashley Killough
Research Fulbright to Armenia
Journalism

Am I eligible for a Fulbright grant?

Fulbright has basic eligibility criteria for its U.S. Student Program grants. (Other Fulbright programs have different requirements.) Consult the Fulbright website or your campus Fulbright Program Adviser for the most up-to-date list. Past eligibility requirements have included the following:

- Applicants must hold U.S. citizenship at the time of application

- Applicants must hold a bachelor's degree by the date the grant begins, but cannot already hold a doctoral degree at the time of application (having a JD does not make you ineligible). In the creative and performing arts, four years of professional training and/or experience may substitute for a BA

- Applicants cannot have previously received a study/research Fulbright Student Grant or Fulbright-Hays Doctoral Dissertation Research grant

- Applicants must be in good health

- Applicants cannot be a U.S. Department of State employee, an immediate family member of a U.S. Department of State employee, or an employee of an agency under contract to the U.S. Department of State to perform services related to exchange programs

- Applicants cannot have lived abroad for five or more consecutive years in the six-year period preceding the date of application

- Candidates may not apply to the Fulbright U.S. Student Program and the Fulbright U.S. Scholar Program in the same competition cycle

- Candidates may not apply for more than one type of Fulbright U.S. Student grant in a given competition cycle

If you don't like learning languages and learning about other cultures, you've got no business applying to the Fulbright Program. If you're not interested in people and don't like people, you're really kind of missing the point of Fulbright. And there are those who are antisocial, who prefer to work from language textbooks. That's fine, as long as they're making that effort to respect their host language and culture. That's an important thing.

Nic Wondra
Research Fulbright to Georgia
Political Science

Based on my experience, the Fulbrighters who had some professional experience before they went on their Fulbright were better able to work the system, take initiative, and push to be more engaged. Whereas those who had come straight out of school from undergrad were less likely to do so. I attribute this to lack of experience in a professional environment. They were more hesitant to step on other teachers' toes. We had fifteen Fulbrighters in the ETA program in our year. The majority came straight out of undergrad, but there were several of us who had some work experience and I think it helped.

Natalia Ksiezyk
ETA Fulbright to Argentina

What does the Fulbright Program look for in an applicant?

Assessing your qualifications

The Fulbright Program Adviser at your college or university can help you most by honestly assessing how qualified you are for the Fulbright Program. Advisers see a new batch of Fulbright applications every year and over time they get a feel for what works. This does not mean you should throw in the towel if your adviser predicts long odds for your application, however. If you are excited about your idea, never let anyone tell you that you can't do it. Listen to them, understand the basis of their assessment, and then ask the most important question: *What can I do to make this happen?*

Fulbright aims to send America's best and brightest overseas as cultural ambassadors, so a certain level of academic or professional accomplishment is expected from all candidates. But Fulbright is looking for more than just a strong GPA. Here are qualities the Fulbright Program looks for in its applicants:

- Serious commitment to your field
- The experience and language skills necessary to complete your proposed Fulbright work successfully
- Clear personal and professional goals for both Fulbright and beyond
- Diplomatic acumen
- A desire to build relationships and engage local communities
- Leadership potential
- A desire to find solutions to issues of international or broad social concern
- Resourcefulness, curiosity, and a willingness to dive in
- Flexibility and the ability to thrive overseas in an immersion environment
- A desire to serve your community and country

Part of developing a strong application is focusing your energies on preparing yourself for your Fulbright work. This will only strengthen your candidacy. With enough time and dedication during the application process you can develop relationships with experts in your field, sharpen your language skills, organize an internship at an organization relevant to your project, or even visit your host country beforehand to get the lay of the land and make connections. It takes time to acquire the qualifications needed to meet your goals—sometimes lots of time—and this is yet another reason to start your application early. You can't learn to speak Chinese in a month, but if you are passionate about doing a Fulbright project in Beijing, a year of intensive Mandarin study will move you closer to your goal.

What does a strong Fulbright candidacy look like?

Strong candidacy checklist

___ Specific goals for your Fulbright work and beyond
___ Awareness of how Fulbright will fit into your larger career trajectory
___ Significant academic and/or professional background in the field
___ Advanced proficiency in the language of the host country
___ A well-researched, detailed, and realistic proposal
___ Demonstrated commitment to social issues, community, or volunteerism
___ A proposal that clearly supports Fulbright's mission of exchange
___ Strong relationships with professors and mentors (for letters of recommendation)
___ Demonstrated leadership potential
___ Demonstrated passion for the subject matter
___ A proposal that clearly conveys why your project is important

Average candidacy checklist

___ Specific goals for Fulbright, but larger career trajectory is less clear
___ Established academic and/or professional experience in the field
___ Some language proficiency with a clear commitment to improving
___ Demonstrated interest in the subject matter
___ Demonstrated interest in leadership and community engagement

Weak candidacy checklist

___ Goals for Fulbright are vague
___ Boilerplate letters of recommendation indicate weak relationships with mentors and professors
___ Interest in the subject is declared but unsupported by academic or professional experience
___ Poorly researched proposal
___ Poorly written proposal
___ Proposal does not demonstrate awareness of and interest in the Fulbright mission
___ No proficiency in the language of the host country
___ No experience with the host country culture

Do I need to be fluent in a foreign language to receive a Fulbright Scholarship?

You don't have to be fluent in a foreign language to apply for a Fulbright Scholarship. For most applicants, however, being able to speak the language of your host country will strengthen the chances of being selected. Fulbright is most interested in whether your language skills are developed enough to pursue your Fulbright work and the Fulbright mission successfully. If you want to study Russian literature at Moscow State University, for example, you need to be able to read in Russian at an advanced level. If you plan to work closely with an English-speaking mathematician in Amsterdam to develop English-language articles for international publication, having a high level of spoken proficiency in Dutch may be less important. Language requirements vary widely from country to country; consult Fulbright's **Country Summaries** for specific requirements.

Don't underestimate the value of language proficiency in your application. Even if you don't need local language skills for your Fulbright work (as is the case with most English-teaching assistants), your role as cultural ambassador will demand it. All Fulbright applicants, and especially English-teaching applicants, should state in their application how they plan to engage their host communities outside of their Fulbright work. This is a critical part of the Fulbright experience and one of the main reasons why foreign language proficiency is so important to your candidacy.

If your language skills aren't what you would like them to be, address this explicitly in your application. Mention how you plan to improve your proficiency while overseas, and what you are doing now to move you closer to this goal (classes, tutoring, language clubs, etc.). If your college or university doesn't offer classes in the language of your host country, talk to the department head about arranging an independent study or check out what's available at nearby schools or community centers. Even if English is spoken widely as a second language in the country you are applying to, making an effort to learn the country's first language shows your commitment to Fulbright's mission of exchange. This can go a long way toward balancing out other weaknesses in your application.

There was an orientation in southern Germany. All the ETAs were together for the first three days or so. I was initially a little shocked because at orientation the guy was joking around in German and I hadn't spoken German in over a year. I felt like I was coming into it not as ready. If I had known six months before that I was coming to Germany I would have been working on my German, but I felt that in terms of language I wasn't ready. Most people had spent a semester there before, or lived or worked there, or done something related to Germany. At least more so than I had.

Lakshmi Eassey
ETA Fulbright to Germany

I've met Fulbrighters going to Russia who had no experience with the Russian language whatsoever. And Fulbrighters going to Poland with no experience in Polish whatsoever. It depends on what the project is. If you're going to be out in the regions, language is more important. If your going to be working with an NGO and getting a lot of support from them, language is less important. Regardless of the situation, the applicant still has to come up with a plan to learn the language on a more formal basis. In some cases there are funds available to help gain that language experience.

Nic Wondra
Research Fulbright to Georgia
Political Science

If elements of your project require language proficiency beyond your current level (conducting interviews in a specific dialect, for example), outline how you plan to deal with this. Hiring a local interpreter for specific aspects of your work is not necessarily a liability in an application: It lets your readers know that you are informed about the situation in your host country. It shows that you are realistic about the needs of your project and resourceful about how to get it done. Genuine interest and enthusiasm for learning the language can often make up for less-developed language skills.

There was a language requirement for Fulbright applications to Poland, but I didn't speak Polish, though I had been taking some private language lessons. I contacted the Polish Fulbright Commission during the application process to find out what I should do if I'm not fluent enough. They said that I should get a letter from my affiliate professor—the guy that's sponsoring me—to say explicitly that even though my Polish isn't good, he still has confidence that I can complete my project. It was like giving me a pass for not yet being up to an intermediate level of Polish.

The original host affiliation letter he wrote was more general, so I wrote him back asking, "Could you please write another letter that specifically addresses this language issue?" He was happy to comply. I knew I would be working with subjects who either spoke English or didn't have a problem working with a translator. That all worked out exactly as I described it.

Mike Seely
Research Fulbright to Poland
Filmmaking

For the ETAs in Romania in my year, you didn't have to have any previous language skills. To some extent that's an added benefit for your students, not knowing any Romanian. English is so prevalent in that country, so widely spoken. Most people learned their English from television and movies and cartoons. If you ask almost anyone from my generation where they learned English, they will inevitably say, "Oh, watching cartoons." As a whole, people in Romania have very extensive English language skills. But they're funny because they know all sorts of things from TV and movies, but they don't know other practical applications of English.

Hannah Halder
ETA Fulbright to Romania

Fulbright Scholarships are more accessible than most people realize. The program's prestigious reputation, distorted in part by a handful of persistent myths, has discouraged many otherwise well-qualified candidates from exploring what Fulbright has to offer. Many applicants are surprised to learn that a Fulbright Scholarship is within reach.

Myth #1: Fulbright Scholarships are only for students at Ivy League universities

Ivy League colleges and universities often have higher numbers of Fulbright grantees not because Fulbright prefers their students, but because these institutions invest more resources into helping students and alumni apply. The Fulbright Program is interested in accepting a diverse cohort of applicants from colleges and universities across the United States.

Myth #2: Fulbright Scholarships are only for academic research

Fulbright uses the term "research" in a very broad sense. Most Fulbright research projects have a clear academic element, but many do not. It is not a requirement. Fulbright grants in the fine arts, for example, often focus on creating a body of work. Often the most productive Fulbright grants are those with practical, tangible, non-academic results.

Applicants to the English Teaching Assistantship program are strongly encouraged to pursue extracurricular activities or volunteer service in their host country. You should outline how you plan to spend your time outside the classroom. For ETA applicants it is even more important to explain to Fulbright explicitly how you will pursue your role as a cultural ambassador. It's not just about teaching English.

Myth #3: **Fulbright Scholarships are only for students with perfect 4.0 GPAs**

You don't have to have perfect grades to qualify for a Fulbright. A mediocre grade point average can be a liability, but it's not always a fatal one. Fulbrighters with low GPAs are rare, but not unheard of. If your grades aren't what you would like, address this directly in your application and be sure to include strong support from your academic advisers. They can address your grade deficiency by speaking to your ability to succeed at the project, course of study, or teaching program you propose. Professional applicants should emphasize the training and experience they have received since finishing school. A balanced application with clear goals and a well-developed plan often carries more weight than a pristine GPA.

Myth #4: **Only graduating seniors can apply for a Fulbright**

The Fulbright U.S. Student Program encourages younger applicants, but there is no official program-wide age limit. Some host countries do have age-specific criteria for U.S. Fulbrighters, so you should check Fulbright's **Country Summary** for your host country early in the application process. You don't have to be enrolled in school to apply for a Fulbright Scholarship, and you don't need a master's degree to apply. In some exceptional cases, particularly in the fine arts, you don't even need a bachelor's degree to apply if you underwent serious training or an apprenticeship.

I was not the most outstanding student in my class. I was by no means the favorite of the faculty. I had some people in my corner, of course, because it is necessary to be able to send in an application and have people support it. I just had experience in the region, a clear idea of what I wanted to do, and I had people who were supportive enough to get behind it. There are a couple Fulbrighters out there who are perfect students, goody two-shoes, who have never been abroad before. They are your 4.0 students. They sail through the system and get a Fulbright. But 95 percent are people who have travelled abroad before, know what they want, and know how they want to get there.

Fulbright isn't just for students from Ivy League schools, nor is it just for students at the very top of their class. I had good academic credentials, but they were not the most outstanding. Professionals should be aware that you don't have to be a professor in order to have the opportunity. Students need to be aware that they don't need to be the leading student in their school to be a real candidate.

Nic Wondra
Research Fulbright to Georgia
Political Science

I think that sometimes the academic community says, "Hey, you need to be one of the elite to be able to get one of these. You have to have the good grades, be articulate, be able to propose something new and cool and different." But the Fulbright is fundamentally an exercise in cultural and social exchange. I don't think the government and IIE misrepresent Fulbright at all, but I think the academic community in universities sometimes does.

Tim Slade
Research Fulbright to Benin
Public Health

It's funny: Even though I applied for the Fulbright, I never thought in my wildest dreams I would get one. Fulbright was always something for those really smart people. I was a good student, graduated with honors from my college, but I really didn't feel that I had done anything that would warrant a Fulbright.

Hannah Halder
ETA Fulbright to Romania

A lot of students are intimidated by the Fulbright Program. I always encourage people to apply, but many say, "No, I would never get it. I'm not smart enough." Don't let that stop you. If you have a strong interest in something and want to do a project related to that interest, I think it's definitely worth applying. Even if you don't feel totally confident but are still passionate about the topic. You'll learn as you go.

Ashley Killough
Research Fulbright to Armenia
Journalism

What type of Fulbright grant is right for me?

Traditionally, Fulbright's two largest and most popular grant programs for young American students and professionals have been the study/research fellowship and the English Teaching Assistant (ETA) Program. Both are part of the **Fulbright U.S. Student Program**, although you don't have to be a student to apply and most grantees are not students during their fellowship. The Fulbright Program awards over 1,200 of these grants yearly to young American citizens to go abroad.

Regardless of which grant you pursue, your Fulbright work will be the beating heart of your overseas experience. It will give structure to your professional development, a community to build on, and a platform for engaging your host country. In Fulbright's eyes it is the principal tool you will use to promote its mission of encouraging mutual understanding between Americans and the people of your host country.

Applicants should choose which of these two grants is best for them based on their goals and qualifications.

The Fulbright study/research grant

The Fulbright U.S. Student Program's research grants are project-based fellowships: they provide support to pursue specific academic or professional goals over an eight- to ten-month period in one of the more than 150 countries Fulbright is active in. Even projects that don't seem to offer much in the way of exchange (some hard science research projects, for example) still serve as a platform for you to engage your colleagues and professional community. If your project offers limited social opportunity, it is all the more important that your application address how you will engage communities and build relationships outside of your work.

What Fulbright calls "research" doesn't necessarily mean academic research. It could mean working with a local organization to re-engineer aqueducts in rural Nicaragua or producing a collection of photographs about the impact of a new oil pipeline in Azerbaijan. Nor does "independent" research mean the grantee must work alone. It simply means that the project is largely of your own design.

If you are committed to the Fulbright mission of cultural ambassadorship but don't know what field to pursue a research project in, consider applying to the Fulbright English Teaching Assistant Program instead.

Overview of Fulbright study/research grants for young U.S. citizens

- Usually 8–10 months in duration, with possibility of a short extension

- Some flexibility in the grant's start date (per funding availability and host country guidelines)

- Applicants submit proposals for a self-designed research project or course of study in one of the more than 150 countries Fulbright is active in

- Grantees receive a monthly stipend to cover basic living and research costs

- Candidates are asked to submit a letter of support from a local organization they plan to collaborate with in some capacity

- Language requirements vary by host country, but applicants must possess sufficient proficiency in the host language to carry out their proposed project

- Applicants must have at least a Bachelor's degree to apply, though candidates in the arts may substitute four years of training and professional experience. Applicants cannot have already received a PhD (those who have should explore the Fulbright U.S. Scholar Program)

- Selection is merit-based and highly competitive

Examples of past Fulbright research projects

- Researching pollution control efforts on India's Ganges River

- Studying performance piano at the L'Ecole Normale de Musique de Paris in France

- Investigating past patterns of wind and ocean circulation in New Zealand in order to enhance climate models that forecast global climate cycles and changes

- Examining how global health initiatives are translated into health promotion and disease surveillance in Malawi

- Conducting an in-depth archaeological and ethno-historical investigation to define the undocumented shrines that link ritualistic pathways once used by the Inca in Peru

- Developing distributed renewable electricity generation systems for villages in Maharashtra, India

- Translating the poetry of Zen Buddhist monk and teacher Muso Soseki in Japan, with attention to the interplay between religion and poetics

- Evaluating school-based deworming programs in the islands of Luzon in the Philippines and exploring how to implement these initiatives

- Studying multicultural interpretations of Shakespeare through research at the Asian Shakespeare Intercultural Archive and an internship at a theatre company in Singapore

- Assessing water quality in streams in the northwestern Ecuadorian Andes and investigating how these results relate to urban development, agriculture, and mining

- Developing bio-fortified rice to combat iron deficiencies in the Philippines

- Examining the effect of technology entrepreneurship incubators on economic development and EU integration in Poland

- Researching the relationships among citizenship, marriage, and kinship in Jordan through exploring the effects of nationality laws on mixed families

- Evaluating the effectiveness and reproducibility of a grid-connected solar panel system in Kathmandu, Nepal—specifically whether this system can help alleviate Nepal's energy crisis

I used this opportunity to conduct the final portion of my dissertation research. I'm a cultural anthropology student. By the time I did Fulbright I was a PhD candidate at the University at Albany, State University of New York. I had done one or two short-term pilot projects with internal grants from the university and used the Fulbright to do some of the more in-depth interviewing and on-site observation that I needed to finish my doctoral dissertation research. I conducted my Fulbright field research in a place called Senahú, Guatemala, in the province of Alta Verapaz, which has a long history of coffee producing. Senahú, the municipality I lived in, was basically founded on the economic structure of an emerging coffee culture.

Winston Scott
Research Fulbright to Guatemala
Anthropology

I studied a group of crustaceans called manta shrimp. Nobody knows what they are, but they are really cool. They happen to produce one of the fastest movements in the animal kingdom. They have a predatory appendage that they use to smash hard-shelled prey because their fast movement provides very high forces that allow them to break the shells. It turns out that although they have this specialized appendage, they actually eat many different things, which is counter to what we would expect. So I'm trying to figure out exactly what they eat, how much time they spend eating, and how much time they spend doing other things. In Panama, on my Fulbright, I actually put an underwater camera next to their homes and tried to film them and figure out what they are doing.

Maya deVries
Research Fulbright to Panama
Biology

My project revolved around seeing what was going on with children's libraries in the Republic of Georgia. What issues they were facing, what was working for the programs and what wasn't, and what the major challenges were. The project did evolve while I was there and ended up being more about collaborating with librarians and discussing ideas that might work in their libraries. This gave me some ideas that I could use at work here in the U.S., especially regarding programming and things like that.

Heather Wakefield
Research Fulbright to Georgia
Library Science

I have a funny story. We all met with the U.S. ambassador at some point at the embassy. All the Fulbrighters in the country were there. He's going around the room asking about our projects and he asks me, "What's your Fulbright?" I said I was working on a water quality project in my community. He said, "That's a Fulbright?!" At the time I was very embarrassed but I realized that the range of Fulbright projects is extremely large, to the point that the ambassador wasn't even aware of the breadth.

Matt Wesley
Research Fulbright to Nicaragua
Public Health

The Fulbright English Teaching Assistant (ETA) Program

Fulbright ETA fellowships give grantees the opportunity to serve as cultural ambassadors by working as an English-teaching assistant in a primary school, secondary school, college or university, or professional program overseas. Because the ETA experience can vary widely from country to country, it is important for ETA candidates to check Fulbright's **Country Summaries** before beginning a proposal. Not all Fulbright countries host ETA grantees.

Although a candidate's proposal must specify the country where he or she would like to teach, Fulbrighters have little control over which the city or institution they are placed in. In some cases the grantee is provided accommodation, sometimes in the form of a homestay, but usually Fulbrighters are expected to arrange their own housing.

Although ETA Fulbrighters are technically teaching assistants, in practice many ETA Fulbrighters find themselves with considerably more teaching responsibility—and opportunity—than anticipated. ETA grantees are also encouraged to pursue individual study/research plans and extracurricular activities in addition to their teaching responsibilities. In the past ETA Fulbright alumni have been eligible to apply later for Fulbright study/research grants, although in general Fulbright tends to prefer applicants who have not previously received a Fulbright Scholarship.

Overview of the Fulbright English Teaching Assistant Program for young U.S. citizens

- 8–9 months in duration (one academic year)

- Grants typically begin in September, per the host country's academic schedule

- Applicants apply to teach in a country of their choosing, but typically are not able to choose which city or teaching institution they are placed in

- Applicants are strongly encouraged to engage in volunteer or extracurricular activities in their host communities

- Applicants must have at least a Bachelor's degree to apply

- Selection is merit-based and highly competitive

Using your Fulbright grant to study at an overseas university

I spent a year in Toronto studying second-generation South Asian immigrant identity development. I was at the University of Toronto working with a professor there in the psychology department. I was in his lab, but technically I wasn't a student at the university. I wasn't taking classes and I didn't have to apply to the university. The professor took care of that from his end and said it wouldn't be a problem. And it wasn't a problem. I got all the library cards and those kinds of things, but I wasn't technically a student.

For me it was not an option to do my Fulbright outside of a university setting. Having just a BA in psychology, even though I did an honors thesis and received highest honors, I definitely was not prepared to take on a full psych project by myself without having someone advising me on things like the IRB [Institutional Review Board], the statistical analysis of it, and publishing. I had published with the help of my professor in college, but you need all that support when you're doing a project that's so specific. I really needed to be part of a university setting in order to do that. I'm not sure how else it would have worked.

Laila Plamondon
Research Fulbright to Canada
Psychology

Most Fulbright research grants are for independent projects, but some Fulbrighters use their scholarship to pursue advanced degree study at a college or university overseas. This may be part of a dissertation or master's thesis, or in a dedicated one-year degree-granting program. Grantees attend classes and lectures but typically focus on a specific research topic or project that will anchor their coursework.

Being selected for a Fulbright Scholarship does not guarantee acceptance into a university program. Applicants interested in graduate study must apply for admission just as any student would. Candidates with projects like these should plan far in advance: If you wait to be selected for a Fulbright grant before you apply for admission to the college or university, it will be too late. Unless specifically stated in the country summary, the cost of tuition is not covered by Fulbright. Your application should address how you intend to pay for it.

If you want to use your Fulbright to study at a college or university overseas, be sure to check Fulbright's Country Summary for your destination. The Fulbright Commission there may offer a different kind of Fulbright Scholarship for exactly this kind of study. Consult your campus Fulbright Program Adviser early and contact the host country's Fulbright Commission before you move ahead with this type of proposal.

It is worth noting that many Fulbrighters pursue academic research in a university setting without officially matriculating as students. They receive no credit towards a degree, but they also pay no tuition. These grantees typically contact specific professors about their research plans and arrange to work with them or their research teams on an independent basis. The Fulbrighter's official status at the university can vary, and you should negotiate with your contact there regarding how much access to the institution's resources (libraries, laboratories, etc.) you will have. Many professors seek qualified assistants to help with their research or to take their work in new directions, and Fulbrighters are often attractive candidates to fill these roles. This can be a productive arrangement for the Fulbrighter, but much depends on the relationship with the adviser.

Examples of other Fulbright grants available to young U.S. citizens

The traditional study/research and ETA fellowships are not the only opportunities Fulbright offers to young Americans to go overseas. The following is a small sampling of grants the Fulbright Program has sponsored in the past:

____ **The Fulbright-mtvU Fellowship**

Provides a small number of grantees the opportunity to pursue projects about an aspect of international contemporary or popular music as a cultural force for expression. Past grantees have documented songs and stories of war-time sexual assault survivors in Kosovo, investigated how musicians in Botswana confront social issues like the country's AIDS epidemic, and explored the relationship between children's music and cultural identity in Indonesia.

____ **The Fulbright-Clinton Public Policy Fellowship**

Places young American scholars and professionals in foreign government ministries or institutions to gain hands-on public sector experience while also carrying out an academic study/research project. Past fellows have worked in the Guatemalan Ministry of Education, in the Ministry of Justice in Côte d'Ivoire, and in the Ministry of Health in Bangladesh. Applicants must already hold a master's degree or JD, or be currently enrolled in a PhD program.

____ **The Fulbright-Hays Doctoral Dissertation Fellowship**

Offers pre-doctoral U.S. students awards to support research and training that focus on non-western foreign languages and area studies.

____ **Fulbright-National Geographic Digital Storytelling Fellowship**

Provides opportunities for American citizens to participate in an academic year of overseas travel and digital storytelling in up to three countries. Grantees will create multimedia stories on globally significant social or environmental topics, including biodiversity, cities, climate change, cultures, energy, food, oceans, and water. Fellows will share their stories through National Geographic's platforms using a variety of digital storytelling tools, including text, photography, video, audio, graphic illustrations, and/or social media.

Fulbright and the arts

The Fulbright Program is one of the best ways for young American artists to pursue training, research, or a specific project overseas. Proposals for artistic projects can cover a wide range of subject matter as long as they fall within one of the accepted disciplines. Past projects have included architectural painting in a squatter community in Turkey, the production of a documentary film about a township in South Africa, and the research and writing of a novel in China.

Applicants in the arts must have training to support their candidacy and are required to submit a creative portfolio that will be evaluated by experts in the field. Candidates with strong artistic inclinations but no formal training should know that they will face stiff competition. Example: A recent biology graduate who never got a chance to pursue his love for drawing while in college would have a difficult time formulating a strong arts application without first taking some studio art classes. Arts candidates will compete against recent graduates who majored in artistic fields, graduate students in dedicated studio programs, and professional artists.

Artistic disciplines that a Fulbright grant can support

- Architecture
- Creative Writing
- Dance
- Design & Crafts
- Filmmaking
- Installation Art
- Music
- Painting/Printmaking
- Performance Art
- Photography
- Sculpture
- Theater Arts
- World Music/Ethnomusicology

Fulbright for artists

Deanna Fei
Research Fulbright to China
Creative Writing

I came very close to not applying for the Fulbright because I didn't know that it could be used to support creative projects like mine, and also the project was still so embryonic in my own head that it didn't seem to merit anything as official as a Fulbright. I applied mostly because I didn't know of any other opportunities that would not only allow me, but *require* me, to be in the country I was writing about, doing pretty much nothing but working on that project. The sense of immersion I would get from it—I knew there was really nothing else out there that could offer that kind of experience. I applied and was pretty surprised to get it. In looking back, I know that I wouldn't have been able to write my novel if I hadn't gotten the grant.

My Fulbright project was to research and write a novel about a family of Chinese-American women who reunite to tour China together for the first time. The story deals with the family history and present family drama that unfolds over the course of that trip. So my research was always meant to be on the more informal side. It was mostly going to consist of traveling to the cities that my characters were traveling to, seeing the sites through their eyes, and exploring their personal histories. I also wanted to do some research on certain aspects of contemporary Chinese history that I knew would play some part in the narrative, such as the Chinese feminist movement, the Civil War, and the Japanese occupation. I had planned to form some kind of relationship with the Chinese writers association where I had a couple of contacts. I wasn't sure if I was going to take classes, but I was affiliated with Fudan University.

Five things to know about being a Fulbright English Teaching Assistant

Antonio A. Mendez
ETA Fulbright to Andorra

1. **Your role in the classroom will depend on your institutional placement**

   In some countries, Fulbright ETAs are assistants to classroom teachers and are primarily used in a support role (think "in-class experts"). In other countries, you are the only teacher in the classroom. Both systems have their benefits. If your primary function is that of teacher's assistant, it is important to develop good communication with your teacher. Start by researching local customs and the role of the teacher in the community, and develop a communication plan with the teacher. If you are the sole classroom teacher, start by developing classroom expectations, guidelines, and grading policies, as well as behavior management strategies for your class.

2. **Expect multiple languages in the classroom**

   We live in a globalized world with lots of immigration. Do not assume that all of your students will speak the national language of your host country. Many countries use multiple languages. In Andorra my students were taught Catalan, Spanish, and French, with English being their fourth language! There were Portuguese-speaking immigrants as well. Do some research into the most commonly spoken languages in that country and among the students at your school. Being able to communicate with students is key.

3. **English teachers teach more than English**

   ETAs are not just English teachers, but also cultural ambassadors. Many of my students had never met an American before they met me and their understanding of our culture came predominantly from American movies and stereotypes. This led to many conversations in class about subjects such as race, gender, foreign affairs, and diet. I always had to be careful not to generalize, and to indicate that my experiences were my own and that other Americans might well have had different experiences. Start thinking about your own cultural narrative, and the narrative of the country as a whole, to be able to educate students about some of their misconceptions.

4. **Much of your Fulbright experience will depend on the age of your students**

   It's difficult to overestimate how profoundly the age of your students will impact your experience. ETAs are placed at all levels of education, from kindergarten to professional schools. Some countries, like Spain, make it clear during the application process what age you will be working with, while others inform you only when you arrive in the country. During my Fulbright I worked with students as young as 13, while other Fulbrighters I know worked with students who were 17 and older. Four years may not sound like much of an age difference, but it's a big difference in the classroom. Think about the students' age when developing your classroom policies and curriculum.

5. **American English is more unique than you might realize**

   European English teaching curricula teach the language from a British perspective. This can be jarring for an American, as there are words we do not use (queue, lorry, etc.). Several of my lessons were spent on these vocabulary differences. I used Spanish to teach them that regional vocabulary differences are present in multiple languages. I had multiple e-mail exchanges with the previous Fulbrighter at my school about what she had taught students. This collaboration ultimately benefits the students.

I applied to the Fulbright ETA program with the intention of understanding education better. I'm not a trained teacher. I studied international relations and European studies in college, but I'm interested in education systems and how they're set up: How civil society is affected by education, especially in the post-communist context. How education has worked, not worked, or changed since communism ended.

My plan was to get some background and actually teach before I went to graduate school so that I would have some basis for talking about education. I think there's a lot of people who are in the field of education who have never actually taught. That's why I pursued a Fulbright.

Hannah Halder
ETA Fulbright to Romania

I was at a university that has the best English teaching program in Argentina. Their purpose is to train teachers of English, and the professors in that department knew how to utilize a Fulbright grantee. Several of them had gone on a Fulbright themselves. I had great working relationships with the people in my department. I was able to teach some classes, contribute content, and then do some extracurricular things with students based on my background, like teach a professional communication mini-course that I designed and host some sessions on American culture. So the placement worked really well for me.

I know that for some people who were placed in other cities, the experience was not always positive. Some people were placed in very small towns where the local English teachers felt very threatened by the presence of the Fulbrighter, and so that created a lot of tension and didn't result in positive relationships. So their ability to contribute to that community was very limited.

I don't think Fulbright is looking for people who have teaching experience. It's not a requirement. Most of the people in our group didn't. There were several who had some ESL teaching experience—if not full certification, then they had done some volunteer work or community service that was centered around English teaching. I think that Fulbright is more focused on people who will be good ambassadors of American culture, and they look for that in the Personal Statement in the application.

Natalia Ksiezyk
ETA Fulbright to Argentina

I was interested in second-generation populations, looking at their cultural identity, and there were three places that I was considering for Fulbright: London, New York, and Toronto, because they all have such large immigrant populations. Of course New York was out, and millions of people apply for Fulbrights to London. But Canada, you don't have as many applying to Fulbright to go there. I sort of hedged my bets in that sense. I knew there wouldn't be many applications, so I'd have a better chance of getting in.

Laila Plamondon
Research Fulbright to Canada
Psychology

If you're trying to find a country and a project that you think Fulbright will fund, that means that you aren't really driven by your connection to the world as a person, but rather by ambition for finding economic resources. Because if you think of the Fulbright as just a nice label that's going to get you a job later, it's hard to really enjoy the experience. You should be guided by your questions about a subject you're deeply interested in, because that's going to be really important to your experience. If you're just trying to fill a gap because you think there will be less people trying to do that, then I think you're going to have a rougher time than if you're motivated by what inspires you.

Blake Scott
Research Fulbright to Panama
History

How competitive is the Fulbright Program?

Fulbright publishes award and application statistics online for each country it operates in. For the 2012–2013 grant cycle, for example, there were 69 applications for Fulbright study/research grants to Jordan, of which 19 were selected. There were 60 applications to Russia, with 14 awards, and 164 applications to China, with 55 awards. Statistically the most competitive Fulbright grants are often those to Britain, Australia, and France.

The most important thing in considering your odds is this: If you are committed to your project and serious about developing a competitive application, your interest and excitement in your field will show through in your materials. If you are excited about a project idea but feel you aren't yet qualified to develop a competitive candidacy, take the time to get qualified. Work or volunteer for a company or organization operating in your field. Take an intensive language course. Visit the country beforehand for research and to broaden your network. These are all viable ways to strengthen your candidacy.

It's also worth noting that many Fulbright research projects can be undertaken in one of several countries that the applicant's experience and language skills apply to. If you want to study the evolution of the Russian language in Central Asia, for example, Kazakhstan, Uzbekistan, Kyrgyzstan, and Tajikistan might all be viable destinations. Choosing one country over another because it awards more grants per number of applicants can be a shrewd application strategy, but keep in mind that there are ultimately far more important variables to consider: the strength of your host affiliation, the resources and network you would have available in the country, and how much you would enjoy living there, to name just a few. It will be very difficult to create a rewarding Fulbright experience in a country you don't want to live in.

Some fellowship advisers take this strategy a step further. They advise applicants to choose their field, project, and host country according to the odds. The theory is simple: If France received 185 applications for 19 spots last year, and Togo received two applications for one spot, find a way to apply to Togo if you want a Fulbright. There is something to be said for being tactical with your application, but if you choose to play this numbers game, be sure you aren't putting the cart before the horse.

Trust your gut. If you studied zoology in college, are

fascinated by migratory bird patterns in Chile, have contacts at a bird sanctuary outside Santiago, speak fluent Spanish, and dream of becoming an ornithologist, then you are an excellent candidate for a Fulbright Scholarship to Chile. These kinds of natural fits usually lead to the strongest Fulbright applications and the most productive experiences. If you decide instead to apply for an ETA fellowship to Moldova because the ratio of awards to applicants there is more favorable, you may do yourself and your career a tremendous disservice. Your school's Fulbright Program Adviser can be a huge help during the application process, but in the end you are the best expert on what you want. Remember: The goal of a Fulbright grant is not to get a Fulbright grant.

Great Fulbright experiences and the level of achievement that accompanies them are built on the passion of the grantee, not the prestige of the award. It is fine to consider the Fulbright competition statistics when choosing a host country, but beware of giving them too much weight.

I applied to Fulbright the year after I finished my undergraduate studies. I knew what I wanted to do and I knew I wanted to be in Latin America. To be honest, I looked at the countries I could go to and the odds and competitiveness of each country, and then was able to develop a project that I was really enthusiastic about in Panama. I wanted to do a photo-documentary about how the Panama Canal had affected locals. It's a waterway that benefits the rest of the world, but I was interested in seeing how Panamanians interact with the canal. I ended up focusing on one particular community, the Afro-Antillean community there, and the descendents of people who had come to Panama to build the canal.

Rose Cromwell
Research Fulbright to Panama
Photography

Serious Fulbright applications are built on serious intentions

Do you want to apply straight out of college, or do you want to apply a couple years down the road after you've really thought about it and it's part of a bigger plan?

I went on a Fulbright at the same time as another good friend went on a Fulbright to Germany. She felt the same thing, that she didn't quite know how it was going to fit in with her overall research plans, her overall academic plans. She worked with a professor there who she had not met before, and she ended up having such a horrible time that she decided to come back to the States. She basically called it quits. She's a super bright girl—very passionate about her field—but she just couldn't make it work.

My experience wasn't so bad that I considered coming home and calling it quits, but it just didn't fit in with my overall plans. If I had known that it would be good to look at the Institutional Review Board process beforehand, that I might have to do some waiting in the middle of my grant, and if I had had a back-up plan during those months, even if it was something that fit in with interests other than academic interests, I think those things would have really helped me better plan those ten months, to make the most of those ten months.

Laila Plamondon
Research Fulbright to Canada
Psychology

The decision to apply for a Fulbright has as much to do with your goals as with your qualifications. With enough time and dedication you can always strengthen project ideas, credentials, and application essays, but crafting a competitive proposal will always be a challenge if your goals are unclear. Fulbright application readers look for vision and clarity of purpose in your proposal because these qualities consistently prove critical in creating a successful Fulbright experience.

The strongest applications and most rewarding overseas experiences most often come from Fulbrighters who view the grant as a means to an end, not as an end in itself. Fulbright can be a powerful tool for pursuing your goals, but only if you have an idea of what those goals are. This concept, which seems simple enough on paper, is ignored by hundreds of candidates each year and is often where many otherwise well-qualified applications go wrong. The farther you can see beyond Fulbright, the stronger your application and Fulbright experience will be. Your qualifications are important, but Fulbright often takes more interest in what you plan to accomplish than in what you've already done. *Identifying your goals is the single most important Fulbright research you will ever undertake.*

Many of the most successful Fulbrighters know long before they begin their application what kind of project they want to undertake. They know how they want to pursue it and how it will bring them closer to achieving their larger personal and professional aspirations. They are passionate about their work and deeply invested in its impact, and Fulbright is usually just one of several vehicles they are considering to make it happen. Applications from these candidates are often stronger because they demonstrate well-formulated objectives not only for the grant work itself, but for their career trajectory as a whole.

But what about the rest of us? Not everyone has this kind of clarity of purpose, especially when just leaving college. If you have an interest in a particular field but lack a detailed plan for your career, you are not alone. The good news is that the process of developing a successful Fulbright application asks you to explore what is important to you, what you hope to accomplish, and how you would like to pursue these goals. Take the time to think about what you want before diving

The strongest Fulbright applications and the most rewarding overseas experiences come from Fulbrighters who view the grant as a means to an end, not as an end in itself.

into your proposal. Be passionate about your ideas and the Fulbright work you propose, not about getting a Fulbright grant.

Is this soul searching really necessary? Some applicants skip this process and rely on salesmanship alone to carry their application. But this approach invites risk. What all Fulbright application readers look for is clarity of purpose, and they are practiced at spotting attempts to disguise its absence. At least three groups of readers will screen your application, and if you undergo a campus interview, you will almost certainly be asked about your larger ambitions.

Fulbright wants candidates with clear goals because grantees without them often find themselves adrift when they hit bumps in their Fulbright work overseas. Bumps are inevitable, but not knowing where you are going makes it difficult to course-correct mid-grant. Alumni who talk of mediocre or disappointing experiences almost always regret that they didn't have clearer objectives before they started their Fulbright. It takes discipline to stop yourself from diving into the application without first exploring what you want in the bigger picture, but this exploration is critical for a strong Fulbright candidacy. This step often separates serious candidates from the rest of the pack. Invest your energy in figuring out what you want, not in trying to cover up the fact that you haven't.

Fulbright's rules say that they don't directly fund films. I was trying to figure out a way to pitch my project in a way where I would get funding to do research for the film but then use my time to shoot documentaries with resources that I already had, and the minimal amount of gear and crew necessary. I wanted to research Polish film history by making documentaries that emulated the styles of prominent documentary filmmakers in Polish history. That was a better approach than saying, "I want to make this movie. Help me make the movie."

Mike Seely
Research Fulbright to Poland
Filmmaking

Don't just do it just for your CV. You're missing a great opportunity if that's the way you're looking at it. In my opinion somebody that pursues it for that reason isn't taking full advantage of what the Fulbright has to offer. Yes, the academic side is fine—I'm writing my dissertation now—but the things that stayed with me more than anything are the people.

Winston Scott
Research Fulbright to Guatemala
Anthropology

When I was trying to write my final grant report I read some of the final reports from the year before. It was just so obvious who the Fulbrighters were that came in with a clear idea of what their goals were, even if those goals changed, and those Fulbrighters who were just out of undergrad and still figuring out what they were doing.

Take the time to understand Fulbright before applying. Know what the program can offer. If you're writing your project to fit the program, then I don't think you're going to get as much out of it as you could otherwise. I knew my goals and I knew the goals of the Fulbright Program. Basically I said, "OK. I'm going to figure out how I can make those two work together.

Maya deVries
Research Fulbright to Panama
Biology

Beware the Application Trap!

Don't be seduced by Fulbright's prestige and résumé-boosting promise. If your end goal is just to get a Fulbright grant, you're missing the point of Fulbright. The objective is not the grant itself but what you can accomplish with the resources, opportunities, and community it provides. Not sure what's possible? Contact some Fulbright alumni and chat about their time overseas. Alumni are often the best source of inspiration for applicants and new grantees.

Interviews with program alumni reveal an interesting trend: Those who admit pursuing a Fulbright grant primarily for its prestige—to validate their work as a student, to impress their parents and peers, or to appear more successful to future employers—often had more complicated and less rewarding experiences in the field. If you find yourself applying to the Fulbright Program for these reasons, stop and step back from the process. Take the time to explore what you really want, even if that means postponing your application.

It's embarrassing to admit, but I was more focused on getting the Fulbright than on what I was going to do with it overseas. Part of it was the idea that Fulbright is something that you can put on your CV to justify what you did the year after college. And really that's not what it should be about. It's about the opportunity to do the research. To live in another country. To meet all the people that you'll meet in that country. To have a year when you can just explore without being graded, when you can try new projects without any pressure to produce something, when you can test out whether you want to be a graduate student and experience the workload that you'll have in graduate school.

To make it the rich experience that Fulbright really has the potential to be, one has to look at it as more than a line on a CV and really approach it as an opportunity.

Lilith Dornhuber deBellesiles
Research Fulbright to Germany
Philosophy

I don't know if anyone else would admit this, but I designed my project for the purpose of earning a Fulbright. I did not have a project in mind that I thought would be super cool and exciting that I wanted to get funded. I sort of put the cart before the horse in that I was mostly interested in the CV-boost that would come from having one of these types of awards. This is a personal failing, and I don't lay this on anyone but myself, but I feel like it's instructive if it keeps anybody else from having the same experience.

I have often heard people say, "If you really want one of these prestigious awards like the Fulbright, find something that you're passionate about. Find something that you really deeply care about and that will shine through in your application and you will get funded." I did have a project that I thought would be pretty cool to do, but I wasn't really invested in it. I proposed it and I guess I wrote convincingly enough about it that I received the award. But because I wasn't strongly invested in my project in the first place, I didn't think as creatively as maybe I should have when things started to go to pot right off the bat in my host country. I didn't explore as many other options as perhaps I should have to help me get to the same place.

I don't think the only way you can earn a Fulbright is if you've found your passion and your heart's desire, but I do think that if you're going to go after it for the sort of cynical reason that I went after it, then it behooves you to do a little bit more thinking up front about how you're going to deal with the obstacles that come up.

Tim Slade
Research Fulbright to Benin
Public Health

Managing your expectations:
What *not* to expect from a Fulbright Scholarship

_____ **Close supervision and hand-holding**

Fulbright goes to great lengths to select applicants who are mature and resourceful enough to pursue their work independently. This is not a study-abroad program: Fulbright Scholars are left largely to their own devices to pursue their work. If the idea of having to arrange your own housing in a foreign country paralyzes you with fear, you might reconsider whether the Fulbright Program is right for you. Finding housing, after all, is the easy part.

_____ **Guaranteed mentorship**

Some Fulbrighters are successful in forging close relationships with a professor or adviser in their host country who is helpful in guiding their work, but many are not. Plan on being the primary engine behind your research project. Reach out to your adviser, host affiliation, and fellow teachers, but don't expect them to move your project or your teaching work along for you. If you need deadlines, set them yourself. This lack of supervision might seem daunting at first, but most Fulbrighters find that the freedom it allows is well worth the trade.

_____ **A competitive salary**

Accept the fact that you will not be making as much money as your peers back home. In fact, you will probably not be making much more than you spend each month overseas. If money is your chief concern, the Fulbright Program is probably not for you.

_____ **Guaranteed language fluency**

Many Fulbrighters come home from their year abroad asking themselves why they don't speak the language of their host country more fluently after so many months living there. The hard truth is that an immersion environment alone does not lead to fluency in a foreign language, especially if your starting proficiency is less than advanced. If your goal is to speak the language well, you must do two things: study every day and avoid hanging out with other English-speakers.

_____ **A guaranteed job when you return home**

There is often an expectation among Fulbrighters that their grant experience will translate into immediate professional advancement. After such an intense intellectual experience, how could it not? Ironically, the most successful and productive Fulbrighters are often too busy to search for work while on their grants.

I expected a little more structure, which is something I should have given myself. That was probably an unreasonable expectation. My adviser and I didn't have as many meetings as I expected. There wasn't the checking in that I expected. That's not to say that the people at the Fulbright Commission weren't fantastically supportive. When I was unsure of whether I could abandon my supervisor and switch topics, the country leader—and he really was wonderful—he sent me daily e-mails when I was going through that process and asked, "Have you made your decision?" Or, "How is it going?" So when you reach out to Fulbright, they are there and they are supportive and they are wonderfully generous. But they're not going to take that first step, which is probably good for some students who need to do it on their own. It's not what I was expecting.

Lilith Dornhuber deBellesiles
Research Fulbright to Germany
Philosophy

It's really easy to get sucked into being lonely and focusing too much on the cultural and language differences. "I miss my family." Or, "I can't go to this party because I have to talk to my boyfriend tonight." I've known Fulbrighters who have done that, who sat at home and talked to their boyfriend back in the U.S. and weren't taking full advantage of things. I would say you shouldn't necessarily apply for a Fulbright if you're the type of person who needs a lot of hand-holding. Of course it really depends who you are and what stage you're at in your life.

Hannah Halder
ETA Fulbright to Romania

I think certain people have the expectation that a Fulbright Scholarship is going to get you into better jobs and is going to put you so far above the rest that you'll be set for life. I don't believe that's true, actually. You do become part of this great community and the Fulbright experience is something you share with people from many other fields, but it's not a professional development program. It's not aimed at getting you a better job. If you go on a Fulbright with those expectations, you're going to be disappointed.

I do think that in academia having a Fulbright on your résumé is a very strong thing, but in the corporate world most people don't know what a Fulbright is. And if all you have going for you is a Fulbright, it's not going to be enough to get a job. You still have to have the skills and relevant experience necessary to get that job. The Fulbright is definitely an advantage, but it's not the end-all, be-all of your life. And it shouldn't be.

The Fulbright was a very enriching experience for me. And I do think that it gave me some professional skills that are useful as well, but that's in the bigger context of other things that I've done and other opportunities that I've pursued. They all work together.

Natalia Ksiezyk
ETA Fulbright to Argentina

I think that a really good tip for someone preparing to go do a Fulbright is to think about learning in the broadest sense. You have to recognize that you can learn in so many different directions, and it's not just about the specifics of your project. Have that as your focal point, but also be able to imagine and creatively engage other aspects of the place that you're at and learn from it. I walked away from the Fulbright feeling like I could create my own questions about life and the world, and then figure out how to begin to address those questions. You're sort of set up to think about the world on your own.

Blake Scott
Research Fulbright to Panama
History

Strong reasons to apply for a Fulbright:

___ You are passionate about your field

___ You want to expand your proficiency in a foreign language in a practical context

___ You want to serve your country and help make the world a better place

___ You want to develop relationships with international colleagues in your field

___ You want to strengthen your leadership skills

___ You want to teach

___ You are interested in the ideas of civic engagement and social entrepreneurship

___ You are interested in expanding your work internationally

___ You have a professional or academic interest in a specific region of the world that you would like to develop further

___ You believe in the power of community and in giving back

___ You have a great idea for an overseas project

___ You are interested in representing the United States overseas

Weak reasons to apply for a Fulbright:

___ You've wanted a Fulbright scholarship since you were in high school

___ It will look good on your résumé

___ You think it's a great way to get paid to travel the world

___ Mom and Dad will be proud

___ You think it will give you a chance to figure out what you want in life without looking like you don't know

___ "It's free money."

___ "It will let me do whatever I want."

___ It will let you spend time with friends or family who live overseas

___ It will help you get into graduate school

___ "It beats flipping burgers for a year."

Chapter 2

The Habits of Successful Fulbrighters

Twenty years from now you will be more disappointed by the things you didn't do than by the ones you did do. So throw off the bow-lines. Sail away from the safe harbor. Catch the trade winds in your sails. Explore. Dream. Discover.

Mark Twain

Fulbrighters are by and large a driven and intelligent bunch. It comes as no surprise that so many Fulbright projects—from transcribing Taiwanese folk songs to teaching English in rural Vietnam—are inspiring in their scale, resourcefulness, and impact. But even among Fulbrighters there exists a small group of grantees who enjoy exceptional success in what seems like every aspect of their lives overseas—professionally, linguistically, socially, and academically. People, projects, and opportunities seem to constantly seek them out, and they often assume leadership positions in whatever they do. The number and impact of their projects are inspiring, and the influence of their work and relationships frequently catapults them onto a career track whose momentum continues long after they return home. These Fulbrighters seem, at first glance, like the beneficiaries of incredibly good fortune.

In reality, luck has little to do with their success. Or, put differently, they manufacture their own luck, partially through hard work and preparation, but also through the philosophy by which they pursue their goals. These Fulbrighters often embrace a common set of strategies in managing their Fulbright experience. These strategies help create a positive, inclusive, and fundamentally productive relationship between their work, their lives overseas, and the communities they interact with. This relationship lies at the heart of the Fulbright experience.

These strategies are not unique to Fulbrighters: They are present to some degree in every instance of great innovation and achievement in history. But what makes them so valuable in the Fulbright context is that they so directly support the program's mission and methodology. They help Fulbrighters build relationships, seek out positive opportunities in challenging circumstances, and remove the ceiling on what is possible to achieve.

These strategies can positively influence every aspect of your Fulbright application and overseas experience. They can influence the type of research, teaching, or study you propose; the side projects you initiate; and how you invest your free time. For most people, learning to incorporate them consistently takes time, but the decision to begin doing so can happen right now. Study these strategies. Embrace them, as they will pay spectacular dividends in your Fulbright work and far beyond.

The Habits of Successful Fulbrighters

1. Dream big

Many grantees are surprised to learn just how few limits there are on what a Fulbright Scholar can achieve while overseas. Making the most of this opportunity, however, requires that you allow yourself to dream big about what's possible and then be fearless in pursuit of your goals. When it comes to transforming ideas into action, it is vision, confidence in your abilities, and a willingness to dive in that guide the most successful Fulbrighters.

When we consider our goals and what we are capable of achieving, we are often our own worst enemy. How often have you talked yourself out of a good project idea by focusing on challenges that might get in the way? This reaction is natural, but it often asphyxiates ideas before they get the chance to thrive. Fear is almost always our biggest obstacle, and learning how to overcome it is the first step in letting yourself dream beyond what you think is possible. First think about what you want to accomplish— *then* worry about how to get it done.

If you are passionate about forestry and interested in the cultures of Central Asia, allow yourself to visualize your dream job in that field. Is it managing the regional offices of an environmental organization in Kazakhstan? Teaching forestry conservation at a university in Bishkek? Writing the field's authoritative guide on Central Asian flora? A Fulbright Scholarship could help you take important steps toward these goals. It could enable you to study endangered tree species in Kyrgyzstan, track deforestation trends in central Russia, or document evolving perceptions of conservation on the Mongolian steppe. For candidates with the right motivation and experience, Fulbright is designed to make projects like these happen. Dream big, plan ahead, and explore how the Fulbright Program can help you get there.

I've talked to other Fulbrighters about their projects and I don't think they set their goals high enough. They come in thinking, "I'm only here for a year. I'm just a recent college graduate. I don't really know anything. There's nothing I can really do." They settle for the convenience that everything's just too complicated to get anything done. I think this is what is limiting not just a lot of Fulbright Scholars, but a lot of people in general. They need to figure out not just what's good enough, but what is ideal, and then go for it. If you set your goals higher, you will end up higher than if you settled for mediocrity.

With the Fulbright you have almost a full year, but only a year. You get funding to do basically whatever you want. That's why people apply for the Fulbright, so they can do a project that they really believe in. That kind of opportunity is extremely rare. Don't set a glass ceiling for yourself.

Jared Sun
Research Fulbright to South Africa
Public Health

2. Take action, take initiative

The main factor that separates those who accomplish great things from those who don't is not education, training, wealth, or privilege, but rather the courage to act on your ideas. Making the jump from theorizing to putting an idea into practice is often the most difficult part of any project. The Fulbright Program excels at helping grantees make this leap.

Any project worth doing will involve risk, and the more ambitious your goals, the more intimidating these risks may seem. But a Fulbright grant doesn't just open doors, it invites leadership and action from grantees. Rarely in your career will you have so much opportunity to act on your ideas. If you want to organize an international environmental conference while overseas, organize one. If you want to plan a trip to study wine-making in a remote mountain village, plan it. If you want to interview the Minister of Energy in your host country, ask your Fulbright Commission how you can make this happen. With Fulbright's reputation and resources, and enough polite persistence, you can get a meeting with just about anyone.

There is a vast difference between dreaming and doing. Dreaming is safe and comfortable, while doing requires the courage to take risks, overcome our fears of failure, and venture into the unknown. Never underestimate your abilities or the capacity of the Fulbright program to help you reach your goals. To act on a big idea requires risking failure, but not acting on it guarantees defeat.

This is never going to happen again, so seize the moment. At least, that's what I kept trying to remind myself. I'm never going to have the opportunity again to do 100 percent outreach for a week if I want, and then 100 percent research the next. It's just not going to be like that ever again. I'd remind myself of that, and that even though I often felt like I hadn't done a lot, that really I had.

I did a really good job of keeping a field notebook. Every day I wrote just a little bit about what I did. Whenever I thought, "Oh my God, it's been eight months and I can't believe it's gone by so fast! I haven't done anything!" I'd look back and say, "Wait a minute. Actually, I did do a lot."

The freedom Fulbright gives us is an asset. It is absolutely the main advantage of the Fulbright Program. But I had to teach myself how to give myself more self-affirmation than I usually do. With less structure, you have to remind yourself that, yes, you are doing a lot.

Maya deVries
Research Fulbrighter to Panama
Biology

You will always miss 100 percent of the shots you don't take.

Wayne Gretzky

3. Don't wait for permission

Most people who change the world do it by doing things differently. Charlie Parker and Thelonious Monk broke the harmonic rules of jazz and redefined the genre. Einstein, Galileo, and nearly every great scientist in history questioned the infallibility of established belief. Big ideas aren't just helped by breaking the rules, they require it.

The freedom to innovate and improvise is one of the biggest gifts of a Fulbright Scholarship and one of the main reasons Fulbrighters accomplish so much. As long as your motives are honorable and your methods hurt no one, never wait for permission to act on your ideas. If somebody takes issue with what you've done, you can apologize later, but chances are you will never need to.

There will always be someone telling you that you can't or shouldn't push ahead with your vision, and the bigger your ideas are, the more resistance you will encounter. The best response is to smile, thank them for their feedback, and then push their doubts aside. Conventional wisdom is just that—conventional. It rarely leads to innovation. Moving forward with a good idea could define what convention looks like tomorrow, and then no one will care that you broke the rules.

The Fulbright Program wants you and your work to succeed. Many Fulbrighters who are nervous about the grant's official rules are surprised to find out just how supportive their host country's Fulbright Commission can be. As long as you remain a responsible ambassador, nobody is going to take your grant away for doing your job well. They might even offer to help. History shows that fortune favors the bold.

I planned to examine the effects of secondary school reform in Georgia. When I arrived I was hoping to look at a large selection of schools, speak with lots of people, and observe classes. For the first six months, nothing at all happened because I was working on securing permission to go into schools and interview professionals. In the end I got the runaround from the Ministry of Education.

Then I thought, "Maybe working through the ministry is not the way to go here. I just need to show up and gate-crash." In the end, that's what we decided to do. We would just show up at schools and say, "This is who we are, this is what we're doing, and we would like to speak with you and your colleagues." We always had someone who could introduce us to the school director. In the end, that's the model that worked, just going to schools directly. I should have come to that conclusion earlier.

Nic Wondra
Research Fulbright to Georgia
Political Science

I said yes to any opportunity that came up. As much as I possibly could, anyway. I was just so thrilled to get this opportunity. I'm going to do everything. Everything from going to Carnival, which is a big thing in Panama, to saying yes to helping my host institution organize a recycling program. I would just do it. It was a way that I could learn the culture, meet my goals and the goals of the Fulbright Program, and help out in a couple communities that I had fostered strong connections with.

Maya deVries
Research Fulbright to Panama
Biology

4. Embrace failure

Failure is amazing. It feels like crap when it's happening, and I was definitely down in the dumps many, many times during my Fulbright, but when I look back on it I learned so many things. I learned from a lot of mistakes that I will never repeat. I learned by doing. I put myself out there and looked like an idiot so many times, and did things I normally wouldn't do. I was the only person there. I didn't have someone to rely on like in the U.S. I couldn't Wikipedia something when I was in the middle of this rural community. I had to improvise and go outside my personal boundaries, my technical skills, and my formal training. That's a unique experience that you will never get in the United States. It's a unique experience and I feel very grateful for it. Fulbright was kind of a testing ground for my personal skills and my social skills.

Matt Wesley
Research Fulbright to Nicaragua
Public Health

In philosophy, every time someone points out a fallacy in your argument you learn how to build a better argument. Failure is an important learning tool, which is why Fulbright is such a great opportunity. You are going to fail again and again, living in a different place, speaking a different language, embarking on a research project that may not have a lot of support.

Even when learning a language, having people laugh at your attempts is invaluable. It helps you admit that, yes, you are failing every minute in that language, but that's not a reason to stop. The laughter tells you that you're using the language incorrectly, and you can use that failure to learn.

Lilith Dornhuber deBellesiles
Research Fulbright to Germany
Philosophy

Fulbrighters tend to be overachievers by nature and many aren't accustomed to the idea of failure as a stepping stone to success. The stigma surrounding the idea of failure is so pronounced in our society that it's easy to lose sight of its incredible value. Success doesn't come from avoiding failure; success comes from failing at bigger and bigger things.

The career of every great athlete, inventor, author, and statesman—of every great visionary and leader in history—has been built on failure. Babe Ruth retired with a record 1,330 career strikeouts. Steven Spielberg was twice rejected from the University of Southern California's film school before enrolling elsewhere. Michael Jordan, one of the greatest basketball players of all time, was cut from his high school team. "I have missed more than 9,000 shots in my career," he later said. "I have lost almost 300 games. On 26 occasions I have been entrusted to take the game winning shot and I missed. I have failed over and over and over again in my life. And that is why I succeed."

Failure is how we grow, how we develop as leaders, and how we become true experts in our field. The trick is to learn to fail forward, to push through disappointment and study where you went wrong. If you let it, failure will allow you to grow strong from your defeats. Experience is the name we give our mistakes.

There will never be a better time to fail than during your Fulbright grant. Thousands of miles from home, far removed from the judgment of peers, and responsible to no one but yourself for the success of your work, as a Fulbrighter you have a rare opportunity to make spectacular mistakes. Seize it. You will never have another chance to fail so magnificently with so few consequences. If during your Fulbright you discover that you're not consistently failing, it's a sure sign that you're not reaching far enough.

Would you like me to give you a formula for success? It's quite simple, really. Double your rate of failure.

Thomas J. Watson, Jr.

I saw it as part of my role as a Fulbright English teacher to not just sit around and wait for someone to tell me what to do, but to come up with ideas and work with the resources I had, or that I knew the institution had, to make something out of it. I created a professional communication course that focused on communication at work and in the grant application process. It started with résumé writing, cover letters, and interviews. I also administered a Myers–Briggs personality assessment. It was a comprehensive hands-on course that helped students understand what an application process in the U.S. might look like.

As a Fulbrighter you have to take a lot of initiative and be a self-starter. If you just rely on the host institution to plug you in and tell you what to do, you're going to miss out on a lot.

Natalia Ksiezyk
ETA Fulbright to Argentina

Everybody was happy to say they would help me in terms of meeting with me and letting me interview them, but I really had to follow up on that, to stay on it. I just learned not to take no for an answer. I didn't have a hard time calling people two, three, or four times. Or just showing up, because that seemed to be the most effective way to get what I needed. Sometimes I would just go to their office and hang out, or talk to their secretary and find out when they would be around. In the meantime I also tried to find other people who knew them, to see if I could get to them through other people. Trying to figure out if there was any way I could come in face-to-face contact with them. That was really the most effective way to get things accomplished.

Renee Brown
Research Fulbright to Croatia
Political Science

If you want to go fast, go alone.
If you want to go far, go with others.

Ancient African proverb

5. Reach out

No one has ever succeeded in changing the world by themselves. Simply put, the deeper and more collaborative your connections are with others, the more rewarding and productive your Fulbright pursuits will be. Successful collaboration is powerful because it often leads to results that are greater than the sum of their parts. Two heads brainstorming equals more than twice the brainpower. The amount of input, support, and resources at your disposal as a Fulbrighter will increase exponentially as your relationships grow.

For a program steeped so heavily in community and exchange, Fulbright attracts remarkably independent-minded applicants. Fiercely resourceful and self-sufficient, many Fulbrighters fall into the trap of believing these qualities are all that's necessary to succeed in their Fulbright work. But the myth of the lone genius is just that: a myth. Working alone may seem faster or more productive, but avoiding opportunities to share your life and your work inevitably limits what you can accomplish and how much of your experience you are able to enjoy. Resourcefulness and resilience don't preclude collaboration, they empower it.

But strong relationships do not form by themselves overnight. It takes initiative and patience to cultivate the mutual trust and understanding they require. Don't wait for these connections to come to you: Seek out and nurture new relationships. Embrace these opportunities with passion both within and outside of your Fulbright work, because there is no surer way to make the most of your time abroad.

What I wish I had done more of—and this would have helped add structure and deal with the stress of worrying about the project—was I wish I had asked for help more often. People in Armenia are so nice and they want to help you. They were always offering to help, but I felt bad taking their help. In America people offer their help but don't always mean it. It's more of a polite thing. I wish I had just not worried about what they were thinking and taken them up on their offer.

Fulbright is billed as this independent program and I felt that if I was asking for help, then I wasn't doing it on my own. But that's silly. I probably would have gotten more done if I had approached people for things. And I know they would have helped. They would have done it in a second.

Ashley Killough
Research Fulbright to Armenia
Journalism

Never say no when someone invites you somewhere, or invites you over to their house for a meal. My philosophy was to say yes even if I didn't know someone very well, even if I just met them.

One of the secretaries at the university called me and wanted me to talk to her nephew who is Romanian but had lived in Chicago for the last few years. She wanted me to meet with him. I thought, "I don't know why I'm meeting with this kid. But sure, I'll talk to him." I ended up making so many connections and having an amazing afternoon in the mountains with a Romanian family. These types of experiences come from taking chances and leaps of faith. You don't know who you're going to meet, or the type of people you're going to talk to. It's easy to get caught up a lot being in academia, if you're based at a university, and you forget to get out of that bubble sometimes. It's important to take the academic side seriously, but you're not only an academic. You're there for the cultural experience as well. You're going to lose out on a lot if you only focus on just one or the other.

Hannah Halder
ETA Fulbright to Romania

When your Fulbright project is collaborative and you work with a broader group of people, or more closely with a smaller group of people, it fulfills both your project goals and the goals of the cultural ambassador experience. You learn more about the culture, about the people, about true everyday life when you're working with someone and exchanging ideas. If you treat it as an equal exchange where you both have something to bring to the table, then you can have the fulfillment of both sides being rewarded.

I learned while I was there that the more I asked for help and the more I reached out to other people, the more willing they were to share information, and the more ideas I got for my project. The more you explore the ideas of the people around you, whether you use them or not, the more opportunities you will have to expand your work and make it more meaningful.

Heather Wakefield
Research Fulbright to Georgia
Library Sciences

Know what you want to get out of the Fulbright before you go in. The situations vary from country to country, but you need to have enough initiative on your own to make it successful. No one is going to hold your hand. You have to go do what you need to do. Be determined. Not aggressive, but determined. You need to have the wherewithal to roll with the punches and make it happen.

Courtney Doggart
Research Fulbright to Turkey
International Relations

Setting up a new emergency response system in South Africa

Jared Sun
Research Fulbright to South Africa
Public Health

The project I was working on was an extension of something I had been working on my junior year in college when I was overseas in Cape Town. I was in one of the townships and we were getting a tour of the Amy Biehl Foundation site. Being interested in emergency medicine, I asked, "Well, what happens when someone gets beaten or stabbed or shot in the townships?" The guy giving us the tour said that nothing really happens because the ambulance takes too long to show up. It's kind of a mess. People don't really know what's going on. I had been one of the teaching assistants at an EMT training course at Stanford, and hearing him say that gave me the idea to start teaching people in the townships emergency first aid skills. So that when they see someone shot or stabbed in front of them they don't just have to turn their heads because they think there's nothing they can do. So I started teaching them, and I proposed to continue that for my Fulbright project.

South Africa is very bureaucratic in the sense that they always want you to go through certain offices to get something done. I realized that to get anything done I just had to do it on my own and apologize later. It took a lot of entrepreneurship. I really had to trick myself into the sense that I could do anything, and I had to do whatever it took to get it done. My project was quite ambitious: setting up an entirely new layer of the emergency medical system in a year. Not only was I not a doctor, but I was only 22 at the time. I would literally sit in

meetings where head doctors would look at me and say, "I don't think you can do this." And I would have to stand my ground: "I will do it. I can do it." They would say things like, "If this is something that was worth doing it would already have been done." And I said, "I think that's why it hasn't been done yet, and I'm here to do it." I really had to tell myself to always just keep trying to do what was necessary for the people I was trying to serve.

The Fulbright for me was a springboard to jump into this field. Because of the Fulbright, people recognize me for my work. Ever since I've been back I've been contacted by people from organizations in other countries. "We heard that you did this in Cape Town. Would you be willing to help us do something similar?" A team of doctors from Tufts asked me if I could help them do something in Haiti. Some other public health researchers want to do something in Guatemala. The head of emergency medicine for Ghana asked me if I could help him replicate there what I did in South Africa. Not only have I already created a niche for myself, but because I'm young, people see that I'm in this for the long haul. The Fulbright opened doors for me. It basically was an investment. I will take everything I learned on the Fulbright and use it for the rest of my life to keep giving back to society in this way that I think I'm good at, which is working in international emergency medical systems.

6. Go in with a plan

Success, the old adage tells us, is what happens when preparation meets opportunity. The Fulbright Program gives grantees such spectacular opportunities that it is difficult to overestimate the value of preparation. Planning allows you to refine your goals, optimize your methods, and gain perspective on the best path to your objective. The most influential Fulbright projects are planned meticulously beforehand. Some of the most committed candidates even travel to their host countries before applying to scout things out and lay the groundwork for their Fulbright. Thorough preparation pays dividends once projects are underway, because you can never fully make up for insufficient preparation once you're in the field.

But a plan is only valuable if you are willing to adapt when circumstances change, which is inevitable. This evolution is a normal part of fieldwork. All plans require change once they're put into action. How flexible you are in adapting your plans to new conditions is what will define their success. And remember, this is how ideas and projects grow. If your plans are not challenged at all, you're probably not reaching far enough.

But what about the value of *not* planning? About learning to let go, to improvise, and to trust your instincts? Despite what many believe, preparation doesn't preclude improvisation—it empowers you to improvise productively. Your abilities to plan and improvise will work in concert to keep you and your work on track. The best plans anticipate change and prepare you to be creative in how you adapt.

In preparing for battle I have always found that plans are useless, but planning is indispensable.

Dwight D. Eisenhower

Another thing that was really helpful for me was that I actually went to Panama while I was writing the application. Coincidentally, my mom had some business down there and I was able to stay in a hotel with her. It was totally worth my time and effort to go to Panama. I hadn't been there before and I was able to visualize what my project would be a little better. I was able to meet with the person who was writing my letter of affiliation and even make some contacts that were helpful when I came back to Panama. If you have the opportunity to visit your host country beforehand, I would definitely recommend doing that. Meet with the person you want to write the letter of affiliation.

Rose Cromwell
Research Fulbright to Panama
Photography

We make a living by what we get. We make a life by what we give.

Winston Churchill

7. Pay it forward

The Fulbright Program attracts applicants who are committed not only to their work, but also to the idea of making a lasting contribution to the world around them. The idea of giving back to one's community is a key element of the Fulbright experience. Many of the most successful Fulbrighters, however, take this idea to the next level. They ask not only how their contributions can benefit the community, but also how these contributions can continue to benefit the community long after they leave their host country. They reach for sustainability. They seek ways to *pay forward* the opportunities Fulbright has given them.

That's great, but isn't there more?

GIVING BACK

PAYING IT FORWARD!

Yeah!

Chapter 3

What You Should Know about Fulbright Before You Apply

The big question is whether you are going to be able to say a hearty Yes to your adventure.

Joseph Conrad

The strongest Fulbright applications often come from candidates who view the Fulbright Scholarship as a means to an end, not as an end in itself. The grant can be a powerful tool for achieving your goals, but only if you have an idea of what those goals are. How do they fit into the larger framework of your career? How do they contribute to Fulbright's mission of exchange? The Fulbright Program wants to invest in tomorrow's leaders, and the farther you can see beyond your Fulbright Scholarship, the stronger your application and overseas experience will be.

If you approach it properly, the application process can be an important tool to help refine your plans and build a support community around your Fulbright work. Many elements of the application process—letters of recommendation, letters of support from organizations in your host country, language evaluations—are opportunities to develop the foundation of your Fulbright community in very real and powerful ways. Never underestimate how central the ideas of community, collaboration, and exchange are to the Fulbright experience.

For some candidates the application process is complicated by misunderstanding the Fulbright grant as a reward. They see it as a prize for one's professional and academic achievements to date. What these candidates overlook is that a Fulbright Scholarship is more about your future than your past. What you aim to accomplish with the grant is often more important to application readers than what you have already done. Your qualifications are important, but strong vision combined with solid research and a realistic blueprint for your project are the hallmarks of a successful Fulbright candidacy. Identifying your goals is the single most important Fulbright research you will ever undertake.

Serious Fulbright applications are built on serious preparation

I don't really understand how people can develop a strong proposal without visiting the country. If you can afford to do it, or if you can get funding through your university, I recommend going to the place you're applying to the summer before you apply. Go there and check it out. Build relationships. The people who will end up writing your letter of support, the affiliation letter, will see that you went to the country, that you care about the project, and that you're really dedicated to seeing it though. I went down in August and December the year before and developed a relationship with the NGO I would be working with. So when I started my Fulbright I wasn't learning the ropes. I wasn't spending all my time getting acquainted with the country.

I know people that got the Fulbright who had just spoken over the phone beforehand with their affiliate organization in their host country. That's fine, but it's not the same. You need to go and see it and get a feel for it. If you don't visit the country or the site before you go, you might end up not liking it. That would be unfortunate.

Matt Wesley
Research Fulbright to Nicaragua
Public Health

We've all heard about Fulbright Scholars having incredible adventures in remote reaches of the globe. These achievements make great stories, but the truth is that successes like these are built on months or even years of meticulous preparation. Research and groundwork make the difference between mediocre projects and life-changing experiences with Fulbright. Time spent on preparation before departure can save you weeks or months once your project is in motion. The flexibility that results from planning is what allows projects to adapt and to persevere, because circumstances in the field are never exactly what we expect.

Many applicants fall into the trap of focusing too much energy on selling themselves to Fulbright and not enough on preparing for their time overseas. "If I can just get the grant," they tell themselves, "*then* I'll have time to figure out a way to make it work." This strategy may seem sound in theory, but the reality is otherwise. To get the most out of Fulbright opportunities you must first get the most out of the application process.

If you allow it, the application can be a powerful tool to prepare you for your Fulbright experience. It's one thing to propose living with a jungle tribe while you research flora changes in the Brazilian Amazon, but laying the groundwork needed to make that happen is a different story. A strong applicant would contact organizations in the region early on to see whether this kind of living arrangement is possible. They would find out who can help organize it and what challenges they should plan for. If this sounds like a difficult phone call to make with someone you don't know in a language you may not be fluent in, you're right. It is. But this kind of initiative separates strong applications from weak ones, and rewarding Fulbright experiences from those that could have been more.

Many Fulbright alumni who feel that they could have gotten more out of their time overseas regret not committing more time and energy to preparing for the experience. Their hindsight emphasizes an important lesson: Your application is more an opportunity to plan your Fulbright experience than an exercise in salesmanship. If you prepare well, your qualifications, groundwork, and enthusiasm will show through in your application. If you don't, you will spend your energy trying to hide your lack of preparation instead of doing what's necessary to take advantage of the opportunities Fulbright offers. Applying for and preparing for your grant should be part of the same process. In fact, the application *is* your preparation. Thorough planning, more than any other factor, defines the strength of your application.

Your application strategy

As tempting as it is to get started right away, don't dive into the application process and hope to figure things out as you move through it. Take the time to make a schedule and a plan—it will save you countless hours of work. Use the following strategies to apply structure, style, and consistency to your application. They will help ensure that each element fits as seamlessly as possible with the rest of your materials.

1. Start early, start often

The application process is a marathon, not a sprint. Those who sustain a steady flow of attention to their application over many months will submit far stronger applications than those who wait until the final weeks. Applications thrown together at the last minute—even those with perfect spelling and grammar—have a way of feeling rushed. Application readers have a knack for spotting this a mile away.

Good ideas take time to mature. What seemed like a brilliant idea last month may be completely infeasible today. This process of revision is a normal, healthy part of any serious candidacy. Some Fulbright applicants are content to put in a minimum amount of last-minute effort and take their chances on a long shot. By contrast, serious candidates understand that the strongest applications are the product of months, and sometimes years, of work.

2. Treat it as a proposal, not an application

Despite what the name suggests, the Fulbright application is a proposal. Like all good proposals, it must answer five basic questions:

1. What is your goal?
2. What is your plan for achieving your goal?
3. What are your qualifications?
4. Why should we care about what you are proposing?
5. How will your work further Fulbright's mission?

Definitely do not wait until the last minute. Applying for a Fulbright takes time. Even before I began the application process I would go to information sessions on campus and hear that you should be preparing your essays at least a year in advance. I thought, "Wow, that seems like a lot of time to get an application together." But as I was going through the process I realized why that recommendation was given. It takes time to be able to express yourself in the Personal Statement essay, and then to write about your actual research proposal in two single-spaced pages. That's just not a lot of space to concisely and eloquently talk about yourself and why you would be great as a Fulbrighter. And to describe your research project, why it's important, whether anything like this has been done before, what the timeline is, and what methods you will use.

It really takes time to be able to start out with just an idea in your head and get to a finished proposal. What that means is a lot of revisions and having a lot of people look at your essays to give you feedback. And reworking the essays again and again. And that's why giving yourself plenty of time from the beginning is so important in that process.

Tiffany Joseph
Research Fulbright to Brazil
Sociology

I really saw the proposal as a chance to get other people as excited about my project as I was. That might be something that's more particular for people who are in the arts. I think it's important to argue for the necessity of your project, especially when other people are applying for projects in urban planning, public health, and other fields that may seem much more socially useful. I knew that what I had to do was win people over and show them what moved me about what I wanted to write. If you don't capture that sense of excitement, or a sense of the broad insight that you're hoping to gain, or the joy of exploration . . . you have to capture that in your essay. It can't just be, "This is what I want to find out and this is how I'm going to find it out."

I think that people who are reviewing these applications are fully conscious of the fact that whatever field you're applying in, your questions are going to change and your research is not going to end up being what you thought it was going to be. The situation is going to change daily when you're living abroad. You can't really count on anything panning out the way you hoped that it would. And this is even more relevant when you're talking about a creative project. It's important to captivate people with your project, not just argue for the importance of what you're going to find out.

Deanna Fei
Research Fulbright to China
Creative Writing

Your answers to these questions should be crystal clear in your application materials, particularly in your essays. When friends ask, you should be able answer each of these questions in one sentence or less. If your goals, methods, or qualifications aren't clear to application readers, it is unlikely you will be selected for the Fulbright Program.

3. Keep it simple

Most good ideas appear simple in their final design. This is not by chance. Simplicity allows people to access your ideas, and the more accessible your ideas are in your application, the more attractive they will be to your readers. If you propose to research a complex subset of string theory at a laboratory in France, one of your biggest application challenges will be to reduce the essence of your work to concepts that laymen can both understand and appreciate. Assume that most of your application readers do not have experience in your field. They will be educated, intelligent people, but you must write so that the layperson can grasp your proposal.

4. Get your readers excited about what you propose

There are a small number of Fulbright proposals that application readers know instantly they will recommend for selection. These applications reflect a kind of easy harmony, a perfect fit between the candidate's goals, their qualifications, the project details, and the objectives of the Fulbright Program. More importantly, they reflect the candidate's genuine excitement for their work, and this kind of excitement is infectious.

Selection committees know that Fulbrighters who are truly passionate about their work are less likely to get bogged down by adversity. They are less inclined to throw in the towel when their host organization suddenly closes for lack of funding, when they are asked to develop a school's entire English-language curriculum, or when an armed conflict requires that they evacuate the country. (These have all happened.) People who are driven by their ideas don't quit—they persevere. This determination is a very attractive quality in a Fulbright candidate.

If you are on the fence about the Fulbright work that you propose, stop now and take the time to develop it into something that excites you, or find a new idea that will. Fulbright is too valuable an opportunity to waste on something you're not excited about.

5. Be specific

A certain amount of big-picture idealism in your application is healthy, but only if it's backed up with specific, practical details about what you propose. Your application essays should leave no questions about the "who, what, when, where, why, and how" of your Fulbright.

It's tempting to hide behind vague but important-sounding descriptions of your work to mask a lack of planning, but this won't fool your application readers. If you plan to produce a documentary film about Laotian youth culture that you hope will change how society views that community, tell us what specific issues or questions you plan to address. Will you be shooting interviews? If so, how many and with whom? How will you find subjects? What is your production schedule? What is your distribution plan? What kind of equipment will you need? Listing details like these isn't as sexy as waxing eloquent about cinema as an engine of social change, but your application will be stronger. You can adapt your project to circumstances on the ground once you arrive in your host country—indeed, you will be required to—but you still need a detailed plan. When in doubt, err on the side of providing too much detail.

6. Build a support community around your Fulbright

Successful Fulbright applications are never the product of the candidate's efforts alone. They include contributions from a team of advisers: area experts, language specialists, academic mentors, campus Fulbright advisers, recommendation writers, proofreaders—the list could go on and on. Every person you talk to, consult, ask for advice, and brainstorm with about your Fulbright application has the potential to be a member of your Fulbright community, but only if you choose to nurture these relationships. The community you build throughout your Fulbright is one of the most valuable assets you will take away from the Fulbright experience.

If you recognize its potential, the application process can be an excellent tool to build your Fulbright support community. When you ask someone for a letter

I agree with the general piece of advice that the more planning you do the better your experience will be. And I think that goes for any grant application. The Fulbright committee wants to see projects that are very well thought-out and contain details and specifics.

Natalia Ksiezyk
ETA Fulbright to Argentina

I was very lucky because I was still in school when I applied and had a great adviser who worked very hard with me. The hardest part for me was the host affiliation.

Just start early. I started thinking about the application more than a year before it was due. I started networking and looking for host affiliation about ten months before it was due. That's the key, starting early.

Ashley Killough
Research Fulbright to Armenia
Journalism

For me the application was manageable because I could draw from other grant applications I had written in the past. But I made sure that I was discussing the goals of Fulbright. I also had to make the language a lot less scientific, and that was kind of the challenge for me. How do I fit this very esoteric topic that I've chosen for my dissertation into a broader proposal? I ended up talking about how a specific type of shrimp fit into the coral reef food web. Writing the application forced me to think about my work in new ways. That was pretty cool, actually.

Maya deVries
Research Fulbright to Panama
Biology

of recommendation or for feedback on your proposal, you aren't just asking for help with the application. You are inviting them to be part of your Fulbright experience. When they agree to help, they are investing in your project and your career.

When you encounter difficulties in the field, these are people you can turn to for advice. If you have questions about publishing your research, your academic adviser can point you in the right direction. If you are frustrated by language barriers, your language evaluator can recommend tutors or curricula. When you need career advice, the experts you consulted are already there to help. These are invaluable resources but only if you choose to grow these relationships beyond the application process.

Ideally, these advisers' input shouldn't be one-off contributions to your application. They should launch much larger, more fruitful relationships that can be resources throughout your Fulbright work overseas, and beyond. People want to be part of this experience. They want you to succeed.

7. Don't forget the Big Picture

Intense focus on a specific research question or teaching assignment is important, but be sure to take a step back and tell your readers about your work in a broader context. Why is it important? What will your Fulbright work mean for your career? Your ability to put your Fulbright proposal in the larger context of progress and development will demonstrate your leadership potential. Think of Fulbright as a means to an end: *What can Fulbright help me accomplish?*

8. Remember Fulbright's mission

Fulbright wants you to build relationships and engage communities in your host country. Your application must address how you will do this.

Don't just write that you look forward to engaging the local community in your spare time. Tell us how. Do you plan on playing sports? Volunteering for an organization that helps local women entrepreneurs? Starting a book club? An environmental club? A design collective? If you find yourself shying away from details because you don't know what's available in your host country, you need to do more research.

Some Fulbright applicants are content to put in a minimum amount of last-minute effort and take their chances on a long shot. Serious candidates, by contrast, understand the simple fact that the strongest applications are the product of months, and sometimes years, of work.

Applying through your school vs. applying "at large"

I knew the professor who worked with Fulbright applicants and I figured it would be easier to apply through the school. I definitely think it's a good decision to have a little extra support with everything application-related. They helped me make sure I had all the different moving parts of the application in place.

Lakshmi Eassey
ETA Fulbright to Germany

One of the things that benefited me most was looking at past application essays—seeing what essays were successful and using those as a model for my own. That was one of the biggest things. None were projects just like mine, but I got an idea of what kinds of outcomes Fulbright likes to see and what kinds of research methods could work.

Heather Wakefield
Research Fulbright to Georgia
Library Science

The Fulbright Program maintains a network of more than 1,200 campus Fulbright Program Advisers (FPAs) at colleges and universities across the United States. These advisers help guide candidates through the application process and shape their application materials into stronger, more Fulbright-friendly proposals. If you are a student, Fulbright encourages you to apply through your school's fellowship office. Each school goes through a campus interview and evaluation process before submitting its students' applications to Fulbright. This process helps ensure that the candidate is a good fit for the Fulbright Program.

Applicants who are not students may apply independently to Fulbright as "at-large" candidates. These candidates are not required to do a campus interview and their deadline for submitting materials is typically three to five weeks later than the institutional deadlines. Many colleges and universities allow alumni to apply through their fellowship office, even if they've been out of school for many years. Applying through your institution can be a valuable resource.

Advantages of applying through your school

- More easily accessible information about the Fulbright Program

- Access to a Fulbright Program Adviser who can help assess your competitiveness as an applicant, guide you through the application process, and provide informed feedback

- Institutional infrastructure offers better access to the alumni network, academic advisers, and research facilities

- More options to publicize your award if you are selected

- The possibility of feedback on your application through the campus interview process (some schools allow candidates a few days to incorporate interview feedback before submitting their applications to Fulbright)

Advantages of applying as an at-large candidate

- Later application deadline

- No on-campus interview requirement

- Freedom to work on your own schedule

Anatomy of a Fulbright application

Check with the Fulbright Program Adviser at your school or alma mater, or Fulbright's website, for up-to-date application requirements. Also check the Fulbright **Country Summary** for your host country before starting your application. Past applications for the traditional study/research grant and the English Teaching Assistant Program have required the following elements:

1. Online application form

2. Letters of recommendation

3. Official academic transcripts

4. Letter of host country affiliation (for study/research grants)

5. Foreign language evaluation

6. Statement of Grant Purpose essay

7. Personal Statement essay

8. Creative submission (for arts candidates)

9. Campus interview (if applying through your school or alma mater)

It was really crucial to have contacts already in place in my host country. I know the other Americans who were there would agree with me on this, that it's really difficult to get your teeth into things when you're an outsider. It helped that I had previously spent a year there working with the International Rescue Committee and volunteering at an orphanage. It was through doing that and going to an academic conference in Dubrovnik, where I was able to meet other academics, that I actually met my adviser, my mentor, and what became my host institution during my Fulbright stay. I found that being able to be on the ground for basically a year before going on my Fulbright was hugely important to my ability to carry out my project.

I was a little concerned that my previous experience would be a liability in Fulbright's eyes for my application. I don't know how they viewed it. But after having talked with a person who works at the embassy, a local person who was really in touch with the Fulbrighters, I think she really appreciated that I was going to be one less person whose hand she would have to hold. I don't know how much say she had in my acceptance to the program, but I think for her that was probably attractive.

Renee Brown
Research Fulbright to Croatia
Political Science

Project ideas for Fulbright research grant applicants

The best proposals begin with good ideas. If you come to Fulbright with a specific project in mind you're already ahead of the game. Much of your application process will involve fleshing out the details of your proposal and packaging them in a way that demonstrates your preparation and motivation for your work.

For applicants who don't yet have a specific research project in mind, now begins the process of identifying your goals and exploring possibilities. Whatever its theme or

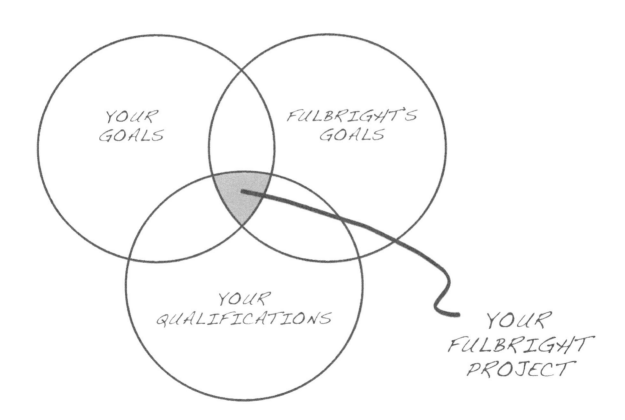

structure, your Fulbright project should be designed to meet three broad criteria:

1. The project should further Fulbright's mission of exchange within an academic, artistic, pedagogical, or social entrepreneurial context

2. The project should be realistic and feasible given your experience and language skills

3. The project should move you closer to your professional and personal leadership goals

The best way to learn what Fulbright projects look like is to research what past Fulbrighters have done. Start by speaking with your campus Fulbright Program Adviser, reading Fulbright blogs, and talking directly with recent alumni. Brainstorm ideas you are excited about. Start by asking yourself: *If I could pursue any project I wanted overseas, what would it be?*

Project development for English teaching applicants

If you are applying to the Fulbright English Teaching Assistant Program you have the advantage of already having your core project picked for you—your teaching assignment. As an ETA applicant you aren't expected to provide project details the way research applicants are. But be very explicit about why you want to teach English. Why you are you interested in teaching in your host country? Most importantly, how will you pursue your role as a cultural ambassador outside the classroom?

Many ETA candidates pursue community engagement by developing a small research or volunteer project to pursue outside their teaching work. These projects should never eclipse the importance of your teaching work in your application. That could compel Fulbright to ask why you aren't applying for a research grant. Also remember that you will have no input on the location of your teaching institution or the age of your students. In the past, Fulbright's website has offered information about the range of possible assignments for ETA Fulbrighters in specific countries.

Tips for finding your research project idea

- **Start with preliminary research**

  Do some basic topical research on the country or countries you have an interest in, particularly those places where you have proficiency in the local language. Make sure Fulbright has an active program in these places and read the **Country Summary** to learn about specific program parameters. Check Fulbright's online database to see what kinds of projects grantees have done there in the past.

- **Can you build on previous work?**

  Many candidates choose to continue previous work or an international experience that they found inspiring. Consider expanding a term paper, thesis project, or study abroad experience that resonated with you while you were in school.

- **Seek feedback on your favorite ideas**

  Choose your top three ideas and write a few sentences about each that cover the basic questions of "who, what, when, where, why, and how." Consult with your academic adviser and the Fulbright Program Adviser at your school for substantive feedback on your ideas (the FPA can tell you how good a fit it would be for Fulbright). Which projects resonate with them? Which hold the most potential? What challenges do they foresee? Much of developing a strong project idea is about learning to ask the right questions.

Frequently asked questions about Fulbright research proposals

_____ *I understand that I need to include project details in my proposal, but many of these details won't become clear until I begin work in my host country. Surely Fulbright understands this?*

If you want someone to give you money for a project, you have to show them that you know what you're doing. Fulbright understands that the trajectory of your Fulbright work will change—this is a normal part of any fieldwork—but it's important that they see that you're prepared. Don't wait until you've been selected to begin planning in earnest; it will be too late. The time to plan is during the application process, and details will lend credibility to your proposal.

_____ *I'm an artist and many of my ideas don't translate well into writing. That's why I work in a visual medium. Is it OK that the description of my project is a bit vague?*

If you're applying for an arts or performance-based research grant, it is even more important that your proposal be as specific and detailed as possible. Don't hide behind art-speak: If your ideas don't make sense to the non-artist readers who will evaluate them, your application will not be selected. Artist or not, you must find a way to write about your work. This is true for the Fulbright proposal, and it will be true for every grant proposal you complete over the course of your career.

_____ *Can I submit a proposal for a project that I will do in multiple countries?*

Fulbright allows multi-country grant applications for certain areas of the world, but these grants are rare and require considerably more work from the applicant. The candidate must justify why his or her project must be regional in nature. Multi-country applications must also be approved by each country involved, which increases the possibility of rejection. Though these grants exist, the Fulbright Program is really designed so that grantees can focus on one country.

_____ *How do I know whether my project idea is one that Fulbright would be interested in?*

The Fulbright Program Adviser at your college or university is the best source of information about what Fulbright is looking for. If you are no longer a student, contact the fellowship office at your alma mater and ask if they accept applications from alumni. Most do.

I recommend that applicants go somewhere they've never been before. By that I mean a place where they would be most challenged in a new situation. Somewhere that they don't have friends or family. Somewhere that they speak the language is probably a good idea, but also somewhere that there aren't a lot of Americans.

There was another American volunteer with the NGO that I was associated with. My Spanish was horrible while he was around. I would run to this person to commiserate about being American. I didn't have to confront a lot of problems. I could just go and talk to him about it. When he left I was the only American there and after that I started integrating and learning a lot better. I think being by yourself and being independent is very valuable.

Matt Wesley
Research Fulbright to Nicaragua
Public Health

My project idea developed from studying East European politics and history. I was interested in ethnic cleansing. Both these geographic and thematic areas fit Croatia, and I had lived there before on another grant. My Fulbright project was doing research on the policies enacted to facilitate minority return to Croatia. So I was looking at the Serbs returning to Croatia who had been displaced during the war. The project idea and my contacts there really came from the year that I had spent there previously. So the Fulbright gave me the opportunity to further explore those things that I was interested in.

It would be good for applicants to know beforehand what kind of projects Fulbright is interested in funding in that country. What issues are trendy and current? Once I got to Croatia and got to know the woman in the cultural attaché's office, she told me that she's tired of projects that have anything to do with the war. Even though she felt very strongly that way, there have been two projects since mine on a very similar theme, and they were funded. It seems strange to me.

Before being granted the Fulbright I would not have thought of reaching out to the embassy or Fulbright Commission, but that's something I would definitely encourage people to do. Reach out to the cultural affairs divisions and try to start up a conversation. Maybe they will give you that kind of information. You don't know until you start asking. They want to give money to things they are interested in, so why wouldn't they want to talk to you?

Renee Brown
Research Fulbright to Croatia
Political Science

How do I know if my research topic is a good fit for Fulbright?

- Does it contribute to your larger career trajectory?

- Does it facilitate engagement with communities and colleagues in the host country?

- Is it feasible and can it be completed in the Fulbright time frame?

- Is the project supported by your academic and/or professional experience?

- Are you excited about the project (and not just about living abroad)?

- Is it clear why your project must be undertaken in the host country?

- Do you have the background and language skills to carry it out successfully?

- Does the project reflect serious pursuit?

- Does the project reflect an element of social consciousness, academic curiosity, or sensitivity to questions of international concern?

- Will the project provide opportunities for academic, professional, or personal leadership?

- Have you received postitive feedback when discussing the idea with Fulbright alumni and your school's Fulbright Program Adviser?

What research can English teaching candidates do for their application?

- Research the educational system and pedagogical traditions of your host country. Explore curriculum possibilities and teaching methodologies that fit the host culture and education system. You might be assigned to teach children, so research what discipline techniques are common in your host culture.

- Contact American English teachers, Fulbright and otherwise, who have taught in your host country. What approaches do they recommend? What challenges should you expect teaching there?

- Research the history, cultural traditions, and current events of your host country.

- Regardless of how well you speak the host language, keep studying it.

- Evaluate how this teaching assignment will contribute to your larger personal and professional goals. Think in terms of leadership development. Be as specific as possible.

- Contact organizations in your host country that can facilitate your plans for community engagement and exchange outside of class.

- Read the Fulbright **Country Summary** for your host country to ensure that your project and plans for community engagement are feasible.

Host country affiliation

Research applicants are required to establish affiliation with an organization, institution, or government entity in their host country. For candidates undertaking a course of study at an academic institution, the college or university will be your affiliation, although a letter of support from a specific professor you will work with is a good idea. For independent research, affiliation should be arranged with an organization or individual working in your field. This can be an academic institution, arts collective, professional mentor, theater troupe, think tank, non-governmental organization, or even a government ministry. It's up to you to identify and make contact with an organization that can provide a letter of support for your Fulbright application.

Establishing a relationship with a local organization is an important step in ensuring you have as many opportunities as possible in the field. Not every host affiliation relationship is as productive as the Fulbrighter could hope, but having that point of contact when you arrive can be a huge help in getting settled and getting your project up and running. When contacting potential affiliates, don't just seek a letter of support. Seek possibilities for collaboration.

Many Fulbrighters successfully establish affiliation through cold e-mails or phone calls, but introductions are always easier through a mutual acquaintance. Start by asking for ideas from the contacts you already have—your application mentor, professors, colleagues, and past Fulbrighters. If you have no leads, try e-mailing the Fulbright Commission in your host country or the Public Affairs section at the U.S. Embassy there. Tell them about your Fulbright proposal and ask what they recommend.

Tips on finding affiliation in your host country

- Leave yourself at least two months to secure a letter of affiliation.

- Ask your application adviser for ideas, recommendations, and introductions.

- Unless you've already established a relationship, keep your initial contact with potential affiliates short and sweet. Don't include lengthy descriptions or attach any files—there will be plenty of time for that later. Be prepared to follow up with a copy of your project proposal.

- Propose collaboration. Don't just ask for a letter of support.

- Make sure that letters of support are given to you on the organization's official letterhead, with a signature. The text of an e-mail is not sufficient. Have them scan the letter and e-mail it to you or send you a hard copy.

- Make writing the letter of support as easy for them as possible. Offer to provide a draft of the letter. Remember that English might not be their first language.

When it comes to finding your host affiliation, don't just seek a letter of support. Seek opportunities for collaboration.

Finding host affiliation was the hardest part of the Fulbright application. I sent out a bunch of e-mails and tried to network as much as I could. I asked Armenians in the States if they knew somewhere I could work. I spent about six months looking for something. Then one day it just came down to who I knew. I had an Armenian professor who sent an e-mail to a colleague there, and I sent him an e-mail too, and he agreed to let me work with his organization. It wasn't pure luck, but it was helpful that I knew somebody.

Networking is important. Telling people about your Fulbright plans is important. When you meet someone new, regardless of whether they have anything to do with your country, say "I'm applying for a Fulbright to Iceland," or wherever you're applying to. You never know who might know somebody in Iceland. I was in D.C. interning and I got to meet so many Armenians that way. They would say, "Oh, I know this person. You should talk to them." While many of those didn't end of leading to a host affiliation, it still helped build a network that prepared me for going there. You might get tired of hearing yourself talk about this application that you're working on, but it really does wonders for building your network.

Ashley Killough
Research Fulbright to Armenia
Journalism

I encourage people to start early, seek out a partnership with an organization in their host country, and get letters of support from them early on. Even if it's not required for your application, I think it's a huge advantage to have. Research the organization. Make sure they are viable and not politically connected in some weird way to something you don't want to be connected with. There are Fulbrighters who didn't end up working with their organizations, and there are those whose organization ended up being kind of a scam.

Evan Tachovsky
Research Fulbright to Azerbaijan
Political Science

For applicants looking for a host institution, don't be afraid to reach out to your professors. If you're in an African studies department, chances are pretty good that the professors in that department have contacts in Africa. Go make those connections.

Winston Scott
Research Fulbright to Guatemala
Anthropology

One of the things that I did wrong on my Fulbright, and then did wrong again on my Boren Scholarship a couple of years later, was that I chose to work only with local NGOs. I really felt that development has to be led by host nationals, that it can't be led by external forces. I did not work with anybody that had an international presence. This was great in terms of trying to keep up my view of how things work in Benin, but it's spectacularly shortsighted if you want the Fulbright to help catapult you into your career.

Practically speaking, you get less networking benefit out of having worked with a local NGO. What I found was, after having spent the year in Benin I didn't actually have anybody who could vouch for me as a professional, for the kind of things I had learned and done through the project. I wish I had been more deliberate about trying to force connections with the international NGO expat staff who I met while I was there and tried to parlay those connections into job opportunities, or at least stronger networking opportunities. I regret that.

Tim Slade
Research Fulbright to Benin
Public Health

For my first Fulbright application I was able to contact a host organization in Sri Lanka and get support from them, which definitely helped. I just used the Internet. Through books I had been reading I found out about organizations and e-mailed people who were involved with them. I basically explained my project idea and eventually got a couple of responses and was able to start a conversation about my plans. "This is what I'm interested in doing. Would your organization be able to support me?" That type of thing. I found an NGO that had done work bringing women journalists together in Sri Lanka, which was exactly what I wanted to do: to talk to journalists, specifically women, about how they were covering things, and about peace-building.

Lakshmi Eassey
ETA Fulbright to Germany

I had two contact letters. One was from the head of emergency medicine and the other was from a township community worker who was kind of the health person in the community. She was from the slums so she didn't really have proper grammar or spelling, so I wrote the letter for her and had her check it. My boss, he's kind of a cowboy and doesn't want extra work, so any time I needed him to write anything he told me to write it and he'll look it over. When I wrote a draft of the support letter the first time, I didn't know him very well. My language was kind of soft. It said, "Jared is a great person, blah blah blah." When I sent it to him and he edited it, he changed everything into absolute terms. "Jared is the one to do this. He will have the support of me and my team of 50 doctors and 200 medical students." He was very clear. It definitely helped.

Jared Sun
Research Fulbright to South Africa
Public Health

Sample e-mail query for research project host affiliation

Dear Dr. Pasha,

I am a U.S. Fulbright Scholarship candidate preparing a ten-month project to ~~study~~ research beetle migration in Azerbaijan. I am intrigued by the work your organization is doing in the field of beetle habitat conservation and would like to discuss ways we might <u>collaborate</u> during my research there next year.

If your organization is interested in hosting an American Fulbright researcher, I would like to tell you more about the project.

Best wishes,

Grantee McFulbright

Avoid language that paints you as a student or intern. You will be a U.S. Fulbright Scholar.

Writing in English is usually acceptable for international organizations or big universities, but be prepared to write in the local language if necessary. Investigate which is appropriate. If you write the letter in a foreign language, make sure someone proofreads it before you send it.

Don't just ask for a letter of support. That comes later.

Be very clear about what you are asking.

Fulbright for filmmakers

Kristin Pichaske
Research Fulbright to South Africa
Filmmaking

Kristin Pichaske is an award-winning filmmaker and professor of documentary filmmaking at Columbia College in Chicago.

A Fulbright Scholarship is one of the only grants available to young emerging filmmakers that will give you nearly an entire year's worth of funding at the outset of your project. It is truly one of the best ways I can think of to get your first big independent film off the ground. That said, getting a Fulbright isn't easy and neither is completing a film once you've been selected to the program. Here are things you should consider when applying:

_____ **Find a local partner that cares about your story and can connect you to the right people**

I was caught off guard by the resistance I encountered working on my first film in South Africa. The subject matter was politically charged and because I was an outsider many locals immediately questioned whether I had a right to tell their story. I would have had a hard time overcoming that bias without my host institution, a grassroots organization that was entrenched in the local community. If you're producing a documentary, making connections with interviewees and subjects can be much harder to pull off in a foreign country. Having an "in" is extremely helpful.

_____ **You will probably need more than a Fulbright grant to make your film**

Think realistically about what you can accomplish in 10 months and be honest in your application. Do you have gear? A crew? Other sources of funding? Are you able to shoot and edit your own work? Can you provide evidence of these abilities in your portfolio?

If you're working on a bigger project, don't assume that you can finish an entire film in one year. You will encounter many surprises and setbacks. Think about how you will acquire the funds to finish after your Fulbright has ended. Don't plan to spend a year just doing research so you can figure out a production plan later—try to get your film shot during your Fulbright year so that you have sample work or a trailer to show prospective funders.

Think about your target audience and the Fulbright mission

Is it just an interesting story, or do you have a clear sense of how your project might impact behavior or policy at home or abroad? Keep in mind that you will be competing against Fulbright proposals in other fields that involve serious research and community work designed to provide direct, tangible results.

Involve as many community members in your project as possible

Don't be the kind of foreign filmmaker who parachutes into a community, nabs some footage, filters it through his or her American lens, and then vanishes. Find local collaborators and make relationships a priority. I trained local teenagers who had no experience in film to record sound, work as production assistants, and assist me as translators. They became invaluable in countless unforeseen ways, from helping me overcome power outages to bridging cultural gaps between me and my subjects. Most importantly, the community got to know me and gained a stake in the project's success through these partnerships. This wasn't a part of my original Fulbright proposal but I wish it had been because it fit nicely with Fulbright's mission of ambassadorship.

Build a professional network

Get to know the Fulbright Commission and the public affairs staff at the U.S. Embassy or Consulate in your host country. They often sponsor screenings and visiting filmmaker programs, and can provide valuable relationships to help you stay connected to your host country beyond the end of your Fulbright grant. These people are generally well-connected and may even be able to help you find additional sources of funding for your work.

Have lunch with some folks from the country's Ministry of Culture or the national film commission. Meet as many local colleagues as you can, from producers and directors to crew members and arts organizations. Take in every local screening and community event you can. Volunteer on other filmmakers' projects. One of the great things about a Fulbright is that it sets you up to do ongoing work in your host country and these connections will almost certainly prove valuable down the road.

Use your work as a platform for teaching or lecturing

If you need a test audience for a rough cut of your film, partner with a local university or media organization to host a lecture. People want to hear about your work as a Fulbrighter in their country, and teaching is a valuable part of any long-term career as a filmmaker.

Just after my Fulbright year ended, I taught a five-day documentary workshop at the University of Cape Town. That soon led to a semester of thesis advising, and then an adjunct faculty position, and eventually a full-time faculty appointment. It was a terrific experience that allowed me to spend three more years in South Africa, complete a PhD, and land a tenure-track teaching job in Chicago before I moved back to the States. Opportunities like these abound if you to take the time to look for them.

Multi-country research grants

Fulbright grants are typically designed to enable grantees to live and work in one specific country. In rare circumstances Fulbright offers multi-country grants in select regions of the world. Candidates interested in a multi-country grant should consult the Fulbright website for the latest list of participating regions.

Multi-country applications require considerably more work from the candidate. Not only must you justify why the project requires a regional approach, but you also must secure host affiliation in each of the countries. Your letters of recommendation should speak directly to the multi-country nature of the project and why it is necessary. Be prepared to justify why your project cannot be undertaken in just one country.

If a multi-country application advances beyond the first stage of the selection process (the National Review Board), it will go on to be evaluated by committees in each of the countries you are applying to. If one of the countries rejects it, you may or may not be allowed to revise your proposal. ETA applicants are not eligible for multi-country grants.

Many candidates fall in love with the idea of a multi-country project. But in the Fulbright framework, broader scope does not necessarily lead to a more rewarding experience.

Institutional Review Board (IRB)

Fulbright projects that involve interviews, tests, examinations, or behavioral studies of other people may need to be approved by an Institutional Review Board (IRB). This is especially true if your work deals with vulnerable populations (children, inmates, refugees, disabled persons, victims of abuse, etc.). IRB review of your project can occur at your home institution in the United States or at your host institution overseas, but it must be completed before research can commence. At-large Fulbright applicants should arrange their own ethics review to ensure that their project meets internationally accepted ethical standards for research. If you've never dealt with the IRB process before, ask you school's Fulbright Program Adviser or application mentor how to proceed.

At one point I started applying for a multi-country Fulbright grant to China, Japan, and Hong Kong. I got pretty far along in the process until someone said that since an MFA is not a terminal degree there might be a problem. There was some technicality about whether an MFA or a PhD is a terminal degree for creative writing. So I ended up having to change the whole thing at the last minute and make it just a China application. In the end I'm really glad I did that because for me navigating all the bureaucracies of daily life in China, before even getting into the research and travel, was probably about what I could handle while still making some good progress on my project.

Deanna Fei
Research Fulbright to China
Creative Writing

The Critical Language Enhancement Award

The Critical Language Enhancement Award (CLEA) is a supplementary grant that has in the past been offered to some Fulbright grantees. It provides recipients of research and ETA Fulbright fellowships the opportunity for three to six months of intensive study of the language of their host country. CLEAs are available only for select languages, and the list sometimes changes from year to year. Past CLEAs have funded study of Arabic, Azerbaijani, Bahasa Indonesia, Bangla/Bengali, Chinese (Mandarin), Gujarati, Hindi, Marathi, Punjabi, Russian, and Urdu. Check the program website for the latest list.

Interested applicants should apply for the CLEA in conjunction with their Fulbright application. Candidates should reference the CLEA in their Statements of Grant Purpose and address specifically how this additional language training will benefit their Fulbright work and long-term career.

Applicants will have an opportunity to suggest their own language training programs and duration of study. In some countries, CLEA-funded language study must be completed before the Fulbright grant starts. In other cases it may be set up to include intensive study before the grant begins, followed by tutoring or coursework done concurrently with the Fulbright. Intensive study is typically defined as 20 hours per week of classroom study or 10 hours per week of tutoring. Grantees must complete pre- and post-grant language evaluations and submit a final report.

You should really consult with your school's or your affiliate's IRB [Institutional Review Board] if you're going to be doing an interview-based project. That's crucial. The IRB is going to be able to give you the guidance you need to make sure your methods are sound and that you're abiding by ethical standards. My IRB was at Smith College. I actually didn't do my IRB application until after I was awarded the Fulbright. Before the end of the school year I got the IRB to approve my methodology because the methodology that you give to the IRB is far more in-depth than the one you're asked to give Fulbright. Once your methods are approved by the IRB you will have a lot more weight behind your research for publishing purposes. That's also really handy.

Read about similar projects that have been done and look into the methodology that was used. Really think through your questions before you start doing the interviews. Think through how you're going to ask questions and what questions you're going to ask, because once you start your interviews, if you really want the data to all work out, you're going to need to ask the exact same questions to different people. Or at least have a methodology that has some structure to it so that all the data is reliable. I wish that I had had more standard questions that I asked everyone.

Jessie Rubin
Research Fulbright to Nicaragua
Political Science

Navigating the IRB process in researching second-generation immigrant identity development

Laila Plamandon
Research Fulbright to Canada
Psychology

I was a senior in college when I applied to the Fulbright Program. I started my application the summer after my junior year. I was quite young. I found an adviser just by e-mailing professors that seemed to be in my field and might be interested in helping me. I was looking at cultural identity development and I found a professor at the University of Toronto who had very similar ideas and interests, so that was a good match for me. But it was pretty much a cold call, e-mailing professors whom I hadn't met before. I did make a trip out there to meet my adviser before I submitted my application, just so that it would be a solid bond, so I knew what I was getting into. Everything went pretty smoothly.

There's such a huge time period between when you actually apply to Fulbright and when you find out that you've been accepted. I wasn't really thinking about the Fulbright anymore when I was accepted. But as soon as I found out I e-mailed the professor and said, "I'm coming now, for sure. I'm really excited. Can we get started working on the project? What would you like for me to do in terms of the IRB?" He said, "No, no, no. Just wait until you get here. Enjoy your summer." So that's what I did. I waited until I arrived in Toronto. If I had to do it again, I'm not sure I would have taken that advice.

Getting approval from the Institutional Review Board is really important for anyone who's doing research in psychology, sociology,

or anthropology. You send your proposal to the board and they make sure that you're not harming anybody or putting people through anything that the school could get sued for. In retrospect I think I would have tried to reach out to more master's or PhD students in his lab. I would have asked them, "How long does an IRB application usually take? What is it like to work in the lab?" I might have even started the IRB application process, because I think it would have pushed the professor a bit to get things rolling before I came. I knew what I wanted to study, but I didn't have a solid IRB proposal yet because my advisor wanted me to wait for his input. If I had been able to hand in the IRB application before I got there, even if I had spent a month there waiting for it to come back, I would have had so much more time to actually work on the meat of the research, which I was so excited to do. But the approval didn't come until months after I was there.

I handed in the IRB application in November, but because it was such a huge university I didn't realize what a big deal it would be. I didn't get my proposal back until the end of January. So I had two and a half dead months out of my ten Fulbright months. And that was really difficult because it pushed me back so far. I wasn't allowed to do any interviewing or actually move forward with my research until I received an OK from them. That was frustrating. I wasn't expecting this, having come from a small college where things like this get turned around much faster.

I just kept reading and preparing to actually do the interviews and learning as much as I could, hoping that it would be helpful later in the process. I found it pretty stressful. Because I was so busy at the beginning of the year, I decided not to take classes in order to focus on the research. But I wish I had taken the classes because it would have given me something to do that's productive and tangentially related. I didn't negotiate it very well at all. I think it was just difficult.

I finally started interviewing in February, and once I got started it was great. I was studying Bangladeshi immigrants (I'm part Bangladeshi). I was able to get into their club and I would go to their social events and meet people that way, and they would help me find Bangladeshis to interview. So the social aspect of it was great. By March I had all my interviews done. I spent the month of April transcribing and then in May I started to learn to use the software I needed to actually do the analysis. But by the end of the month it was time for me to go, so I never actually finished my project, which was so unfortunate. And because I wasn't moving on into a PhD program, because I had to start working, I haven't had time to dedicate to finishing my Fulbright project.

I have one big piece of advice for anyone looking to do a Fulbright: It's such a great opportunity, you should really be prepared to hit the ground running. Know what you're doing. Get approval to do everything beforehand if you can. There will always be things you just don't see coming.

Budgets and fundraising

It is not uncommon that Fulbrighters require additional capital to realize the full potential of their Fulbright work, whether for teaching materials, travel expenses, conference fees, art supplies, or any other costs that Fulbright doesn't explicitly cover. Fulbright doesn't ask applicants to submit a budget with their proposal, but candidates whose projects involve significant expenses will do well to create one for themselves.

It's helpful to mention in your application what you plan to do with your Fulbright work, whether it's host a gallery exhibition, organize an international conference, produce a documentary film, or something else entirely. You should address how you plan to pay for these things if they involve serious cost. Be sure to include a list of the funding organizations you've been in touch with about your plans. If any of them express interest in providing support, include a letter of support in your application saying as much. As a Fulbright Scholarship candidate you are well positioned to ask people for funding. Don't be shy about doing so.

Fulbright allows outside funding to be applied to your Fulbright work as long as it doesn't overlap with expenses that the program already covers. Costs that Fulbright covers include travel to the host country, housing expenses, and language study through a CLEA grant. Fundraising isn't just for research fellows: If you are an English teacher, think about what materials you will need in the classroom, what excursions you might want to organize, and how much capital you'll need to create the teaching experience you want your students to have.

Was the Fulbright stipend enough? Yes, it was. I had to be prudent with it, especially with rent, which was probably the biggest expense. Especially in a big city. Be careful with money and make sure you're budgeting carefully, but don't go to the extreme of wanting to live like a local and feeling like hardship has to be part of the experience. Of course living abroad necessitates some of that, but I think some people go a little too far and find themselves stuck in a position that actually only makes their research and work harder. You do need some comforts that help approximate your home life. I think the Fulbright budget allows for that to a reasonable degree.

Deanna Fei
Research Fulbright to China
Creative Writing

Apply for outside grants. I wish I had. I didn't even know I could do that. There are tons of opportunities out there. I would have even contacted my local women's department. I would have found more opportunities for funding. Even if it's only a little, it adds up.

Saving money is another thing. Having a very realistic expectation of how much things cost. But I would apply for more financial grants. Even if one lives very frugally, you want to make sure you have all options in front of you to do it the way you want to do it.

Shadi Khadivi
Research Fulbright to Turkey
Architecture

Fundraising for a water sanitation project in Nicaragua

Matt Wesley
Research Fulbright to Nicaragua
Public Health

In December of the year I applied I made a trip to my host country, funded through my university, to test out the project I planned to do there. I toured two or three communities to test it out and it seemed to work out very well. I had no idea whether I was going to get the Fulbright at this point, so I applied for outside funding. I raised $25,000 though outside grants and through my university. There were huge material costs associated with my project that Fulbright didn't cover. I went to Nicaragua early to get a head start, right after I graduated.

Fulbright didn't have any problem with my raising outside money. They encouraged it, actually. I was very careful to make sure the funds were designated specifically for materials and not for living expenses. If you declare that you have other funds to pay for your food and living expenses, Fulbright will deduct that from the stipend. I ended up having my incoming flight paid for, so I reported it to Fulbright and they deducted about $400 from my stipend. You can earmark certain outside funds for materials, if that's what you need, so that it doesn't overlap with your Fulbright funding. It's just wasted money if it overlaps.

I had worked with Engineers Without Borders for four years at Rice University and I developed some contacts for funding. The university knew that I had done good work with Engineers Without Borders and they were very willing to help out. I was awarded a number of fellowships—one for $10,000 and another for $12,000. There were a few interviews to go through to get the funding, and it had to go through a committee at the university, but mostly I needed to demonstrate a history of conducting responsible projects and programs. Being able to demonstrate that when you're applying for funding is a good thing.

Local organizations love it when college students have an idea and they can sort of experience the project by supporting them financially. I already had a relationship with a Rotary Club chapter. I contacted them in the middle of the project saying I was short of funds, and they helped out. So there are a lot of opportunities that people don't know about and don't take advantage of. I basically applied to everything I could to get funding.

I think that part of the reason I got a lot of funding was because I was already in my host country and had no logistical costs. Fulbright was already paying for my food, transportation, and other basic expenses. For people who want to donate and support projects, Fulbright is a very, very attractive opportunity.

Fulbright's selection process

After your application is submitted to Fulbright it will be reviewed in a three-step selection process. At each stage a different group of readers evaluates your materials:

Stage 1

Applications are first referred to Fulbright's **National Screening Committee**, which is composed of area specialists who meet in November and December to assess the strength of the candidates' materials. Subcommittees organized to assess academic proposals are generally grouped by regions. For example, a subcommittee for western Europe will review a mathematics application to Norway. Proposals in the creative or performing arts are often reviewed by specialists working in the applicant's field. These may be photographers, painters, architects, etc. In the past the committee has typically recommended at least 1.5 to 2 times the number of candidates as there are grants available in each country. Applicants are notified by January 31 whether their application has been recommended for further review.

Stage 2

Applications recommended by the National Screening Committee are forwarded to staff at the Fulbright Commission and/or U.S. Embassy in the host country. Screeners at this stage include American staff and host country nationals who are able to gauge the candidate's strengths and weaknesses, assess the feasibility of their proposed Fulbright work, and weigh options for ETA placements and research affiliation. Host country committees recommend principal and alternate candidates for advancement to the next stage of selection.

Stage 3

Based on the recommendations of the selection committee in the host country, final selection of Fulbright candidates is undertaken in the United States by the **J. William Fulbright Foreign Scholarship Board**. The board's 12 educational and public leaders are appointed by the President of the United States. Candidates are usually notified of their selection status—accepted, alternate, or "non-recommended"—between April and June each year.

If you are serious about the Fulbright Program, plan on applying more than once—chances are you won't be accepted on your first try.

What does it mean to be put on the wait list?

So I got wait-listed. Then I moved to New York City and I had a job. I was working and the Fulbright was just sort of in the back of my mind. And one day I get a call from the State Department. This was six or seven months after the whole thing. "Remember me? We want to offer you the Fulbright. Somebody declined and we want to see if you're interested in going." I asked, "What is the last day I can go? My project is being built and I need to be here through construction." They told me I could leave as late as March of the following year. So I left much later than everyone else in my year. When I arrived it was a very disorienting experience for me because I didn't get the benefit of the orientation.

Shadi Khadivi
Research Fulbright to Turkey
Architecture

Candidates designated as "alternates" wait the longest—sometimes well into summer—to find out whether they made the cut. A candidate may be promoted from the wait list two ways: when an accepted candidate declines the award, or if additional funding becomes available, which Fulbright typically finds out about in late spring.

The plight of the alternate can be a very uncomfortable wait. Fulbright isn't able to shed any light on the candidate's status until it changes. (There's no use calling IIE for news.) To complicate matters, those eventually promoted to full acceptance are often asked to make a speedy decision, sometimes within mere days.

If you have been wait-listed, all hope is not lost. Fulbright keeps alternates on the list until August, and late-hour promotions do happen. Most grantees who have experienced the wait list recommend that you forget about the Fulbright and move on with your life. If you do get the call, you can make the decision then.

Applicants who do not advance to award status should not give up on Fulbright. If your application got you as far as the wait list, at least some readers found attractive qualities in your candidacy. If you are serious about the Fulbright Program, plan on applying more than once—chances are you won't be accepted on your first try. Despite the large number of Fulbright Scholarships awarded each year, the selection process remains extremely competitive. Many candidates apply several times before being accepted. Persistence is often what separates Fulbright grantees from unsuccessful applicants.

The first time I applied I found out in May that I was wait-listed. It was kind of torturous. Because I was wait-listed, I wasn't sure what to do or when I would be told "no." They kind of string you along. I never got anything that officially said, "No, we cannot take you." It just gets increasingly less likely that you'll get it as time goes on. Eventually it was clear in September or October that they weren't able to accommodate me.

I was wait-listed for my second application as well. This time I kind of forgot about it. "Well, I'm wait-listed. It may or may not come through, so I'm not going to wait around for it." I actually started working for the Obama campaign in Florida, and then I got a call about a month before I was supposed to be in Germany asking, "Would you like to go?" I was initially a little bit shocked because there was such a quick turnaround for me. I had barely a month to get everything together and move.

My advice is to carry on with life. If it comes down to it and you can and still want to go, then you'll go. If the time has passed and you no longer want to go, then that's fine too. Carry on with life, because you don't know what's going to happen. Don't wait around for them to tell you that they want you to go there.

Lakshmi Eassey
ETA Fulbright to Germany

If you don't get the Fulbright, don't call it off. I've seen too many people, very close friends, who did not have a positive application process. They say, "I'm never doing that again. Blah blah blah." Well, why not? They just throw in the towel.

Personally, I didn't think I was going to win a Fulbright the first year. And I didn't. That to me was part of the process. I expected that. I was going to get my foot in the door, my name into the committee's minds, and put together the best damn proposal I could put together at that point in time. I just came in expecting that if you critique me, it's not because you hate me, but because you can see something that's worthwhile, something that can be better, that can be improved. That's the way I always looked at it. I tried not to get discouraged about things.

I don't know many people who win a grant on their first go-around. It's a process. There are a lot of smart people out there with a lot of really good proposals. That became apparent to me at the mid-year Fulbright conference. Just in the Central America pool, we got together fifteen or so Fulbrighters and there were so many good proposals.

It helped me to keep close to my dissertation committee. Two of them had conducted research through Fulbright fellowships. One took three years and the other took four years to get it. I tell people not to get frustrated. Go get that critique on your application where you can. Get it from your professors. Get it from your peers if you have that opportunity, and from your campus Fulbright representative. That's only going to make your application better. Too many people don't like critique. They say, "My proposal was good. They're off their rocker if they didn't like it." Well, it probably was good, but it can be better. Don't just come in the next year and turn in the same proposal.

Winston Scott
Research Fulbright to Guatemala
Anthropology

Chapter 4

Building Your Fulbright Application

If I had eight hours to chop down a tree,
I'd spend six sharpening my axe.

Abraham Lincoln

B uilding a competitive Fulbright candidacy isn't just about presenting yourself in a way that application readers will find attractive. It's also about developing your goals, your project, and your credentials so they will benefit from and support Fulbright's mission. Think of the application process as the design phase of your Fulbright experience.

The most valuable Fulbright research you will ever undertake is to explore your long-term goals and then assess how Fulbright fits into the big picture. Talk to experts in your field. Contact Fulbright alumni. Go to professional conferences. Read voraciously. This soul searching can be challenging, but it is often what separates strong Fulbright candidacies from all the rest. Don't be seduced by the Fulbright name: Ask yourself honestly whether this is the right time to apply for a Fulbright Scholarship. The program will still be available to you in a few years, and you will only be more qualified then. Many candidates who received a Fulbright right after their undergraduate work wish they had waited a few years before applying.

If you decide the time is right to apply for a Fulbright Scholarship, commit to that process with focus and discipline. It takes time and energy to develop a good application, but it takes far, far more time and energy to develop a great one.

Working with your campus Fulbright Program Adviser

The Fulbright Program and its partners do an excellent job of making information about the application process available. The program's robust outreach includes a comprehensive website, guidance seminars, webinars, blogs, podcasts, alumni interviews, and an applicant newsletter. Between all the application components, deadlines, and requirements, there's a lot of information for the applicant to process.

The best resource a candidate has to help navigate the this process is the campus Fulbright Program Adviser (FPA), the official liaison between applicants and Fulbright Program administrators. The first step of the application process is to check in as early as possible with the FPA at your college or university, or, if you're not currently enrolled, at your alma mater. Their job is to provide information and guidance to potential applicants, and manage the campus application process, including the interview.

The experience of working with a campus FPA can vary widely from institution to institution. Much depends on the adviser's personality, background, and commitment. Depending on their level of experience, your FPA can be a tremendous asset to your application. They can help answer questions about the application process, navigate the complexities of Fulbright's many programs, assess the strengths and weaknesses of your candidacy, and help you prepare for your on-campus interview. Some FPAs are Fulbright alumni themselves, but most are not.

If for some reason the relationship with your FPA isn't working, or if you don't have access to a campus adviser and are applying at-large, you may have to contact the Fulbright program directly with your questions.

I actually didn't have a lot of contact with the Fulbright representative at my school during the application process. They were very responsive every time I did contact them, and most of my interactions with them were really about the details of the application process and making sure I had dotted my I's and crossed my T's. I didn't get any advice from them related to content or the way I should write the proposal, but they did seem very open. If I had wanted my hand held more during the application process, they would have been there for me. That's the general sense I had. And they are curious now to hear how the project ended up. I need to let them know.

Mike Seely
Research Fulbright to Poland
Filmmaking

There's a certain strategy to one's application. One of my big struggles was dealing with faculty who looked at Fulbright as the crème de la crème of grants out there. My original academic advisor, who I had for my first three years as an undergraduate, dissuaded me from applying. He said I had no shot in hell. For students my age, for people who just finished a Bachelor's degree, my advice is to shrug off negative advice from faculty. In my case I had a heart-to-heart with a faculty member who was in my corner who said, "Don't listen to him. It's just like any other workplace. You're going to have people on your side and people against you, and everything in the middle." You just have to go for what you want. So it's about making a calculated decision.

Nic Wondra
Research Fulbright to Georgia
Political Science

Beyond the campus adviser: choosing an application mentor

Regardless of how helpful your campus Fulbright Program Adviser is, they should never be your only source of information about the Fulbright Program or your application. Successful applicants recommend also having someone who can help guide your project idea through the development and proposal stage, an academic or professional mentor with expertise in your field who can advise you on a closer, more personal basis. This mentor is not there to check for spelling errors or to make sure all the application components are in order—your FPA can help with that. Your application mentor helps guide the big-picture development of your proposal. They can give substantive feedback on your ideas, help refine your goals, and share potential contacts that could help with your project. Ideally this mentor is someone with whom you already have a working relationship.

Good mentors are difficult to find, particularly outside of a university setting, and developing and nurturing these relationships requires your care and attention as the mentee. By agreeing to advise you in your Fulbright endeavors, your mentor is investing in your career, and the most successful mentor relationships last for decades. Respect their time: never demand feedback on short notice, and be sure to thank them for their help.

As fruitful as this relationship can be, it is your responsibility to move your application forward. Don't expect someone else to give you a deadline, and never wait for permission to reach out to other people about your application. Take advantage of the extensive online resources Fulbright offers and contact Fulbright alumni directly about their experiences.

One thing I benefitted from is that I had a professor whose abilities I very much trusted who I knew would work with me. I actually got college credit for research I did on my essays because I set up an independent study over the summer before the deadline. The independent study was structured around doing all the research that went into my application essays. I got my professor to be my independent study adviser. We set up regular meetings. I would send him copies of my essays and would then go in and meet with him. He would say, "Well, you might want to look at this paragraph." If I had been taking a full course load that the independent study was not part of, applying would have been much more difficult. I know it's not an option for everyone, but I recommend it.

Heather Wakefield
Research Fulbright to Georgia
Library Sciences

Fulbright application essays

Fulbright requires that research and ETA applicants submit two written essays as part of their application: the Statement of Grant Purpose and the Personal Statement. These essays are your best opportunity to show Fulbright who you are, what you hope to accomplish, and why the program should invest in you. As the core of your application they should work in concert to convey your motivations, qualifications, and potential to achieve great things as a Fulbrighter.

The biggest challenge in writing strong essays isn't poor grammar, syntax, or structure, but rather hubris: We all think we are better writers than we actually are. If you can admit that a college degree doesn't make you a star writer, and that it's worth swallowing your pride and asking for feedback, the challenges of writing a persuasive proposal will become more manageable. Those who underestimate these obstacles, or overestimate their writing ability, often fall into a self-defeating pattern: They wait too long to start, dive in without preparation, don't seek feedback, and spend too little time revising.

Good writing takes time to produce, even for best-selling authors. If you don't have a strong background in writing, or if you come from a field where you don't get much practice, you will need to work that much harder to develop competitive essays. If you are worried about your abilities, take a composition class, sign up for a writing workshop, or work with a writing tutor. Many colleges and universities have writing centers that offer free help. Your essays will compete against those of advanced graduate students and even professional writers.

Take your time with the application. It's rigorous. It's hard. Really be sure about what you want and be able to articulate that. The Personal Statement essay is a huge part of your application because it can really distinguish you from the hundreds of other applications that they're getting. You just need to be able to set yourself apart and make yourself memorable. In a good way, of course.

Hannah Halder
ETA Fulbright to Romania

I knew that I really wanted this grant. I had a whole binder of research materials on Panama. At the time I was kind of obsessed with this. I was working for a photographer at the time in Baltimore and I would work for him in trade for his help editing my writing. I think we worked on the essays for two and a half months. I was writing them all summer. I went through a lot of revisions. The language ended up being very clean in the end, and the idea was pretty solid.

Rose Cromwell
Research Fulbright to Panama
Photography

You're writing to a very educated but very general committee. There can be scientists on it, there can be historians, there can be artists. I just tried to write in a way that I knew everyone could more or less follow. I knew if my mom understood what I was saying, then I was more or less OK. Have your mom read your essay.

Maya deVries
Research Fulbright to Panama
Biology

Essay-writing strategy

Writing a strong application essay is difficult. Use these strategies to help bring out your best work:

_____ **Start early, start often**

It is difficult to overestimate the value of starting your Fulbright application as early as possible. This is doubly true for writing essays. Six months or a year before the deadline is not too early to start. Writing about yourself and your project will show you the weaknesses in your ideas and plans, and starting early gives you time to deal with them. One of the biggest factors contributing to strong Fulbright essays is the amount of time invested.

_____ **Consult the Fulbright _Country Summary_ for your host country**

Many countries have preferences for the kinds of Fulbright projects and applicants they approve. Some encourage independent research, while others prefer that applicants incorporate coursework into their proposals. Some require advanced language fluency. Others have age restrictions. Check these out _before_ you begin writing.

_____ **Know your audience**

Your essays will be read and evaluated by American and foreign readers with widely varying levels of expertise. Your essays must be easy to follow for all of them.

_____ **Consider your goals**

The Fulbright Program gives grantees tools and resources to achieve goals that also further the Fulbright mission. If you don't know what you want from your Fulbright grant, stop now. Spend time soul searching. Don't apply to Fulbright just to get a Fulbright.

_____ **Keep your writing clear and simple**

No matter how complex your ideas, you have to find a way to reduce them to clear, simple concepts that any reader can understand. Don't try to impress readers with fancy terminology and name-dropping—that only weakens your chances. Fulbright wants to know about

---

The Fulbright is probably not the only thing that you've applied for. I know that I drew upon other essays and applications that I wrote. I researched project proposals that were available online. Seeing other people's essays takes a lot of the guesswork out of it. That just sort of got me in the mood of organizing my thoughts and writing my essays.

Renee Brown
Research Fulbright to Croatia
Political Science

you, your plan for your project, and how clearly you are able to articulate these things. If you can't describe your project in one clear sentence to someone outside your field, you need to spend more time developing your ideas before you start writing about them. Your reader should be left with no questions about the "who, what, when, where, why, and how" of your project.

With so little space to articulate your plans, you cannot have too clear a structure for your Fulbright essays. Each essay, each paragraph of each essay, and each sentence of each paragraph should have its own purpose. Don't ramble and don't jump around. If readers must work to understand you, it's not likely they will look favorably on your application.

Seek feedback

Good writing does not occur in a vacuum. Like all endeavors worth pursuing, we need feedback and critique to hone our ideas and streamline their presentation. There is a subtle art to working with feedback, and there's a lot more to it than just proofreading. If you're embarrassed or reluctant to share your proposal, you probably already know that it needs work.

Writing the essays was so mind-wrenching. I think I wrote 15 different versions of the Statement of Grant Purpose. I spent a long time writing it and the project changed a little with each version. I spent about four months writing.

The harder part for me was not the description of the project, but the Personal Statement. I read samples. Some were stories of nostalgia and some were just explanations of why their interests were the way they were. I think reading the samples actually ruined my experience because it took me a long time to get out of the mindset of what I had just read. I couldn't quite find my own voice in other people's writing. Suddenly I had lost my own reasoning for why I deserved the grant.

I suggest explaining things as simply and as clearly as possible for the Statement of Grant Purpose. I would say it's better if you write your own Personal Statement and be really confident with it before you read others. It took me a long time to come to conclusions about what my Personal Statement should be about.

There were a lot of people looking at my essays. The main person was my husband, who spent time with me looking over everything carefully. I would write it and then read it to him. And he would say, "Well, it doesn't sound like this is working here." There was a lot of going back and forth.

Shadi Khadivi
Research Fulbright to Turkey
Architecture

Your Statement of Grant Purpose

The Statement of Grant Purpose is a short essay in which applicants outline the type of Fulbright research, study, or English teaching assignment they propose. More importantly, it tells Fulbright what kind of ambassador you will be. In many ways this is the fulcrum of your candidacy. All other elements of your application—your letters of recommendation, language evaluation, letter of host affiliation, even your Personal Statement essay—work to support this proposal. Both research and ETA applicants are required to submit a Statement of Grant Purpose.

For study/research applicants

Your statement of grant purpose should clearly explain the goals and methodologies of your proposed Fulbright work. In the past Fulbright has limited this essay to two pages of single-spaced text. For many candidates the biggest challenge is fitting their proposal into so little space. Strong essays should accomplish the following:

- Present the "who, what, when, where, why, and how" of your project

- Clearly state your goals for the project, its concrete outcomes, and its measurable results

- Explain how it will facilitate your professional or academic development

- Outline how the project will further Fulbright's mission of promoting international exchange and mutual understanding

- Show that the project is feasible with your experience, language proficiency, and resources

- Tell your readers why the work is important

- Clearly show your qualifications for undertaking this project successfully

- Explain the details and background of your project in a way that all readers can understand

- Outline who you will work with and the kind of support they have offered

Make sure that your proposal reads well to someone who is an intelligent and critical reader but not an expert in your field. It needs to flow. It needs to incorporate broad ideas of exchange: what you're going to give, and what you're going to get back. I don't think strictly academic proposals are the way to go. For the Fulbright student grant, stick with a narrative format. If your project is too complex to explain to your Grandpa, it's too complex.

Evan Tachovsky
Research Fulbright to Azerbaijan
Political Science

In the Statement of Grant Purpose you are supposed to address what led you to want a Fulbright English Teaching Assistantship, and also what projects you could contribute to or be part of. That's a little bit hard to write because you can't talk about a specific research project proposal. If you talked about a specific project proposal they would ask, "Then why are you applying for an ETA Fulbright and not a research grant?"

Hannah Halder
ETA Fulbright to Romania

For English-teaching applicants

Unlike research applicants, ETA candidates are not expected to include extensive project plans in their Statement of Grant Purpose. The primary project, after all, is the teaching assignment. At first this may seem like a gift, but writing an ETA Statement of Grant Purpose can be an even more formidable challenge than a research proposal. Past ETA statements of purpose have been limited to either one or two pages in length, so check the latest Fulbright guidelines before starting. Your statement should clearly address the following:

- Why have you chosen this country?

- What are your motivations for teaching English overseas?

- What makes you qualified to serve as a cultural ambassador in your host country?

- How will this assignment contribute to your professional or educational development?

- How will you contribute to Fulbright's mission of promoting mutual understanding?

- How do you intend to engage your host community outside the classroom?

Explaining how you plan to pursue your role as a cultural ambassador is of particular importance for ETA candidates. You should be very explicit about how you intend to engage your host community outside the classroom (most ETAs don't work more than 20 to 30 hours per week in the classroom). Herein lies what many ETA applicants see as this essay's biggest challenge: While you are encouraged to outline extracurricular activities, community service, or research projects you hope to pursue outside the classroom, you don't know where exactly you will be posted. This makes it difficult to formulate detailed plans, but you should nevertheless contact organizations that might be able to help organize these activities.

Talking about outside projects is important, but don't let them eclipse your teaching work. The priority is to address the pedagogical component of your Fulbright. If you find yourself more interested in a non-teaching project you propose, it may be time to consider a traditional Fulbright research grant instead.

I was applying from the perspective of a PhD student who wanted to get my dissertation research done. I had already written a dissertation prospectus and had that approved by my committee, so I already had a pretty good idea of what I wanted to do. But I had to get the description into two single-spaced pages. I had to figure out how to express what I wanted to do in this small amount of space. This meant being very concise and figuring out what was relevant given the page limitations of the research proposal.

I definitely knew it was essential in my case to talk about what I wanted to do—to study perceptions of the relationship between immigration and race for Brazilians who live in the U.S. and then go back to Brazil. So I needed to 1) provide some background on my research questions, and 2) talk about the specific methods I was going to use to pursue them. Then I talked about the time frame for the nine months. How am I going to go about making sure that I do this? And finally, I talked about the broader contributions not only of the project, but also from me as a Fulbright grantee, and how this project will be relevant in creating mutual understanding between the U.S. and Brazil. I tried to do each of those things in one or two paragraphs within the full two pages that I had to talk about my research project.

Tiffany Joseph
Research Fulbright to Brazil
Sociology

Tips for writing your Statement of Grant Purpose

_____ Be sure you conform to Fulbright's formatting and length guidelines. Don't get fancy—this isn't a design competition. If you can't be trusted to follow those simple instructions, how can Fulbright trust you with an overseas grant?

_____ Check Fulbright's **Country Summary** for your host country before you begin writing. Different countries have different language requirements, affiliation limitations, and even age limits.

_____ Write clearly in well-structured paragraphs. Don't ramble and don't try to hide undeveloped ideas behind effusive prose. Nobody likes being forced to read something twice to understand it.

_____ Make sure that the "what, when, where, why, and how" are all clearly stated in the first paragraph of your essay. You can elaborate in subsequent paragraphs.

_____ Don't leave readers with questions that make them search for information. Your essay may be one of dozens that each reader is evaluating. Convoluted or disorganized writing signals poor preparation.

_____ Don't leave any doubt about the feasibility of your project or your ability to take on this teaching assignment. If you're not qualified to undertake this work, either get qualified or modify your project. If your proposal elicits questions that cast doubt on feasibility, address them directly. Example: "For interviews in the northern regions where a different dialect is spoken, I will hire a translator to accompany me."

_____ Make 100 percent certain there are no grammar, spelling, or syntax mistakes in your essays. Every year essays are submitted with egregious grammatical mistakes. Nothing turns off readers faster than sloppy proofreading. Don't rely on your computer's spell-checker. At a minimum read your final draft out loud to yourself slowly. Hire a professional copyeditor if you have to—just get it done.

I had a separate paragraph in my proposal about community involvement. I recommend that applicants make a list of all the extracurricular activities they engaged in while in college, maybe even in high school as well, and choose two that they think they could pursue in their host country. I should have done that. I should have thought about what I was most passionate about as an undergraduate student and chosen that for my community involvement in Germany. But I thought, "I've done enough of this." In reality, doing them in a different country is going to be a different experience.

If you worked on a literary magazine as an undergraduate in the United States and you do something similar in your host country, you're going to learn a whole different approach to publishing, to the selection process, and to every aspect that you may think you're already very familiar with in the American system.

**Lilith Dornhuber de Bellesiles
Research Fulbright to Germany
Philosophy**

I started by writing very generally in my research statement, then got very specific, and then broadened out again. I guess that's typical proposal writing advice. The more specific you can make your questions and the more you can tie them into current issues in the country, the better. That's hard. I had to do a lot of background research. I talked about the effects of overfishing in general on coral reefs, but then I also made it very specific about how overfishing is affecting Panama in particular.

**Maya deVries
Research Fulbright to Panama
Biology**

If you're going to make a film, be sure to delineate exactly what resources in addition to the Fulbright grant you're going to have with you or available to you to help you complete the project. I wrote that I was going to use a couple thousand dollars of my own money for incidental costs, travel, and things like that. And possibly to pay a day rate for a sound guy here and there. I edited on a laptop and used my own video camera and sound equipment. I kept it super minimal in terms of gear and focused on the story and the process of making a film.

**Mike Seely
Research Fulbright to Poland
Filmmaking**

Your Personal Statement

For the Personal Statement I talked about my personal experiences negotiating race as a black American woman who has lived in other Latin American countries, and how my experience was probably similar to the people that I would be interviewing: Brazilians who come to the U.S. and have to negotiate race and figure out this new racial system. And I talked about how that experience for them was similar to experiences I've had when I traveled in Latin America, and how that was what got me interested in this particular research. How moving across borders changes the way people think about themselves in racial terms and influences the way people think about race and racial classification.

People ask me what the difference is between the two application essays. Your research proposal is exactly that—a research proposal. But your Personal Statement is how you got interested in that country, or that particular research question, or both. What's your personal connection to this? How can you show the Fulbright application readers who you are as a person? How is that reflected in what you want to do? That's how I approached writing the essays.

Tiffany Joseph
Research Fulbright to Brazil
Sociology

The Personal Statement is a short autobiographical narrative that paints a picture of you as an individual. It is not a regurgitation of your résumé or a list of your accomplishments to date, but a way to contextualize your Fulbright experience within your broader professional, intellectual, and creative trajectories. What is important to you? What do you believe in? What influences shaped your convictions? What do you hope to accomplish in your life? The Personal Statement is the best tool you have to paint a picture of who you are and where you are going. Great Personal Statements leave no question about how Fulbright fits into that picture.

Many applicants find that writing the Personal Statement is the most challenging element of the application. It is limited to one page in length and, unlike the Statement of Grant Purpose, there are no clear stylistic guidelines for writing it. The essay is in many ways a blank slate, an opportunity for you to write about what is most important to you. You can write about your family background, intellectual development, ambitions, challenges, opportunities (or lack of them), and how these things have shaped who you are today. What inspires you? What do you hope to inspire in others? What event most shaped who you are now?

The open nature of the Personal Statement is probably intentional on Fulbright's behalf. Not knowing what Fulbright expects can motivate applicants to write about what's really important to them. The Personal Statement is also an excellent exercise in diplomacy. Much of what makes effective cultural ambassadors is how they present themselves to audiences who have no reference point for judging them.

A strong academic record, international experience, language skills, a clear idea of your goals—these qualities should be emphasized in your application. But they do little to tell Fulbright whether you have the hunger for learning, drive for leadership, commitment to service and community, or sense of curiosity that motivate the most successful Fulbrighters. These qualities can be difficult to demonstrate in the Statement of Grant Purpose, and that's where the Personal Statement can help.

Tips for writing your Personal Statement

_____ Don't treat it as a CV. Instead of listing your experience and qualifications, let the reader know why they are important and what they say about who you are. (Other sections in the Fulbright application ask you to list honors, awards, and accomplishments.)

_____ Situate your Fulbright within the larger narrative of your career. What got you to where you are today? Where are you going? If possible, show how your Fulbright project is the natural culmination of your academic and professional experiences to date. Tell us how it will open a new chapter in your career.

_____ Don't talk about the details of your project. The Personal Statement should complement your Statement of Grant Purpose, not repeat it.

_____ Make your essay easy to read. It should flow well and not be too dense with facts or credentials.

_____ Be true to yourself. What drives you? Let your personality shine.

_____ Try to connect your academic achievements with the rest of your life.

_____ Do mention your international experience, but don't waste space talking about how much you love to travel. We all love to travel.

_____ Show your excitement for what you do and where you're going.

_____ Don't gush aimlessly about why you love the culture of your host country.

_____ Write about your background and this Fulbright opportunity in terms of your development as a leader.

I left the Personal Statement for the very end. I had no idea what to write. I went back and looked over some artist statements I had written in the past, and looked over an application I had done for photography school about five years before. And then I compiled to the best of my knowledge what would be a personal statement. I think that's always the hardest part.

Lauren Hermele
Research Fulbright to Romania
Photography

How to get feedback on your application essays

On the recommendation of my advisor I had a different professor look at my essays. She was accustomed to a different type of research so she had all kinds of suggestions for changes to my essays that I really didn't take. They weren't applicable to the Fulbright experience. This goes back to looking at sample essays: If someone is telling you to do something radically different than the other essays, you might have to ignore them.

Heather Wakefield
Research Fulbright to Georgia
Library Science

The most important thing is contacting former Fulbrighters and asking them to look over your essays. Get their input, and get other people to edit. I had six or seven people, professors and professionals, editing my essays. It was helpful to hear their thoughts, but it's still you writing it. They shouldn't change your voice at all. I was lucky to have a good support system around me.

Ashley Killough
Research Fulbright to Armenia
Journalism

Getting feedback on your application essays is critical if you want a competitive application. But not all feedback is good feedback, and you must be strategic about who you ask for critique. Many Fulbright alumni recommend finding three readers who can commit early on to giving you feedback on at least one draft. Remember, you are not asking them just to be proofreaders; you are asking them to join the community of supporters you are assembling around your Fulbright project. You might not phrase it that way when you approach them, but that's how you should treat the relationship. You never know what introductions they might be able to make or what they are capable of contributing to your work. Getting feedback on your essays is a great opportunity to expand your Fulbright community.

At a minimum, consider finding readers who can serve in the following roles:

1. **An expert in your field**

   Ask this person for substantive feedback on your project and proposal. Are the goals well-articulated? Are they feasible? How can you improve on your idea? This reader should provide macro-level feedback on your project and your ideas. Let this reader help you with the big picture.

2. **Someone outside your field**

   Your application will be judged by experts and non-experts alike. It's critical that a layman be able to understand your proposal. Ask this person for general feedback and pay special attention to his or her first impressions. If at all possible, have a scholar or artist from your host country review your proposal for issues of cultural sensitivity.

3. **A proofreader**

   Select a proofreader with an unfailing eye for proper English grammar, syntax, and punctuation, not for their ability to give substantive critique. This person should provide micro-level feedback of your final draft. Bring him or her in at the end of the process: It's pointless to proofread an essay that you haven't finished.

I sent my essays out to several people for review and went through a fairly lengthy editing process because I knew that the writing had to be really top-notch. The more time you have and the more people that can look at it, the better. As an example, when I wrote my Statement of Grant Purpose I wanted to meet with someone who worked in the area of civic engagement in Latin America. That person sort of tore apart the basic ideas of my proposal. It was so helpful, because when you write, sometimes it just makes sense to you and you assume that everyone's going to like it. When you present it to someone who actually has some expertise in that area, they see huge holes in it. That person's contribution was really helpful in thinking through the ideas. Start early and get people who are both experts in your project area and just good editors to review your writing.

Natalia Ksiezyk
ETA Fulbright to Argentina

I was working with the Fulbright adviser at my college and I started investigating the whole application process in May. I worked for several months on my essays. I probably did 10 different drafts of each one. My advice to applicants is to have as many people as possible read your essays. The more people the better. When you're writing it's so easy to forget that people aren't inside your head and can't read your mind. Even if you know what you want, effectively communicating that on paper can be a struggle. I had a ton of people read over my essays.

Hannah Halder
ETA Fulbright to Romania

I really think that selecting a few people who you feel can provide some substantive feedback and who also have experience in grant writing, or writing applications, can help. Be selective in who you choose to look over your application. If you have a professor, an adviser of some sort who is willing to take the time, definitely take advantage of that. One of my professors offered to read my essays, and I also had two other graduate students who were friends read them.

I selected the graduate students because they were people I had had many conversations with. I trusted their use of the English language. I trusted them to find structural problems with what I was writing. They also had experience in applying for grants and fellowships, which I thought was also useful. And after I felt I had their input and had made my revisions, that is when I asked this professor to give it a look-over and provide me with any comments he had.

Renee Brown
Research Fulbright to Croatia
Political Science

Something that I didn't do that I should've done more of, and that I should do more of every time I write any kind of proposal, is get feedback from other people about my writing. I was lucky in that my proposal was successful and that the essay seemed to go over well with Fulbright readers in the U.S. and in Poland, but I really think it would have benefitted from some additional eyes. Not necessarily the eyes of other filmmakers, but of somebody who's trained in writing. That's advice I would give even though I didn't follow it myself. I would do that next time.

Mike Seely
Research Fulbright to Poland
Filmmaking

Tips on working with editors

____ **Always give readers your best draft**

Don't submit material with grammar and punctuation mistakes—it's disrespectful and wastes the reviewer's time. Inattention to detail will cause them to take you less seriously.

____ **Invite honest critique**

If you are committed to making your application the best it can be, you need to hear the honest truth about the state of your proposal. Readers aren't doing you favors by sugarcoating their feedback. Let them know you want hard criticism, and that now is the time to hear it.

____ **Be careful asking friends for feedback**

So much baggage comes into play when you ask friends to critique your work. When possible, stick with professionals who can give you straightforward, informed feedback, and who aren't worried about hurting your feelings.

____ **Don't begrudge readers their comments**

They took the time to read your proposal because they want to help—it's not fair to hold this against them. If they tell you everything is great and talk about how wonderful you are, find a different reader. If they tell you your essays need lots of work, push through the disappointment and find out more.

____ **Set a deadline for feedback**

"Would next Friday be too soon?" Offer to come to their office or wherever is most convenient for them. Make the review process as comfortable for them as possible.

____ **Seek quality in your feedback, not quantity**

Don't e-mail a draft to all your friends with a note saying, "Any suggestions would be much appreciated!" This invites a flood of unqualified, potentially harmful feedback.

____ **Vet your critique**

Not all feedback is good feedback. You are the only person who knows what you want. Compare notes from your readers and trust your instincts. If more than one reader tells you something isn't working, it probably isn't working.

Get feedback. Don't be afraid. My problem was that I didn't want to look stupid, so I didn't ask more questions. I had the opportunity to ask more questions about how to formulate my research and how to carry out my fieldwork and things of that nature. What I would have done differently is I would have talked to more people—to professors and to people who had done qualitative research—and I would have tried to get more information about their experiences working in the field.

Fulbright applicants should be talking to people who have done similar work and to people who have lived in the country they'll be going to. Even better if you can speak to Fulbrighters who spent time in your host country, because that sort of combines the two segments of the experience. Also reach out to locals in that country, because they have a different perspective on Fulbrighters. Knowing how you're perceived is also useful.

Renee Brown
Research Fulbright to Croatia
Political Science

It takes a village . . .

I had professors who would read over my essays. I had a writing center I could go to for some of the more technical elements. I must have rewritten the essays a hundred times, and started over completely at least a dozen times. A guiding principle that I used was to treat it like a letter to another committee at the college, to people who have to be kept abreast of what you're planning and what you're going to do. Use your friends, family, and acquaintances for help. The more eyes that see it, the more people you can count on pleasing with your writing.

Nic Wondra
Research Fulbright to Georgia
Political Science

Even with the help of an application mentor and your campus Fulbright Program Adviser, developing a successful Fulbright proposal requires the support and input of an entire team of contributors. Research applicants in particular need to reach out to experts in their field, both in the United States and in the host country. Writers, journalists, researchers, professors at other institutions, and industry experts could all have something to add to the development of your ideas. Most will be happy to chat with a Fulbright Scholarship candidate.

Research is critical. Even the smallest piece of information can have a tremendous effect on your application strategy. Learning that everyone in your host country goes on a month-long vacation in September, for example, could seriously affect your work, but not everyone thinks to share such casual information.

There is an unwritten etiquette when contacting people for help. Once you've identified someone you'd like to talk with about your proposal, seek out an introduction from a mutual acquaintance. Cold calls, e-mails, and letters should be methods of last resort.

Although it was my project, with all the people involved it felt a lot of times like a very big collaboration. I'm so grateful for the people who were involved and supportive of it. I'm not a natural writer. For me it takes a lot of emotional energy to convey articulately what I want to say. I'm much better at drawing it out visually than I am at explaining it as a proposal. So for me it took a long time. Some people don't have that problem.

Shadi Khadivi
Research Fulbright to Turkey
Architecture

Much of the strength of my application came from the fact that I was more passionate about the project than I was about the Fulbright grant. It was something I believed could contribute back to the world. Getting the Fulbright Scholarship was a plus—it's prestigious and they take care of you—but I could care less about the title "Fulbright Scholar." What was more important to me was getting my project done. I had something I wanted to do.

A lot of my friends who were struggling with the application process, they decided first that they wanted a Fulbright Scholarship and then tried to come up with a project. I was coming at it from the other direction: I already had a project. My application was strong because it exuded this sense of, "I have everything set up. I have the project and everyone's on board to do it. I'm the right person to do it." The Fulbright advisor who was working with me at Stanford, as well as all my contact letters and all my letters of recommendation, they all felt the same way. They saw that I had a lot of passion and drive to do my project, so they wrote in their letters that this guy just wants to do this work. And because he's so passionate about it, he's already thought of everything. He just needs the money.

I think I even said at one point that whether or not I get the Fulbright, I will go to Cape Town and do this project. "Fulbright committee, you can either help me or get out of my way." Of course I didn't say that directly, but that's basically what I was alluding to, that this was something I was going to do. I think when you have that kind of heart and passion for the project you're doing, it makes the application process so much easier.

Jared Sun
Research Fulbright to South Africa
Public Health

Your letters of recommendation

The Fulbright application requires letters of recommendation from people who know you and your work. These letters tell Fulbright about the support community you've built around your project and your career. Acquiring these letters encourages you to seek out experts and develop relationships with them in the context of your Fulbright proposal. Ideally these relationships will stretch far into the project itself. These letters let application readers know who you have on your team. They reveal the resources and expertise at your disposal to ensure the success of your Fulbright work.

Your letters of recommendation are among the best opportunities you have to expand the core of your Fulbright community. Think of your recommendation writers as your project's advisory board. They should know the details of your proposal and your goals. They should be given every opportunity to offer their insight. Ideally, these are people you will turn to for advice when you encounter hurdles in the field. Some will be too busy to help beyond writing a letter of recommendation, but many will expect to be updated about your project and will be flattered by requests for advice. By writing a letter of recommendation they invest in you and your Fulbright work. Remember: You are asking for support, not just a letter of support. Don't underestimate the potential of this relationship.

Tips on Letters of Recommendation

_____ **Be strategic in choosing whom to approach**

Professors, former professors, academic advisers, mentors, work supervisors, gallery curators—these are all potential candidates. Letters from people in prestigious positions can be assets for your application, but only if the writers are available to discuss your project. They should know you well enough to be specific about your strengths and your proposal. The worst thing that can happen is that they hand the task to an assistant. The most important person you know is not necessarily the best choice to write a letter of recommendation.

_____ **Take time to build a relationship**

The real value of a letter of recommendation is the relationship beneath it. Take the time to meet with your recommenders in person to discuss your Fulbright plans.

The value of exchange

Blake Scott
Research Fulbright to Panama
History

I think you really have to embrace the idea of exchange, because ultimately that's the way we're supposed to learn, through an exchange. I went into the Fulbright thinking that I was going to do this research project, and that I was going to learn a lot about my project. But I also was going to embrace the idea of exchange and see where that took me. And so I tried to create as many relationships as I could with people who I felt wanted to have that exchange with me, who I felt wanted to learn about the United States. Because I wanted to learn about them and about their lives in Panama.

I started a language exchange with a few folks that I had met in coffee shops and through mutual friends. We would meet once a week for two hours. We would speak for an hour in Spanish about anything we wanted to talk about, and then we would speak for an hour in English. I learned a lot about the history and culture of Panama from these conversations: how they viewed Americans, how they viewed themselves, how they viewed their government, and how they viewed different people within Panamanian society. How can you study the history of a place without understanding how contemporary people think about it?

Another way I pursued exchange was to play sports. I played flag football and basketball. And anytime anyone invited me over to their house for dinner, I would take them up on their offer. Because I was managing my own schedule, I could decide that from 8:00 am until 4:00 pm, my job was to think about my history project. But in the afternoons, and sometimes in the mornings, I would have exchanges with people. And it was during those times that I probably learned the most.

For me it was a very difficult application to complete. As an architect I had to submit a portfolio, and the portfolio had to tie in to the research. In addition to all the writing, the portfolio was a big visual presentation as well. And tailoring it to people who are not architects is a very challenging thing. Within my own industry we all have a way of talking. I wasn't sure who the audience was when they are viewing the applications.

Shadi Khadivi
Research Fulbright to Turkey
Architecture

Ask their opinion and advice before you request a letter of support. It's important that your recommenders be familiar with you, your past work, and your future plans, both in the context of Fulbright and beyond. The better they know you, the more personal the letter will be. The worst scenario is that they write about you in platitudes.

_____ **Be deferential and respect your recommenders' time**

Students often think professors are obligated to write letters of recommendation, but this is not the case. Writing a strong letter of support takes time. If they agree to help, it is as a courtesy to you and your career. Don't take this for granted. Be clear and straightforward about the deadline and give them plenty of time to complete the letter. A month is good, but less than two weeks is not. Respect their busy schedules.

_____ **Make the experience comfortable for your recommenders**

Give them whatever information they need to write an informed recommendation. The minimum you should offer is literature about the Fulbright Program, your CV, and a copy of your Statement of Grant Purpose. Your statement need not be finished, but it should be close. If they are particularly busy, offer them an outline or draft letter they can build on. Ask them directly, "What can I do to make this process as convenient for you as possible?"

_____ **Send a friendly reminder one week before the deadline**

Sometimes even the most reliable recommenders forget about deadlines. Be sure you have a back-up plan, just in case.

_____ **Express your thanks**

Keep your recommendation writers updated about the status of your application. Let them know that you couldn't have done it without them. Once you've heard back from Fulbright, send them a handwritten thank-you note whether you were selected or not.

Language evaluation

How well you speak the language of your host country is one of the biggest factors affecting the success of your Fulbright work. More importantly, it gives Fulbright an idea of your potential as a cultural ambassador.

Fulbright's foreign language requirements relate primarily to two factors: the country you are applying to and the nature of your Fulbright work. Different countries have different language requirements and these are often outlined in the **Country Summary**. In the past Fulbright has used two methods to gauge your level of fluency: the Foreign Language Evaluation and the Language Self Evaluation. The Foreign Language Evaluation should be completed and submitted by a qualified language instructor at a college or university. Ideally this is someone familiar with your abilities. If one is not available at your academic institution, Fulbright recommends approaching another faculty member with knowledge of the language. Applicants should provide the evaluator with a copy of their Statement of Grant Purpose.

What if I don't speak the language of my host country?

If you don't speak your host country's language at all but are applying to go somewhere where English is not widespread, be proactive about exploring ways to increase your proficiency. Start taking a language course immediately and begin researching language schools in your host country that you could attend during your grant. Don't try to hide the fact that you don't speak the language. Be sure to mention in your Statement of Grant Purpose what your plans are to continue studying the language in the coming months.

The creative portfolio

Fulbright research candidates who propose artistic or performance-based projects are required to submit a portfolio of their creative work. Fulbright provides specific guidelines for the creative submission on its website. Candidates should consult with professionals in the field to make sure their portfolio conforms to accepted layout and presentation standards.

Application readers for arts projects at the U.S. committee level are often discipline-specific: If you submit a photography proposal, professional photographers will likely review it. They often begin their assessment by evaluating candidate portfolios.

Your campus interview

All candidates applying through their college or university, whether current students or alumni, are required to do a campus interview. Usually this panel is led by professors and fellowship advisers, and sometimes Fulbright alumni. Its purpose is to assess your level of preparedness, the strength of your qualifications, and how well you can carry out Fulbright's mission of international exchange. Interviewers evaluate your candidacy by completing a form that has in the past included both a written evaluation and a ranking system. This evaluation is forwarded to Fulbright with your application.

As daunting as it sounds, the campus interview is a valuable opportunity for you to show Fulbright your strengths as an applicant, especially those difficult to convey in a written application. It's an opportunity to expound on your project beyond the written essays and, more importantly, demonstrate your excitement for the work you propose. Your interview also gives Fulbright a taste of your personality and it suggests how well you will be able to engage your host country in challenging circumstances. In short, the interview helps Fulbright gauge how effective you will be as a cultural ambassador.

The campus interview is handled differently at different institutions. Forward-thinking schools treat it as a final opportunity for you to receive feedback from qualified readers. Some schools even give you a few days after the interview to revise your application materials before submitting them. At-large applicants are not typically required to do a campus interview.

Tips for the campus interview

- Make sure you are well-versed in the historical, political, and cultural aspects of your host country. Stay up on current events.

- Practice your interview beforehand with someone who will ask tough questions. Don't go in without preparing.

- Anticipate the possible challenges to your project and the weaknesses in your candidacy. Be prepared to speak to them directly. Don't just cross your fingers and hope that the interviewers don't ask.

- Treat it as a professional interview and dress accordingly.

The whole Fulbright application process was different from other grants. In some ways better and in some ways worse. Better in that you actually got an interview. To have that personal relationship, that contact, was a huge benefit in explaining where I was going with the research and in letting them know that there's a person on the other end of the application.

I never looked at the interview as an obstacle. I always saw it as a positive, as an opportunity for them to make a connection between a piece of paper and the person. It was a chance for me to expound on what I wanted to do and elaborate a little more on everything I couldn't get into the written proposal. Look at the interview as a time when you have access to people who are professionals in their field. They're experienced, they're bright, but don't be intimidated by them. Treat it almost as a dialogue, and use it as kind of an auxiliary to your written application.

Winston Scott
Research Fulbright to Guatemala
Anthropology

During the interview they asked me additional questions about my essays. They asked me about what type of teaching materials I would bring with me, and about cultural differences. Things that weren't included in the application essays. What type of experiences have you had in the past? I specifically talked about a cultural experience in the opening of my Personal Statement, so they asked me a little more about that situation. They just want to make sure that you sound as good in person as you do on paper. That you can articulate and expand on what it is you want. That you're sure about Fulbright. That you're not just applying because it sounds like a cool thing to do and you want to get someone else to pay for it. They want to make sure that if they're putting their name on the recommendation and the letters, that you'll be a good representative for your college, and for the U.S. as well.

Hannah Halder
ETA Fulbright to Romania

I interviewed with a panel at Stanford. They were mostly professors and one or two administrative people who were affiliated with the Fulbright office at the school. It was a little nerve-wracking, but everyone was very curious and nice. I actually came out of it feeling that it was a good exercise for me to answer questions, explain clearly the concepts for my project, and talk about what I wanted to do.

Mike Seely
Research Fulbright to Poland
Filmmaking

Your Fulbright interview:
The view from inside

Tiffany Joseph
Research Fulbright to Brazil
Sociology

*After returning from her Fulbright experience in
Brazil, Tiffany became an IIE Fulbright Ambassador
and served on the Fulbright interview committee at
the University of Michigan.*

___ *From your experience as a campus Fulbright
interviewer, what do the strongest Fulbright
applicants look like during the interview process?*

The strongest interviews are generally those with
candidates whose applications are well put-
together before they get into the interview. We
read all of the application materials beforehand
and before each candidate comes in we talk
briefly about some of the things we want to
address. If the application is strong in the
beginning, that leaves fewer questions for the
interviewers.

We look for candidates who have a clear
sense of what their research project will be.
The timeline of it, the feasibility of it. Does the
applicant have the language skills to do what
they are proposing to do? Have they had any
previous exposure to this country and if so, what
was that experience like? Aside from everything
I've read on paper, I also try to get a sense of
what sort of personality they have. Do they
look like they will be able to go abroad, live in
another country, get by in a language other than
English, and still make it work?

I remember in one interview I was talking
with the applicant about some of my experiences
in Brazil, particularly with regard to language.

I described getting off the plane in Brazil and making the complete switch to Portugese, and how difficult that was even though I had undergone significant language training. And how in the midst of that I had to find housing and do all of these other things. Her eyes got really big as if to say, "I don't know if I can do that!" I try to read people to get a sense of whether they really know what this experience will entail. It's not just going on vacation in another country, but really living in a place, interacting with people, and getting around on your own without some of the things you're accustomed to. It's about being outside of your comfort zone and learning to thrive in another environment.

____ *Many applicants see the interview as an obstacle to overcome, but you seem to see it instead as an asset for the applicant.*

I do. When I think back on the interview process when I applied, I definitely felt the interviewers were critical of things in my application. "How are you going to address these things? We need to have a sense of that for the evaluation." I felt like getting that critique from them helped make my application much stronger in the long run, even though it seemed like a daunting process during the interview.

Afterwards I could see how that strengthened my application. In that actual moment it can be a source of stress, but in the long run, at least for me, the interview ended up having a positive result. I've heard that on some campuses the interview is used to weed out applicants, but at my university it is used to give them valuable feedback on their applications so they can decide to either revise it before resubmitting, or not do anything and submit it as is. That's something that varies from institution to institution.

____ *So you had the opportunity to revise your application materials after the interview before it went to Fulbright?*

Yes. It was maybe a week at the most. It wasn't much turnaround time, but it was enough for me to tweak it based on the feedback I received in my interview.

____ *What advice do you have for applicants who are about to go into their campus interview?*

Go in prepared to get some feedback that could be critical of your proposal. So that you won't feel so flustered when you're actually in the interview, go in prepared to receive some questions that might make you a little uncomfortable about what you're proposing. It can definitely feel stressful. You're already nervous about applying for a Fulbright, and then you go into the campus interview and get these questions about your proposal when you thought you've made your proposal as strong as you possibly could. Try to remember that the people who are interviewing you want to help you. They want to give you feedback to help make your application stronger so that it's more competitive in the larger application pool.

Go in with realistic expectations about what can be done in that year with respect to the feasibility of the project. Know the sort of political system that you're going into. Try to have a good idea of what's happening in the country, the current events there. In the campus interviews that I did with students after I got back from my Fulbright, some students didn't really seem to have background information about the country they were applying to. That suggested they hadn't done their background research and really wouldn't know what they were getting into if they got the Fulbright to that country.

Also, language skills. If you don't currently have the language skills that you need to go to that country, make sure you talk about how you're going to develop them.

___ *After you've interviewed candidates and looked at their applications, you then evaluate their candidacy. Does Fulbright provide guidelines for that evaluation? What does that evaluation look like?*

The evaluation we fill out has open-ended questions that ask about the applicant's attributes, language skills, and the strength of the research project. Would this person be a good cultural ambassador? Does this person have previous experience? Then at the bottom it asks for your recommendation for the applicant: strongly recommend, moderately recommend, or do not recommend. For each candidate that we interviewed we were asked to give a qualitative overview of the applicant based on their interview and their application, and where we thought they would fall on the scale.

___ *What kind of personality do you think Fulbright is looking for?*

I would say you have to be a very patient person who is able to adapt to change very quickly. And be willing to really step outside of your comfort zone. Those are probably the most important attributes that I see. You are an informal ambassador of the U.S. when you're out on a Fulbright, so being able to interact with people and communicate with them is important, even when it gets stressful and difficult. Even when you just want to get on a plane and leave. "Resilient" is another word I would use. And "resourceful." Being able to rise to whatever challenges might occur over the course of the year.

___ *You've read a lot of application essays. What are some of the most common mistakes?*

Simple things like punctuation and grammatical errors. I always tell people to reread, reread, and reread. Those are mistakes you just don't want to see in an essay. There are also a lot of research proposals that aren't very strong or very convincing. Sometimes the applicant isn't very clear about what they want to do in the country except spend time there. They don't really have a research project in mind, or it's not clear how they are going to carry out their research in the time given. Those are three components that are essential to a strong application.

Applicants should also mention how they are going to serve as a cultural ambassador. Why should U.S. taxpayers care about the project you're proposing? Why should people in the U.S. care about this particular issue in the country you are going to? Make sure you're communicating why this project is unique and different, and why we in the U.S. should be concerned about this particular issue. How does it affect us here in the United States? How will being a Fulbright Scholar create mutual understanding on the basis of this type of project?

In my case the campus interview was a formal affair. I showed up in a suit and tie, and I gave a 30-minute presentation about what I planned to do and how I was qualified to do it. I asked for their support. I fielded questions, some of which were critical. Some faculty were supportive. Other faculty said, "I've never heard of you as a student before. I don't know why we should support your application, because you're not an outstanding student. We had one candidate who went to New Zealand and you're nowhere near her caliber." To which I replied, "I'm not going to New Zealand. I'm going to Georgia and I have a lot of experience in the region, so you need to look at this." Of course I was more respectful than that. Depending on your application, it will be received with different levels of support.

Nic Wondra
Research Fulbright to Georgia
Political Science

The application is in. Now what?

Completing a Fulbright application is a huge achievement. You deserve a celebration—and a break. So take a few days to sort out the aspects of your life you neglected in the chaotic weeks before the deadline. Then be sure to take these follow-up steps:

_____ **Write thank-you notes**

Update everyone who helped you during the application process. Let them know that you are honored by their support and look forward to a continued relationship, Fulbright or not. Don't just send an e-mail—buy proper thank-you cards and handwrite the note. It matters.

_____ **Manage your expectations**

Remember that many Fulbrighters apply more than once before being selected. Think of your first application as a test run. If you're committed to the Fulbright mission, start thinking ahead.

_____ **Save your materials**

Take every scrap of application material and correspondence—a copy of your final application, the final essays, the FedEx receipts, everything—put it in a large envelope and store it someplace safe. Make sure you have at least one complete hard copy of your application.

_____ **Make a list of contacts**

Jot down the names and contact info of everyone you interacted with about your project, even if it was just one e-mail exchange. E-mails and their senders tend to be forgotten and lost, but you never know when you'll need to get in touch again down the road.

_____ **Forget about Fulbright**

Try to forget that you ever applied. Don't cruise the online forums to see who has been accepted. Don't call Fulbright asking for news. Don't talk about it with friends and family—they will only ask you about it every time they see you. Just put it out of your mind and ask yourself, "What's next?" Let your acceptance be a surprise.

I think you just have to try to realize what a gift the Fulbright is and make the most out of that time. Read about other people's Fulbright experiences, especially if you're a young Fulbrighter, so that you have more of an idea of what to expect and of all the different ways you can use this time. Because I was a bit younger, it felt more like a freebie.

Laila Plamondon
Research Fulbright to Canada
Psychology

How to deal with rejection

I applied the year previous as well and was on the final list but didn't get it. I went back and got as much feedback as I could through the Fulbright campus representative. I sat down with her and we talked. It wasn't that my application wasn't solid—she always felt that it was—but she suggested that if I did go forward again I should stress this or that point a little more. Or stress my language abilities a little more. We went through some of my recommendations and decided I could speak with my recommenders a little more beforehand to make sure their recommendations were on the same page with what I was writing. And that they stress the benefits that I would bring as a Fulbrighter. It helped a lot to get that feedback.

Winston Scott
Research Fulbright to Guatemala
Anthropology

The Fulbright Program diplomatically calls rejection "non-recommendation." As respectful as this is, it does not remove the sting of disappointment, especially after such a demanding application process. What can help put things in perspective, however, is to remember that Fulbright isn't a small, local scholarship, but a major academic fellowship that attracts the nation's best and brightest candidates. The fact that you even tried out for such a team speaks volumes about your courage, ambition, and perseverance.

Career academics and grant-writing professionals will all tell you that learning how to apply to fellowships like Fulbright requires experience and failure. It takes time to become proficient at pitching yourself and your ideas. The more grants and fellowships you apply for, the more skilled you become at applying. Even the best ideas require packaging that, unfortunately, only experience will help you master. As in life itself, failure is often the best teacher.

Many candidates apply multiple times before being selected. Being rejected on their first try didn't stop them from applying again, and it shouldn't stop you either. A "non-recommendation" letter means you have a decision to make: You can hang your head and toss out all your hard work, or you can explore where you went wrong, how you can improve, and what other means are available to achieve your goals. Most of the work you put in and the relationships you developed can be rolled over into a new plan, but only if you commit to push forward. The most successful Fulbrighters don't take no for an answer.

Action steps for the "non-recommended"

___ **Resist the temptation to respond to the news immediately**

Being rejected after so much work can be an emotional experience. Disappointment can cloud your judgement. Don't send any e-mails until you've had time to process the news and regain perspective.

___ **Meet with your campus Fulbright Program Advisor**

Your FPA can help you assess where your application might be improved. They want you to be selected to the Fulbright Program.

___ **Meet with your advisors and supporters**

The purpose of the meeting isn't to hang your head and say thanks and goodbye. Stay positive and keep your head high. This inspires confidence and shows that you can take a hit and keep fighting. "I want to brainstorm other ways to get this done. What are your ideas?" The important thing is to keep nurturing the relationships you've forged.

___ **Remember: Fulbright isn't the only way to get it done**

Fulbright is a great tool, but it's not the only tool. If you have a project or teaching assignment you want to pursue in a foreign country, start researching other ways to reach your goal. If you find yourself walking away from your project entirely, it may be that Fulbright wasn't a good fit to start with.

Chapter 5

On the Eve of Departure

As soon as you get the Fulbright you need to forget about all its prestige and instead think, "OK, now that I've been given this opportunity, what do I want to make of it?" Ideally you should've figured that out in the proposal, what you want to do with the Fulbright experience as far as what it means for your specific project and your growth as a person.

But there can be a feeling of being a little lost. You're life has been structured for so long, and all of a sudden someone gives you $20,000 and says, "Go live here. I'll see you in a year." And not being really sure what to do with that. You need to recognize that these types of opportunities don't come up that often. Now is the time to think about some things in an intense way and figure out who you want to be at this point in your life, how you want to interact with other people, and then create that as an objective.

Blake Scott
Research Fulbright to Panama
History

The months before you depart overseas are a rare gift in the Fulbright timeline. After so much time away from your original proposal, this period presents an opportunity to revisit your ideas one last time before you put them in motion. Circumstances change and priorities evolve, and from a distance we can often see cracks in plans that seemed airtight when we designed them. This perspective is invaluable for overseas projects and can be very difficult to gain once your Fulbright is underway.

For every big project there's how it's planned on paper, and then there's how you actually get it done in the field. Your application gives you a theoretical blueprint for how your time overseas might unfold in an ideal scenario. The months before departure allow you to reorient your approach to better reflect realities on the ground. Try to identify the practical challenges to your work by speaking with Fulbrighters recently returned from your host country. You developed your proposal for an audience of application readers, but how you prepare before departure is strictly for the benefit of you and your Fulbright work.

When I was awarded the Fulbright I just tried not to get too high. I was happy of course, but I wasn't getting myself into the mindset of, "OK, that's out of the way now." I've seen other Fulbrighters who seem to think that being awarded the grant is the pinnacle. "I've got my money now and I've got this for my CV. I can write down that I'm a Fulbright Scholar." And that's kind of the pinnacle for some people. I thought, "OK, good. Now I can work."

Winston Scott
Research Fulbright to Guatemala
Anthropology

Choosing your Fulbright launch date

There was one thing about Fulbright that I found really frustrating. Our grant lasted eight months, but the school year lasted for a month and a half longer than the grant. And they didn't tell us that before we arrived. I was super upset when I got there and found out. What am I supposed to do? My philosophy, and that of a number of the other Fulbright English teachers, was that I'm being brought here to share my educational values and style. If I leave early and allow someone else to finish my classes, if I can't see this thing through, then what's the point? I had been putting my heart and soul into teaching and making connections with these students, so the idea of leaving early, of having to give up seeing it through to the end—I just wasn't willing to do that. I decided to stay to finish the rest of the academic year, and I paid out of pocket for housing and living expenses to do that. That was really frustrating.

Hannah Halder
ETA Fulbright to Romania

Fulbright English teaching grants and most research grants are timed to begin at the start of the academic year in your host country. Coordinate your arrival dates with IIE and your host country's Fulbright Commission, especially if your orientation takes place overseas (more about orientation soon). You are responsible for making your own travel arrangements, though Fulbright will provide guidance on how to do this. Grantees of U.S. government programs often must comply with specific travel requirements.

If you are pursuing an independent research project not bound to an academic schedule, you might have more flexibility in choosing when to start your grant. Fulbright often allows such projects to begin as late as March of the following year. This flexibility can be convenient, especially for grantees coming from the professional world.

But there are advantages to starting your Fulbright work with your cohort in the fall. Traveling to your host country in synch with other Fulbrighters gives you greater contact with one of the most supportive communities you will have while overseas. Your Fulbright peers can help talk through the challenges of working abroad and set up mutual accountability for the deadlines and goals you set. Also, the Fulbright Program sometimes hosts mid-year conferences for all Fulbrighters in the region. Sharing a similar timeline with other Fulbrighters will help you get the most out of these meetings.

There are a handful of administrative requirements to fulfill before you can officially be awarded the grant. You must submit a medical evaluation, sign the official grant agreement, designate a departure date, and arrange travel visas and transportation. None of this is complex, but do not dally: You can't start your grant until you complete this work. This flurry of administrative housekeeping probably represents your last major interaction with the more bureaucratic aspects of the Fulbright Program. After this, most of your contact will be with your host country's Fulbright Commission or, where there isn't one, with U.S. Embassy staff.

Tips on scheduling your departure

- Think ahead to your return. If you plan to enter graduate school after your Fulbright, plan your grant accordingly. Try not to spend your time overseas applying to graduate schools.

- Check the calendar for holidays in your host country. Many countries have national or religious holiday seasons that last for weeks and sometimes months. In the northern hemisphere many shut down entirely in August while everyone goes on vacation. Trying to schedule meetings while everyone is at the beach tells people you haven't done your homework.

- Consider what you will do with the work you produce while overseas. Will you present a report of your teaching experience at a conference on international education? Take part in a group photography exhibition? Submit your research for publication? All of these require foresight. They are valuable opportunities that can help push your Fulbright work to its next phase, but only if you plan ahead.

- If you're not sure about the best time to start your research grant, ask the staff at the Fulbright Commission or U.S. Embassy in your host country what they recommend.

I felt like I went in there pretty well prepared. But if I could go back and do it over again, I would've focused more on my project and the feasibility of me accomplishing what I wanted to accomplish. I found it difficult not being in a graduate program. I think that having more involved and more invested academic advisers would have been very useful in guiding me through a more realistic project. I had done some research and I had found some other projects that I wanted to emulate, but they were really outside the scope of what I was capable of doing. I think that kind of input from experienced researchers, qualitative researchers, would have been very helpful for me.

Renee Brown
Research Fulbright to Croatia
Political Science

Preparing for the Fulbright economy

Don't let financial issues distract you during your Fulbright. Consider these action steps as you prepare for departure:

1. **Improve your financial literacy**

   None of us was born understanding money. If your financial education is weaker than you would like (like most young Americans), the best investment in your financial future is to start educating yourself now. Read about personal finance. Take a money-savvy relative out to lunch and pick his or her brain. Seek out entrepreneurs whose work you respect and ask for their advice. Talk to a financial planner. Money can be a powerful tool to help accomplish your goals. The more you understand how, the less intimidating it will be.

2. **Pay down debt and avoid new financial responsibilities**

   Credit card companies don't care that you are overseas on a prestigious fellowship, and managing serious consumer debt could prove difficult on a Fulbright stipend. If you can, hold off on buying the new car or new home before departure. It's not impossible to account for them while you're away, but they could complicate your Fulbright experience. The smaller your financial footprint, the fewer distractions you will have to contend with in the field.

3. **Make savings work for you while you're away**

   Most Fulbrighters are able to live on their Fulbright stipends. Many have savings back in the States that sit dormant during their grants. If your nest egg is sizeable, consult a financial adviser about investment options that can work for you while you're away. Just be sure to leave enough cash available for emergencies.

4. Build an emergency fund

For some problems in life, the simplest solution is to throw money at them. This is particularly true when living overseas. Health emergencies, natural disasters, political turmoil—these circumstances can often be best navigated with quick access to American dollars. This might be for a last-minute plane ticket, a midnight surgery, or any other eleventh-hour fix. The less developed your host country, the more you need an emergency fund that you can access quickly and directly, not through a third party like a friend or family member. Speed is of the essence in moments of crisis. If you don't have a credit card, get one before departing and let the company know you'll be traveling overseas.

5. Fundraise

Fulbright allows outside financial resources to be applied to your Fulbright project as long as they cover expenses that Fulbright doesn't cover. You can raise funds for things like additional travel, research materials, language study, and fees to attend conferences. As a Fulbright applicant you are in a good position to ask for support, so don't be shy. The Fulbright name lends credibility to almost any project. Never underestimate its fundraising value.

6. Start thinking about your return to the real-world economy

It's difficult to imagine on the eve of such a big adventure, but the day will come when you must return to normal life and start earning money. You will be a changed person, but your experience and enlightenment alone probably won't transfer directly into gainful employment. It takes planning to recover from a year of low income: Start planting the seeds of financial health now.

I think the real trip-up for me was the money issue. What the Fulbright gave me was not enough. My student loan payments were half of what the Fulbright gave me. While you can defer some student loans, it's not financially beneficial to defer anything. I was conducting my research and still paying my school loans with the stipend I got there. I thought, "OK, I can make it work." There was a time when the currency made it beneficial to buy all my lira at one time, so I changed all my money for four months because the currency had devalued itself. The dollar went up. That helped a little. I would watch the news every day to see where the dollar was. That helped, but it didn't solve it.

Dealing with the financial obligations you have in your own country while you're overseas, that's a big deal. What ended up happening to me was that I came back with more debt, which was a little problematic.

Shadi Khadivi
Research Fulbright to Turkey
Architecture

Expanding your Fulbright community

The pre-departure period is a powerful opportunity to expand the community you have begun building around your Fulbright grant. You are no longer a Fulbright candidate, but a full-fledged Fulbright Scholar. Very few people wouldn't respond to a polite, well-phrased request to talk about your upcoming work. The Fulbright grant gives you a platform for reaching out to experts in your field, potential funding sources, future mentors, and future employers you might not otherwise have access to.

With proper follow-up, these meetings can turn into relationships that open doors for your post-Fulbright career. If you are considering graduate school, get in touch with professors or researchers who are doing work relevant to your Fulbright. Reach out to government offices, non-profit organizations, galleries, publishers, private sector entities, or think tanks you'd like to work with.

Of all the people worth reaching out to about your Fulbright work, some of the most valuable are local Fulbright alumni who studied or taught in the United States as Visiting Fulbright Scholars. These Fulbrighters typically represent some of their countries' brightest minds and all speak fluent English. Like most Fulbright alumni, they are fiercely supportive of the Fulbright Program and the Fulbright community. If you need advice on where to go for language classes, introductions to local colleagues, or even recommendations on where to stay while you look for long-term housing, these Fulbrighters can help. Like many of their American counterparts, they often hunger for contact with Fulbright colleagues. Reach out to them.

It probably would have behooved me to make some more connections in Nicaragua in addition to my host affiliation before I got there. It wouldn't have been hard to do. I know a lot of people who have interests in Latin America, who traveled or lived there, and I could have reached out to find cool people to connect with to show me the ropes. The truth is that once you get there, you can't really count on the U.S. Embassy to do any of that for you. It was pretty clear when I got to Nicaragua that they would change my checks for me, but they weren't going to help me find housing. Before you get to the country, try to reach out to people and make connections outside of the organization or university you're affiliated with. Diversify. Don't put all your eggs in one basket.

Jessie Rubin
Research Fulbright to Nicaragua
Political Science

I spent the first week or two e-mailing people in Panama, old Fulbrighters and other contacts that alumni had given me. I just really tried to make use of the Fulbright alumni who had been in Panama before to make contacts while I was there. It would have saved time if I had contacted Fulbright alumni before I left instead of when I was already in Panama. I think that would have expedited the process of establishing my network.

Maya deVries
Research Fulbright to Panama
Biology

Go in as prepared as you can possibly be. And by prepared I mean have everything in order with regard to your project. Talk to as many people as possible and get as many points of view and bits of information as you can, from housing, to transportation, to other logistical issues. Know what to expect when dealing with landlords. Things like that.

But then once you get there and you have all this information and you're prepared, be flexible and able to roll with things. That sounds very trite and not very useful, but I think that kind of approach will enhance your experience. Be prepared, be open, and be flexible.

Renee Brown
Research Fulbright to Croatia
Political Science

Even if you don't want to use it right off the bat, there's value in doing some groundwork to create a support system for when you arrive. I'm talking about emotional and social support rather than professional support.

There may be other Fulbrighters, especially those who have had extensive experience overseas like I did, who go into it thinking, "I'm going to only work with the host nationals, and I don't need to hang out with expats. I'm going to go native." I'd say to them, "If you're anything like me, you're not as badass and self-sufficient as you think you are." Don't look down on having your fellow countrymen around to help provide some emotional and social support. You'll need it even if you don't think you will.

If you happen to come from a faith-based background, call ahead and find out who from your faith community is doing work in that country. I think that can be worthwhile, especially if the person you wind up in contact with happens to run a hostel. That was the case with us. We could have found some of the missionaries elsewhere and that would have been fine, and I'm sure we would have had a great experience. But the woman that we were connected to, she ran a hostel for all kinds of different folks, so she immediately had her pulse on everything and was very quick to get us plugged in.

Tim Slade
Research Fulbright to Benin
Public Health

Fulbright and your student loans

Most student loan payments can be deferred during your Fulbright, but this doesn't mean you should stop making payments. Here's why: Only subsidized federal loans will stop accruing interest. In other words, if you also have unsubsidized or private student loans, as many recent graduates do, your principal loan balance will continue to grow if you don't make monthly payments. The result could be that you return home with more debt than when you left. Consider these action steps to manage your student loans:

1. **Know your debt**

   Not sure how much you owe or what the interest rate is? Call your lender and get educated. The longer you wait, the more it will cost you. When it comes to debt, ignorance and negligence will only complicate things.

2. **Explore loan consolidation**

   Sometimes consolidating your loans can save you money in the long run. Ask your lender about options.

3. **Set up deferred payments during your Fulbright grant period**

   Not deferring a subsidized federal student loan is like throwing away free money. It will take about 20 minutes to set up and could save you thousands of dollars.

4. **At a minimum, pay all the monthly interest on your debt**

   Find a way to pay off any interest accruing on your loans while you're away, even if this means dipping into your savings account. Coming home is challenging enough without more debt.

5. **Use extra funds to pay down the principal on your unsubsidized federal loans**

   Unsubsidized loans are much less friendly than subsidized loans. If you want to put a long-term dent in your student debt, apply extra money toward lowering your principal balance. Contact your lender to make sure your payment is specifically targeted at those loans. Otherwise they will apply it to your aggregate debt.

6. **Do not ignore your student loans**

   You may forget about them, but they won't forget about you. If you are required to make monthly payments, make the payments. If you can't, call your lender to ask about options. Whatever you do, do not default on your loans.

Nobody can tell you what your goals are—you've got to do it yourself. That's the thing about Fulbright. They say, "We trust you, and that you're smart enough and driven enough to figure out your own goals. And that whatever you come up with is going to be valuable to yourself, to the place you're visiting, and to the place you're from."

Come up with a plan—a very rough plan—of what you would like to achieve during three or four phases of your time overseas. Most of us think about our objectives and our plans within periods of a couple months. What is my goal for the first trimester, the first period of the Fulbright? Then what am I going to try to achieve in the next period? And in the last period?

Blake Scott
Research Fulbright to Panama
History

Planting the seeds for life after Fulbright

Tips on laying the groundwork for your post-Fulbright career

- Ask advisers, mentors, professors, and colleagues if they can introduce you to the people or organizations you want to work with in the future. Your goal is to get five minutes of their time to brief them on your upcoming Fulbright work. Be humble, polite, and persistent.

- Go out of your way to meet these people in person. If the trip requires travel, consider it an investment in your career. Dress as you would for a job interview. If you're lucky, that's what it will be.

- Be prepared to answer three questions: What do you want? Why is it important? And how can it contribute to their work? Don't come to the meeting wanting to know what they can do for you—they want to know what *you* can do for *them*. If you can get them as excited about your work as you are, your meeting is a success.

- Be sure to ask how you can stay in touch and keep them updated on progress. This keeps you connected and gives them a chance to get to know you better as a person, and as a future leader in your field.

For many Fulbrighters the most challenging phase of the Fulbright experience is the return home. Don't underestimate the degree to which preparation and foresight can smooth this transition. The best time to lay the groundwork for your career after Fulbright isn't in the final months of your grant, but before you ever leave the States. As difficult as it might be to think that far ahead, remember that nine or ten months is not a very long time to be away. Forcing yourself to deal with the issue before departure frees you to focus more on your Fulbright work during your grant.

If you want to enter a graduate program when you return home, develop your application now—before you leave the U.S. Don't spend precious time in the field working on applications. Anyone who has done it can attest that putting together a competitive graduate school application while overseas can be frustrating.

If you plan to enter the workforce after Fulbright, the months before departure present an opportunity to network and meet future employers. You are a Fulbright Scholar about to begin important, life-changing work, and this is a great reason to reach out and forge new relationships. Taking the time to introduce yourself to future colleagues over a cup of coffee, or in a five-minute office meeting, will help pave the way for future opportunities. Who wouldn't want to meet a Fulbright Scholar who has reached out to them about their work? Think of this as a way to strengthen and expand your Fulbright community. Not all meetings will lead to relationships, but you waste the potential if you don't reach out.

Looking for the right job is a lot like growing crops: You plant the seeds of connection early on, nurture them, and someday, perhaps, they will yield strong professional relationships, possibly even mentorship. The time to plant these seeds is in the months before your departure.

Sample Fulbright outreach e-mail

Dear Dr. Conway,

always use the appropriate address

I am a U.S. Fulbright Scholar preparing to depart on a nine-month project to study beetle migration in Borneo. Dr. Maureen Johnson, my advisor at the University of Los Angeles, suggested I get in touch to tell you about my project. Your work has been a big influence on my research.

mention a mutual acquaintance or referral

show deference!

Your schedule permitting, I would love the opportunity to brief you on my work, hear your thoughts, and discuss possibilities for graduate study in your department following my Fulbright Scholarship.

Is there a time we could meet to briefly chat about the project?

Best wishes,

Grantee McFulbright

Be clear about what you are asking for

Staying informed about your host country

Hearing domestic news about politics and what people are concerned about gives you an idea of what the main concerns are in your host country. Just as if someone traveling from Europe to America might hear that Americans are concerned about gasoline prices, for example. Knowing what your host community is concerned about, or angry about, when you arrive will allow you to not be shocked when you get there. Sometimes they are minor issues. Maybe it's gas prices. Or lack of poultry in the market. When we first arrived, all of our neighbors were complaining about not being able to find chicken. Knowing more before you get there should always be the goal. Read the news and talk with people there.

Nic Wondra
Research Fulbright to Georgia
Political Science

I thought I had educated myself before going over. I did what I thought was a moderate amount of research to learn some general facts about Korea. I'd never even been to Asia, so I was just trying to learn about that part of the world. But when I got there I realized I didn't really know anything, so I was really glad I had that orientation period.

    Looking back, I wish I'd read a few books. What I did was mainly Internet searches. I found the blog of a previous Fulbright English teacher and I read every single world that she wrote. And I read some other stuff about Korea. It would have been good for me to read some books that had a more in-depth description of the culture and the country.

Bethany Glinsmann
ETA Fulbright to Korea

Fulbright applications ask candidates to spend a great deal of time researching their host country. Avoid the temptation once you've been awarded the grant to relax this research and rest on your laurels. If anything you should redouble your efforts. If you haven't done so already, start incorporating local stories of daily importance into your news consumption. Read newspapers from the region. Check out blogs from both locals and expats who live there—especially blogs by Fulbrighters. Don't just focus on international news feeds. Go right to the source: Read what the locals are reading, gossip and all. Make travel memoirs, scholarly papers, and books about the nation's history part of your pre-departure preparation.

    No amount of reading can fully prepare you for what life and work will be like in the field, but stories of day-to-day significance give you a valuable foundation for interacting with locals. Imagine that first cab ride from the airport after you arrive: Will you cower in the back-seat in silence or chat with the driver about his soccer team's recent victory, the city's new mayor, or the new tax on taxi drivers? Showing interest in your host country demonstrates that you are curious and committed. It engages you more deeply.

I found out in May that I was going and that I would be leaving in September. I read as much as I could about Romania. Blogs. Newspaper articles. I talked to Romanians in the U.S. I spent a lot of time trying to guess what classes I would be teaching. I didn't know what they would be before I left, but I knew I'd be teaching in the American studies department and in the English language department. I did research and read a lot of books. I also spent a lot of time with family and friends. You're so busy and things are so crazy before you leave, if you forget about family and friends it can be more difficult when you're in-country.

Hannah Halder
ETA Fulbright to Romania

I found out at the end of April that I got the Fulbright, so I had about four months before leaving in September. I felt like I had prepared so much already through the application, that during that summer I didn't prepare as much as I should have. I thought I had prepared enough, really.

But there are things I wish I had done more of that summer before I left. I wish I had read more books. I wish I had talked to more people. It would have been helpful to talk to more Fulbrighters who had been to Armenia. There were two recent Fulbrighters at orientation, and that was so helpful. I wish I had prepared more about the cultural things and asked more questions and taken more seriously what it would be like to be a single woman living in Armenia. I was not prepared for that at all. I wish I had prepared culturally for little things like that.

Ashley Killough
Research Fulbright to Armenia
Journalism

Language study

The single most influential factor affecting the quality of your Fulbright experience overseas is the relationships you build with your host community. And the single most powerful tool for building these relationships is your ability to speak the local language.

For those committed to this goal, the immersion environment presents one of the best opportunities to become fluent in a foreign language. It holds more potential for language development than any course of study you will find in the United States. But this doesn't mean it doesn't require work. Here are some things to remember about studying a foreign language:

_____ Unless you are a native speaker, there is always room for improvement. If you are already conversationally fluent, consider focusing on your professional or public speaking skills.

_____ The time to commit seriously to language study is at the *beginning* of your Fulbright experience, not at the end. If you don't think you have time with your busy Fulbright schedule, know this: Every year Fulbrighters return home wishing they had invested more time and energy into language study at the start of their grant.

_____ The benefits of daily, disciplined language study increase exponentially over time. It can be horribly frustrating and unrewarding at first, but sustained attention and discipline will pay dividends down the road.

Things to remember about immersion language study

Lilith Dornhuber deBellesiles
Research Fulbright to Germany
Philosophy

- Language learning does not occur through osmosis. It's not like *The 13th Warrior,* where if you listen long enough one day you'll open your mouth and out will come well-pronounced, grammatically correct sentences. If you want to speak well, you have to work at it.

- Grammar is difficult and it's impossible to be completely perfect.

- You don't have to dream in your host language to prove to yourself or anyone else that you are fluent.

- Knowing grammar and vocabulary is not enough to speak a language well.

- You can learn a language without already knowing the basics when you arrive in a country, but these sure do help.

- When it comes to speaking a foreign language, the perfect is the enemy of the good: It's better to speak with mistakes than not speak at all. *You cannot learn to speak well without first speaking poorly.*

- Gaining professional fluency in a foreign language is a long, difficult process. People who say it's quick and easy either don't speak as well as they think they do or they grew up hearing the language at home. Remember that it's a marathon, not a sprint.

If you're learning a language in which you have no background, the standard advice is to do some sort of immersion, like spending a month there before the program starts. Doing online courses can also be helpful, but I think you do need the one-on-one human teaching space. If it's a language that's common enough in your U.S. community that you can get involved in cultural activities, usually they are very welcoming.

For German, the Goethe-Institut *has plenty of free events for people who want to learn German. I know that for French there's a similar institution. For less schoolbook languages, immigrant communities provide a welcoming place to start to learn a language, or at least listen to it. Advice that I give my students is to watch movies without subtitles. Even if you don't understand it, hearing it and seeing the acting with it is going to start to give you a sense of the cadence of the language so that you can have a better time learning it once you start your formal study.*

Lilith Dornhuber deBellesiles
Research Fulbright to Germany
Philosophy

Whatever country you're going to, if they speak another language do your best to learn as much of the language as you are capable of learning before you go. I think I made a mistake. I should have been more diligent with my language studies.

Heather Wakefield
Research Fulbright to Georgia
Library Science

If it's possible, take a summer language course before you go. If someone spent two or three months sitting with a tutor working on their Spanish or French or Russian, I think that would help. It's hard to do in the U.S., but it's really necessary to help with the acclimation.

If you're in a big enough city in the U.S. you can find Russians, or Azeris, or Georgians and befriend them. It would be possible to understand a little bit more about the people before going out. Of course immigrants in the U.S. have already acculturated a bit, but you could still get somewhat of a sense.

Joshua Noonan
Research Fulbright to Georgia
  and Azerbaijan
Political Science

I brushed up on my language before the Fulbright while I was living in New York. I found a tutor on Craigslist that I met with once a week. She was sort of a starving artist and she was totally beneficial for me. I paid her to speak to me in Turkish two hours a day, once a week, for six months.

Shadi Khadivi
Research Fulbright to Turkey
Architecture

How to get the word out about your Fulbright work

Media relations 101

- Never refer to yourself as a Fulbright "student" or an English-teaching "assistant," and certainly not as an intern, even if that's how your host organization sees you. All grantees are Fulbright Scholars—the administrative differences between the Fulbright Student Program and the Fulbright Scholar Program are lost on people outside the system.

- Don't ever disparage anyone in public. It's bad form and will usually come back to haunt you. No matter how frustrated you are about your work or your professional relationships, always stay positive in the public eye.

- Don't ever say anything publicly that you wouldn't want a future employer to read about, because there's a good chance they will. Treat all interactions with journalists overseas as "on the record."

- Always mention colleagues and organizations you are collaborating with. This is a great way to thank them for their help and support.

- Don't forget to mention the Fulbright Program—it's the least you can do. Send Fulbright a link to published stories or interviews about your work.

Fulbrighters are by and large a humble group and often reluctant to talk about their accomplishments. But like it or not, realizing the full potential of your Fulbright requires letting people know about your work and how excited you are about what you're doing. The more people know about your Fulbright work, the more influential it can be. To get the most out of your time overseas, this outreach should begin before you board the plane.

Most people mistakenly believe that if their work has enough value it will automatically get the attention it deserves. The truth is that good projects and good ideas need help selling themselves. For people to share and celebrate your accomplishments, they must first hear about what you're doing.

Spreading the word about your Fulbright work is a win-win for everyone. It helps the Fulbright Program grow, it inspires future Fulbrighters to pursue their interests overseas, and it dramatically boosts the potential of your project and your career. If you want to be invited to share your work at conferences, have better access to funding sources, or broaden the community that benefits from your work, you must give people ways to learn about what you are doing. Fulbrighters do exciting work, and people want to hear about it.

Action steps to spread the word about your work

____ **Create a web presence for your Fulbright work**

Whether it's an official project page or a personal blog, a website is where people can find out more about who you are, what you do, and how they can contact you. Keep the tone positive and professional, and don't underestimate how many people in your host country will read what you publish. Your website will be their first impression of you. Its quality and style will be interpreted as an indication of your professional acumen.

____ **Spread the news about your Fulbright selection**

Your Fulbright grant is a big deal. At a minimum you should send out a press release about your selection and your project. Be sure to include a web address and how to get in touch. In the past, Fulbright has provided some grantees an official press release to send out at their discretion, but don't be shy about creating your own content too.

____ **Practice talking about your work**

You should be able to describe your work in one sentence in an engaging manner. If somebody wants to know more, move to the more detailed version. Make your project accessible to everyone.

____ **Remember: People *want* to hear what you're doing**

Never turn down an opportunity to talk about your Fulbright work, no matter how insignificant the interview may seem. Show people how excited you are about your project, where it's going, how humbled you are by your colleagues, and how honored you are to have this opportunity. If everyone talked about their colleagues' accomplishments, no one would ever have to talk about themselves.

Force yourself to explain your project to as many people as possible. If you're sitting with a guy who's a consultant for a big oil company and you're trying to explain your project and he's looking at you like you're out of your mind, you need to find a better way to talk about your project. Find what's really interesting about your work. It's not a thing you can just rewrite and rewrite at home and memorize. When you go out and talk about it you have to ask yourself, "Why am I doing this?" It makes you constantly reexamine your ideas.

Evan Tachovsky
Research Fulbright to Azerbaijan
Political Science

Sample Press Release

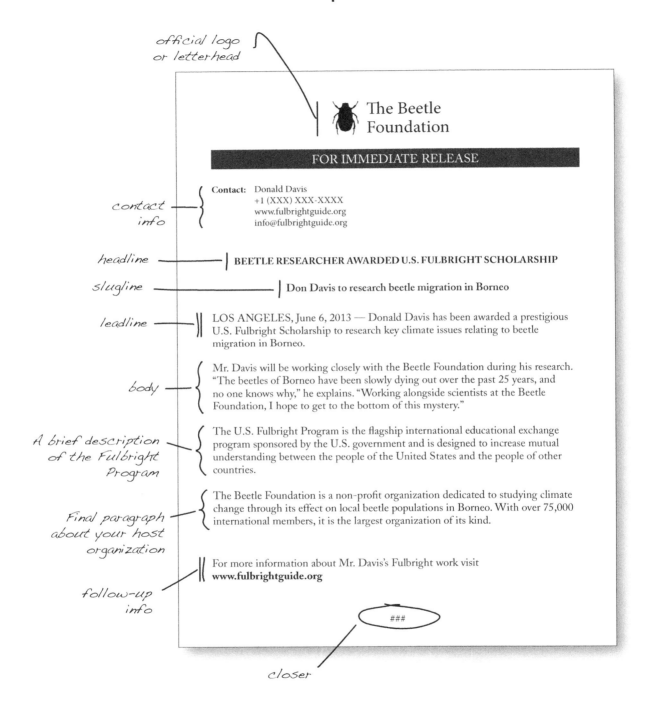

official logo
or letterhead

The Beetle
Foundation

FOR IMMEDIATE RELEASE

contact
info

Contact: Donald Davis
+1 (XXX) XXX-XXXX
www.fulbrightguide.org
info@fulbrightguide.org

headline

BEETLE RESEARCHER AWARDED U.S. FULBRIGHT SCHOLARSHIP

slugline

Don Davis to research beetle migration in Borneo

leadline

LOS ANGELES, June 6, 2013 — Donald Davis has been awarded a prestigious U.S. Fulbright Scholarship to research key climate issues relating to beetle migration in Borneo.

body

Mr. Davis will be working closely with the Beetle Foundation during his research. "The beetles of Borneo have been slowly dying out over the past 25 years, and no one knows why," he explains. "Working alongside scientists at the Beetle Foundation, I hope to get to the bottom of this mystery."

A brief description
of the Fulbright
Program

The U.S. Fulbright Program is the flagship international educational exchange program sponsored by the U.S. government and is designed to increase mutual understanding between the people of the United States and the people of other countries.

Final paragraph
about your host
organization

The Beetle Foundation is a non-profit organization dedicated to studying climate change through its effect on local beetle populations in Borneo. With over 75,000 international members, it is the largest organization of its kind.

follow-up
info

For more information about Mr. Davis's Fulbright work visit
www.fulbrightguide.org

###

closer

Press releases 101

- Join forces with an organization in your immediate Fulbright circle to produce your press release—your university at home, your host organization overseas, or perhaps even Fulbright itself. Letterheads and logos lend credibility and importance to the information that follows.

- Make it interesting. The real story isn't your Fulbright award, but what you're going to do with it. You want to pique people's interest so they redistribute the information, visit your website, or contact you directly for follow-up.

- Present the basic facts in the first sentences. Subsequent paragraphs can elaborate. Don't exceed one page in length.

- Write in the third person, even when writing about yourself. You are reporting an event.

- Try to include at least one quote, even if you quote yourself.

- Dedicate the last paragraph to information about the organization you are affiliated with.

- If you want to cast a wide net, check out online services that will send your release to a much larger audience, including other media outlets.

Don't be shy about talking about your project. Be friendly, be tactful, but be persistent. Just by getting the word out, or by being friendly and making contacts, people will be more willing to share information. If they've already heard of you and already have an idea of what you might be asking, they'll be better prepared when they meet you, which was a plus and a minus for me at times. If you promote your project, you might luck into someone saying, "I know you're doing this research. I have this information." Or, "You might want to contact this person who is doing similar work."

Heather Wakefield
Research Fulbright to Georgia
Library Science

How to make the most of your pre-departure orientation

All Fulbrighters are required to attend an orientation seminar at the start of their grant. For some this meeting takes place in their host country on arrival. But for many Fulbrighters, particularly those with destinations outside Western Europe, the pre-departure orientation takes place over three days in August in Washington, D.C. In the past the Fulbright Program has covered the cost of the grantee's accommodation, meals, and domestic air travel to attend.

After all the application deadlines, medical clearances, and assorted red tape, it's easy to think of the orientation seminar as just one more bureaucratic hoop to jump through. In reality it's much more than that. You will be given a healthy amount of official information about your grant (about the health plan, the stipend, etc.), but the event's real value lies in the vast potential of the new relationships you can form with your Fulbright peers. It is an opportunity to dramatically expand your Fulbright community. Where else can you meet in one place such a driven, intelligent group of your peers who are all specializing in your region of the world and preparing to embark on meaningful projects there? This group is full of tomorrow's leaders, the next generation of experts in their fields. Breakthroughs happen where disciplines intersect, and events like these are where many of these relationships begin.

Fulbright orientation seminars in the States are organized directly by Fulbright partner organizations (usually IIE). Overseas they are often organized by the local Fulbright Commission or U.S. Embassy. Seminars that take place in Washington, D.C., can be quite large (in the past, Fulbrighters heading to Eastern Europe and countries of the former Soviet Union have all attended one orientation). IIE does an excellent job mixing large, formal presentations with small, informal, country-specific meetings led by Fulbright alumni recently returned from the field. These alumni are there to help you, not to toe an official line. You can talk with them about anything, from which neighborhood they recommend living in to language study options and personal safety. Often these alumni returned to the United States only weeks before, so their information is usually fresh.

Tips for making the most of your pre-departure orientation in Washington, D.C.

- Arrange to spend time outside the official orientation schedule with the Fulbrighters who are also heading to your host country. Take the initiative to organize a late-night dinner or drinks at a nearby restaurant. There are opportunities to talk during the orientation, but getting to know each other off-site will lead to deeper connections.

- Learn about as many other Fulbrighters and Fulbright projects as you can, even those not connected to your particular country. These are your peers—they want to meet you as much as you want to meet them.

- Use your time in Washington to meet with organizations that interest you. No other city has as many U.S. federal government offices, foreign embassies, and international organizations. If you are a photographer, arrange to meet with someone at National Geographic to tell them about your project. If you are a public health researcher, have coffee with someone at the U.S. Department of Health and Human Services. If you are a documentary filmmaker, meet with the The Discovery Channel. Ask your congressman or senator for five minutes to brief them on your project. If necessary, arrange your plane ticket to extend your trip an extra day. Washington is full of Fulbright alumni who would be happy to host you for an evening.

- Prepare questions for the Fulbright alumni recently returned from your host country. They can help you hit the ground running when you arrive.

- Stay in touch with your Fulbright peers. Open the lines of communication with a short follow-up e-mail.

Planning your departure

A few tips from Fulbright alumni about the business of departure:

____ Travel smart

Fulbright will not make travel arrangements for you—it's your responsibility to sort out how, when, and by what route you travel to your host country. It's good to be frugal when shopping for airline tickets, but be careful when buying the cheapest deal: Many discount fares allow little or no flexibility on return flights and can involve long, uncomfortable layovers. Paying a few hundred dollars more for a comfortable flight and the ability to reschedule your return is often worth the investment. Don't underestimate the value of arriving in your host country rested and ready to go.

____ Plan for emergencies

International travel comes with risks. Make sure your loved ones back home have enough information to help you if something goes wrong. Give your family a one-page printout of where you'll be, what you'll be doing, and who they should contact in an emergency. Include numbers for IIE, your host institution, the U.S. Embassy, and the Fulbright Commission in your host country. Include copies of your passport, driver's license, and birth certificate. Write out and sign a will and a release of power of attorney, just in case. If you're going to adventure, do it responsibly.

____ Minimize your stateside obligations

Chances are the Fulbright will change your priorities in ways you can't begin to imagine. What seem like inconsequential decisions now could shut the door on life-changing opportunities later. It would be a shame to pass up a great opportunity after your Fulbright because you promised your mother you'd come home to sell the car you left in her driveway.

Check your health

Fulbright requires you to get a doctor's checkup before departure. It's worth the time to get vision and dental check-ups as well. Wouldn't you want to know now if you have wisdom teeth that need to be removed? And don't skimp on immunizations—they are recommended for a reason.

Make time to say good-bye

Nine months doesn't seem like a long time, but you will be surprised how much you will change in this short period. The best way to keep your relationships alive and well is to celebrate your departure. Take your boss out to lunch. Buy your colleagues coffee and donuts at work. Send flowers to the important people in your life. If you have a farewell party, give a speech and print up cards with info on where you're going, what you're going to be doing, and how people can stay in touch and follow your adventures.

Pack wisely

The conventional wisdom for international travel is to bring half the luggage and twice the money you expect to need. Ask former Fulbrighters what they wish they had brought but didn't. What did they bring that was a waste of space? Last year's group might even leave you things you'll need (internet routers, cell phones, power adapters, apartments, etc.). Bring a supply of contact lenses if you wear them, an extra pair of glasses, and any medication you will need. If friends or family will visit during the year, plan for a resupply if necessary.

Fulbright couture

Be smart about the clothes you bring—first impressions matter. Whether you are an independent researcher, student, or English teacher, you are first and foremost a Fulbright Scholar and should dress the part. If you dress like your students they will treat you as their peer, not as their teacher.

All Fulbrighters should bring professional attire beyond what they think they will need for their day-to-day routine. This means at least one formal business suit, even if your work doesn't seem like it will require it. At some point it probably will. Grantees would be smart to bring a "business casual" outfit as well for social functions. When in doubt, overdress. No one will think less of you for being the best dressed person in the room.

Planning your arrival

You cannot completely plan your Fulbright experience—things will begin to change the moment you step off the plane. With sufficient foresight, however, you can make plans that will help mitigate the chaos of arrival. This can go a long way toward starting your project off on the right foot.

____ Transportation from the airport

There's not an airport in the world that won't have a swarm of taxi drivers waiting to ferry you to your destination. There's also a lot to be said for arranging transportation on your own terms, especially after a long flight. Ask your host organization, the local Fulbright Commission, or your Fulbright peers what they recommend. Some Fulbright Commissions and U.S. Embassies offer to meet Fulbrighters at the airport, which is an incredibly courteous service that they are in no way obligated to provide. Public transportation from the airport can be an option, but do yourself a favor and research it beforehand. As a last resort, ordering a taxi ahead of time with a local company will usually be less expensive and less stressful than negotiating at the airport while juggling luggage.

____ Housing

Many Fulbrighters recommend waiting until after you arrive to find long-term housing in your host country. But you will be wise to arrange a short-term place to stay while you sort things out. Reach out to the Fulbright network: Grantees and alumni are generally keen to help each other. You can also ask your host organization, English-teaching institution, or local Fulbright representative for recommendations. If none of these is an option, make a reservation at a hostel, hotel, or homestay before departure.

____ Entry visas

Don't rely on IIE staff in the States to know the latest visa regulations for your host country—they are experts in international education, not consular affairs. When in doubt, ask the Fulbright Commission or U.S. Embassy staff what visa is required for your Fulbright work. When

---

It helps to have a set schedule from the get-go. It provides structure. Lots of Fulbrighters have trouble with the complete openness of the grant. They find it overwhelming. Signing up for a class at the beginning, a language class or something else, is very important right away.

I managed to line up an apartment and a language school before I arrived. Some of my peers spent a month finding an apartment. Doing it beforehand allows you to hit the ground running and focus on your project.

Courtney Doggart
Research Fulbright to Turkey
International Relations

applicable, push for a multi-entry visa that covers the duration of your stay. In many countries renewing a visa can be a frustrating, time-consuming process.

Be aware that getting a visa while still in the States could take weeks and will most likely require that you leave your passport at the embassy or consulate. Always keep a photocopy for yourself. Fulbright often does not cover the costs of visas, but in the past they have provided official letters of support when necessary for the application process. Should you forget this detail until the last minute, companies exist that specialize in helping people acquire visas in a hurry.

Money

Travel with some cash. Unlike credit cards and traveler's checks, cash is accepted everywhere. The only thing worse than an expensive taxi ride from the airport in the middle of the night is needing one when the airport ATM is broken. If you sleep better with maximum preparation, buy some of the country's currency before you leave the States. Just know that the exchange rate won't be anything to write home about.

I have always been an independent person, but being in another country, it was up to me. I had to rely on myself. I didn't have anyone there saying, "Do this now." I had to make these decisions on my own and seek out the best opportunities. And when opportunities present themselves, to take advantage of them.

When you're in a foreign country living on your own, let alone doing independent research, it's good training for trusting yourself, for learning how to deal with diverse people and for learning how to promote yourself. No matter how nervous or worried or fearful you are beforehand, know that you are about to have one of the biggest adventures of your life. Appreciate it. Live it.

Heather Wakefield
Research Fulbright to Georgia
Library Sciences

Managing goals and expectations

Many Fulbrighters underestimate how challenging their overseas experience will be. Although it is impossible to enter into it without some idea of how you would like it to unfold, remind yourself that you will be in unfamiliar territory and often operating far outside your comfort zone.

Many Fulbrighters struggle for months before they hit their stride in their host country. At some point all Fulbrighters experience the need to reassess their expectations and methods in the field. The best way to manage this reassessment is to set clear goals and benchmarks before you leave home. Otherwise it's difficult to track your progress. Ask yourself what you would like to complete by the end of your Fulbright grant. Think in terms of your project's deliverables: What physical result will symbolize success? Is it a written report? A series of twelve paintings? The first chapter of your dissertation? A completed manuscript for your first novel? Even if much of your work is difficult to quantify, a concrete product helps you leverage your Fulbright experience in the larger arc of your career.

I never went into this thinking that I was going to have publishable research, but I do sort of wish I had given more attention to finding a way to quantify my experience. I know that this is kind of opposed to the idea of doing what is culturally appropriate and culturally sensitive in some cases, but at the end of my time in Benin I was not able to say, "I built X number of latrines," or, "I held X number of educational workshops on HIV/ AIDS." Nor had I thought about those things going in. It never occurred to me that I would need to somehow quantify my experience or package it for the sake of the working world. And knowing what I now know about the value of quantifying things on résumés and the like, I would have paid more attention to the things I did accomplish.

Tim Slade
Research Fulbright to Benin
Public Health

I wish that somehow I could have planned out the 10 months a bit better. I felt like there were a lot of times when I was pulled away from my work because people were visiting or other things came up. At some points my outreach work was dominating my time, and at other points the research was dominating my time. I wish that I'd been able to establish a balance between traveling around Panama, doing my research, and doing my outreach. I kind of front-loaded it: The first four months was all research. Then I started to integrate more outreach. Then my family came to visit, and friends came to visit, and it felt like I hadn't worked in a good while. If I'd been able to balance that a little bit better it would have been easier.

Maya deVries
Research Fulbright to Panama
Biology

It's not just that success comes from failure. The real question is, "What are you going to do with your failure?" I wasn't able to finish the research that I had wanted to do. If I had thought about that beforehand a little more, maybe come up with a back-up plan, it would have been better. I ended up feeling slightly jaded, though that's a harsh word. I felt empty. I felt like I had used all my energy for the Fulbright. I didn't feel like there was anyplace else I could go with what I had done.

But if I had asked, "OK, what happens if this fails? What if I'm not able to do this research? What else do I want from my time there? What else am I going to be able to do with these interviews that I've done?" That might have been very helpful. And maybe these questions should be addressed not when you apply, but between the time when you're accepted and when you leave to start the grant.

Use the time before to think about plan A, plan B, and maybe plan C in case something doesn't work out. And what you want from the Fulbright other than the academic aspect of it. Maybe plan a little bit as to how to use the funds, and how long they're going to last you.

Laila Plamondon
Research Fulbright to Canada
Psychology

I wish that I had had stricter requirements for myself. Fulbright didn't demand anything of me. It didn't demand that I publish anything or give a presentation, or show that I'd completed the coursework. I think some self-imposed requirements would have been helpful. Having the expectation before arriving that I'm going to produce this while I'm in the country. Or that I'm going to visit these archives and meet these professors and attend these conferences. I didn't have any goals, and that was a mistake.

Lilith Dornhuber deBellesiles
Research Fulbright to Germany
Philosophy

I think that having sufficient structure is a huge issue. I was better prepared than most, just because I was coming out of a graduate program where there was very little structure. So everything about the daily, weekly, monthly schedule was really up to me. All students at the Iowa Writer's Workshop kind of had to write with the knowledge that if we didn't write it really didn't make a difference to anyone but us, and that was really something that you have to do for yourself.

Going on my Fulbright I already had a clear sense of what my work hours were, how I scheduled them, and how I protected those hours from anything interfering. I think that everyone should probably head out with some idea of how they are going to schedule their days, their weeks, and their months. Because otherwise the time can really just blur by. Which is not to say that you're always going to stick to that schedule, or that it's not going to completely change and shift as your project progresses, but I think it's always good to have that kind of plan and be flexible as much as you need to be.

Deanna Fei
Research Fulbright to China
Creative Writing

At times I wished there was more accountability and structure, so that I would feel more guided. The experience was extremely independent. I didn't really have anyone telling me what to do. It was nice to have that freedom, but at the same time it would have been nice to have at least some direction.

But in looking back I think it was a good approach because I did have that freedom to change and not worry about it. Not having that freedom would have made the experience more stressful. I ended up focusing a lot on developing relationships and living the experience instead of looking at it strictly as a work opportunity. I was able to accomplish something. It wasn't as grand and ambitious as I expected, but because I was able to let go of that expectation I got to experience more of the culture.

Ashley Killough
Research Fulbright to Armenia
Journalism

If I had it to do again I would have adjusted my expectations for my project much more quickly. I would have been more realistic about what could be done in the period of time I was there. Knowing what I know now about Brazilian conceptions of time, I probably wouldn't have been so ambitious. I would have been more realistic about what's doable and not have blamed myself for it. If I had realized this a couple months into the grant instead of four or five months into it, then I probably wouldn't have felt as stressed out about the goals that I had set for my project, about interviewing the number of people that I wanted to interview.

But I recognize that it's a product of the place where I was and that there are just some things beyond your control. You have to get the most out of the experience that you can. Learning how to deal with that by focusing on things that I could control within that process was the biggest issue in trying to do research for my dissertation. I felt like there was a lot at stake for me since I was using it for that purpose.

Tiffany Joseph
Research Fulbright to Brazil
Sociology

You just have to sit down and do the work. Focus on setting a time to do it. For me, getting up early in the morning when I didn't have to, going to the site even if I wasn't scheduled to meet people, and giving myself tasks for the day was a very good way to motivate myself. "I have to finish three paintings and start this section."

I needed a daily calendar of goals, a monthly calendar of goals, and then a nine-month calendar of goals. That was the only way to get the fire growing under me. People want results fast, but a little bit every day gets you far. It's a marathon, not a sprint. If you exercise a little bit of discipline every day, at the end of the day you'll have an accumulation of something that's important for the next task. I came back with nine sketchbooks. Every month I had to finish one sketchbook. I divided up by day how many paintings I needed to have done. If I missed one I had to make it up another day. So it was just very calculated. Sometimes people don't operate that way. But in my experience, a little bit every day goes very far.

Shadi Khadivi
Research Fulbright to Turkey

I definitely would have handled preparation differently. I would have thought a bit more about lesson planning beforehand, but that's hard because you don't know which classes you will be assisting in and what kind of lessons they will be. But I should have thought ahead a little bit more. "If I could teach anything, what would I want to teach?" I wish I had thought more about supplies, about bringing English books. My mom sent me a couple books that were in English about people like Gandhi and Rosa Parks. That was helpful to have with me.

Lakshmi Eassey
ETA Fulbright to Germany

I think that a good way to approach your time during the Fulbright is to be as prepared as you possibly can before you get there, but to also be flexible. Any number of things can change, and any number of new opportunities can arise. That's part of living abroad.

I know that as an American in Croatia I had a lot of opportunities to do things and meet people that I don't get in the U.S. Being willing to do radio interviews because suddenly you're an expert on something, for example. Things like that opened up doors and gave me a more substantial experience with the culture of the country. And that's when I really started feeling as though I was beginning to understand Croatia and Croatian culture on a much deeper level.

Halfway through your grant you should definitely reevaluate what your aims were when you set out on your Fulbright, and where you stand with respect to achieving those goals. And maybe you do need to adjust, refocus, and fine-tune. Halfway through would be a good time to reevaluate and make alterations if necessary.

Renee Brown
Research Fulbright to Croatia
Political Science

Your pre-departure checklist

- [ ] Set up a website or blog for your Fulbright work

- [ ] Contact American Fulbright alumni who spent time in your host country

- [ ] Research and contact Fulbrighters from your host country who are working in your field

- [ ] Set up a place to stay for the first week in your host country

- [ ] Investigate language schools for immediate enrollment

- [ ] Alert the Fulbright Commission or U.S. Embassy about your arrival plans

- [ ] Set up a meeting with your host organization

- [ ] Reach out to new professional or academic contacts in the States about your Fulbright work

- [ ] Send thank-you notes to everyone who helped you with your Fulbright application and update them about your plans

- [ ] Set up student loan deferment

- [ ] Pack a formal suit and a pair of sensible shoes

- [ ] Make of list of short-term and long-term Fulbright goals, with concrete benchmarks

- [ ] Brainstorm ways to showcase your Fulbright work after the end of your grant

Chapter 6

Life in the Field

The contrast between the planning phase and the implementation phase of the Fulbright is almost comical. When you're planning you're trying to imagine nearly an entire year overseas while typing on your computer at home. So much will happen to you, personally and professionally. It will all change. Remember this once you're there. Try to understand where you are failing and where you are succeeding. Just keep going. Don't get waylaid, don't regress and give up.

Evan Tachovsky
Research Fulbright to Azerbaijan
Political Science

At last your Fulbright begins. After all the application hurdles, the waiting, and the preparation, you are finally ready to commence what many Fulbright alumni consider one of the most important periods of their life. As a Fulbright Scholar you will have access to a level of academic, governmental, and professional resources that few people living overseas share. Unlocking the potential of these resources, however, requires initiative and a certain entrepreneurial spirit on the part of the grantee. You alone have the power to build the Fulbright experience you desire. With the right attitude and preparation, there are few limits on what you can achieve as a Fulbright Scholar.

As you start your grant, remember that the Fulbright experience doesn't end when you return home. Your friends, family, and colleagues will want to know about your time abroad, and this is an important part of Fulbright ambassadorship. Your engagement with the Fulbright mission and the Fulbright community have the potential to last a lifetime.

Arriving in your host country

Your first week in your host country will be an exciting and chaotic time. If you've planned well in the months leading up to your arrival, you'll be able to enjoy this honeymoon all the more. One of the most effective ways to launch your Fulbright experience is to invest early on in building relationships and community. The quality and quantity of connections you make overseas will grow exponentially over time.

Your arrival to-do list

- Check in with your local Fulbright Commission. In countries without a Fulbright Commission, your contact will be at the U.S. Embassy. Attend all orientations and security briefings. Be sure you know whom to call in an emergency.

- Check in with your host organization.

- Contact other Fulbrighters, both local and American.

- Take time to get the lay of the land. Map out places you need for basic survival: markets and grocers, metro stations and bus stops, and where to withdraw or exchange money.

- Start language lessons immediately, preferably through one-on-one tutoring. These lessons can be a valuable access point to the community and will help you get settled.

- Set up your modes of communication (cell phone, Internet connection, etc.).

- Take the time to write about your first impressions. You'll thank yourself later.

- Search for housing, but don't settle for the first place you see. Ask past Fulbrighters for suggestions.

____ Housing

Many Fulbrighters recommend not settling for the first housing option you are offered. Talk with locals about actual market prices to know whether you're being given the foreigner rate, and what can be done about it. Invest time in finding a place that is comfortable, safe, and that you won't have to move from halfway through your grant. There will be plenty of challenges during your Fulbright: Your home environment shouldn't be one of them.

____ In-country orientation

Fulbrighters whose group orientation was held in Washington, D.C., before their departure can hit the ground running in their host country. Grantees who didn't attend an orientation event in the States will likely be invited to attend an orientation in their host country upon arrival. Organized by the local Fulbright Commission, this is a valuable opportunity to meet the other Fulbrighters in your host country. If you start your research grant later than your peers, make a special effort to meet your cohort when you arrive. Grantees who attended orientation before leaving the States should still check in with the local Fulbright Commission or, where there isn't one, with the U.S. Embassy's Public Affairs Section.

If you don't have a community already set up in the country because you haven't been there before, then right away start having meetings with professors at the universities. Look on the website and see whose research sounds interesting. Some of them might not have websites. You might have to go the university one day and poke around. Ask administrators how you can find the list of faculty members in your field and their contact information and go from there. My experience in Panama was that the professors at the University of Panama were very excited to talk to me.

Maya deVries
Research Fulbright to Panama
Biology

Since I was a foreigner and didn't have someone to co-sign my apartment lease, the landlord I was going to rent from wanted me to pay six months of rent up front. Fortunately I had brought enough in traveler's checks to be able to do that, instead of having to go to an ATM and make multiple withdraws over the course of a week.

One of my acquaintances in the city where I was living took me around to some of the real estate people she knew to look for housing, and then took me to the bank to exchange traveler's checks. We were in the bank for about four hours because they said, "We don't know how to change these traveler's checks." These are the sorts of things you have to deal with. Things that we consider simple everyday tasks took a lot longer to do in Brazil. I had to learn how to be very patient.

Tiffany Joseph
Research Fulbright to Brazil
Sociology

Rather than jump directly into the project, living in the archives and going through old documents, I decided to approach it gradually and spend a couple months just trying to learn about Panama and the community there as much as I possibly could. Learning the geography, engaging people through language exchange, and playing sports. I always had my project in mind and was taking notes and thinking critically about it, but I knew that I had a lot to learn before I could become some sort of specialized researcher on this one topic. I wanted to see the broader picture of the place.

I think we often fall into the trap of thinking that we're supposed to study one specific thing, and that this is going to be our career. And you forget about all the other aspects of life that really do affect what you're studying, but you're not able to see it because you're navel-gazing so hard. So I feel like the Fulbright taught me how to think broadly and still engage specific questions.

Blake Scott
Research Fulbright to Panama
History

Take time to explore. Take walks. Get the lay of the land. "Oh, that looks like a nice shop if I need glasses down the road." Take advantage of the time you have at the beginning. Fulbright expects you to take some time to get adjusted and settle in. Take advantage of that.

Heather Wakefield
Research Fulbright to Georgia
Library Science

One of the things I did that I think helped a lot in terms of relationships and feeling comfortable, and it seems sort of silly but for me it really worked, was that I found an apartment that was very central in my city. It was easy to walk to and was big enough to host people. I could have people over either for dinner, drinks, coffee, or whatever, and that really worked well. With the group of friends that I made, it sort of became, "If we go out for a drink in the evening we can go to Hannah's afterwards." It was a location that was very central. I think that helped me build relationships with Romanians. I knew some Fulbrighters who found housing sort of on the outskirts, and they were reluctant to go out once they got home after work. I think my location really helped, especially in trying to make connections with people.

Hannah Halder
ETA Fulbright to Romania

Once I got to Toronto they took us to Ottawa for our orientation. There were quite a few of us there. Maybe between 20 and 30 Fulbrighters. It lasted a couple of days. It was really great to meet everyone, to start thinking about what it meant to be an American in Canada. I think it's actually a really interesting experience.

You have to remember that this is when Obama was about to be elected, so it was an exciting time in the States. And Canadians were definitely feeling that excitement. I learned so much about my American identity and how proud I was to be an American.

Canadians are so similar but so different. When I said I was a Fulbright Scholar from the United States people would make mass generalizations. But Americans are from 50 different states. We're not all the same, the same way Canadians aren't all the same. So I felt like I was being an ambassador for the States much more than I expected to be. And I learned much more about being an American than I expected to.

Laila Plamondon
Research Fulbright to Canada
Psychology

When we arrived in Argentina, the people from the Fulbright Commission were there at the airport to meet us and it was very well organized. We had three days of orientation. It was fun and useful to meet with other people in the group and to meet with previous Fulbrighters who they brought in to network with us and to help understand the relationship between IIE, the Fulbright Commission in Argentina, and the Ministry of Education, which plays a big role in the Fulbright Program there.

Natalia Ksiezyk
ETA Fulbright to Argentina

When I called Fulbright in Turkey to see how one finds an apartment, they said, "What's your budget?" I gave them my budget. They said, "We can't help you. There's nothing available for that budget." Wait. What? So I said, "OK, I'll look around on my own."

I found something before I arrived, and the way I found it was very serendipitous. I'm a member of a photo-sharing website. I started searching the tags for the city of Izmir. There was one woman who kept posting all these photos of Izmir. I e-mailed her and said, "I'm moving to Turkey. How does one find an apartment in Izmir?" We became friends via the website. She had an extra room in her apartment. I moved to Izmir and it was so surreal: This woman I had never met came and met me at the airport and I had an apartment that was wonderful. It was very close to the neighborhood that I was researching. That was one of the criteria. So my research began.

Shadi Khadivi
Research Fulbright to Turkey
Architecture

I know other Fulbrighters used the U.S. Embassy to find them housing, but for me I just talked to friends. In Tbilisi, former Fulbrighters helped me find housing. The thing with the embassy is that they aren't going to get you the cheapest place, and I was worried about that, so I did it myself.

Budgeting is important. I had to find money for language tutoring, and it's good to have money to spend on locals to create relationships. For me it was important to have that instead of spending it on an apartment that I wouldn't use that much.

Joshua Noonan
Research Fulbright to Georgia
   and Azerbaijan
Political Science

Acclimating to your new home

One of the big things that helped me adapt to living overseas was reaching out and trying to create a community as fast as possible. Take an activity that you're used to that made you feel good in your previous life—swimming, for example—and see if you can find people to do that activity with in your host country. Find a good place to live where you feel comfortable. Don't settle for the first place you see. Stay in touch with people back home, but don't let that communication dominate your existence. Reaching out and not letting yourself get into an isolated downward spiral, that's super important.

Lauren Hermele
Research Fulbright to Romania
Photography

It's easy to think that culture shock is something that happens to other people. The truth of the matter is that everyone who lives abroad experiences it to some degree. Responses can range from a momentary flash of annoyance to months of loneliness and discomfort. This is a normal part of adjusting to your new environment, and the deeper you immerse yourself in the culture of your host country, the more intense these symptoms might be.

The worst thing you can do when you experience tension with your new environment is to resist. We've all seen Americans who try to live inside an American bubble overseas. They live in American-style houses, eat only at McDonalds, and spend their time exclusively with other expats. This approach can feel comfortable in the beginning but ultimately takes far more energy to maintain. More importantly, it can keep you from acclimating to your host country's culture. As a Fulbrighter you have a chance to immerse yourself professionally, socially, and linguistically. Don't let this opportunity pass you by.

The Stages of Adjustment

_____ **Stage 1: The honeymoon**

The period immediately following your arrival is an exciting time when many people experience a heightened sense of adventure. New discoveries occur every day, and the possibilities seem endless. It is a time of fearlessness and willingness to reach beyond your comfort zone.

_____ **Stage 2: Rejection**

As the honeymoon fades away, many people begin to miss their usual ways of doing things. Relationships seem more difficult. Linguistic challenges become more frustrating. It often feels like you aren't making any progress. You feel homesick, overwhelmed, and critical of life in your new environment. You may withdraw socially, or contemplate going home early. Depression is common during this stage.

_____ **Stage 3: Recovery and acceptance**

With time your view of your new environment will improve as you get the hang of daily life and the language. You begin to feel more relaxed and can enjoy life in your new country. Misunderstandings and mistakes are fewer. You start to form meaningful relationships with locals.

I had a lot of international experience before I went on my Fulbright. I actually moved to the U.S. when I was 10, so I had experience living in another country, plus I had gone abroad and traveled a lot. But the culture shock that I experienced in Argentina was very different and much stronger than at any other time in my life. I wasn't really expecting that, because I felt that I was very adaptable. You never know how it's going to affect you. Each time is different. I was definitely able to cope, but I also had all the symptoms of culture shock. You can't avoid it. You just learn to cope with it more effectively.

Talking with others and knowing that it was normal was very comforting. For me a strategy that works is taking a step back and taking some time to gain more perspective, and then going back and trying to approach that situation again. I had a lot of frustrations trying to find an apartment. This guy was trying to really screw me over. I didn't have the language to express my frustration with him and I sort of had a breakdown with him. But it worked out fine and he didn't screw me over.

Knowing about the process of cultural adjustment is a must. Understand that it's normal to be more emotional and cry, or sleep longer, or have your eating patterns change. I think that having a support group is essential. Being able to talk to others who are going through a similar experience is important. This can be someone back home or someone who is on assignment in a different city. Fulbright's orientation program can be really good for building that supportive network. The rest is left to experience.

Natalia Ksiezyk
ETA Fulbright to Argentina

I have to say that adjusting was challenging in ways I didn't anticipate. I kind of thought I would have an easier time with it than I did since I had already lived as a student in Beijing. I had a really hard time explaining what the Fulbright was to the people at the visa office and at the student office, and getting them to fill out my paperwork and accept that I wasn't going to be a regular student. All that was kind of a bureaucratic nightmare.

I think that most times when you live abroad you'll be surprised and sometimes disappointed in yourself about how the smallest things can take over your entire day. Whether you're trying to pay your phone bill or pick up a package from the post office, you have to navigate a different world. You have to remind yourself that the American way is not universal, and not be too hard on yourself when you get frustrated or when you find that you're stymied every which way. Just chalk it up to being part of the experience.

Deanna Fei
Research Fulbright to China
Creative Writing

There are some pretty savvy people out there who have had the study-abroad experience, who sort of know the ins and outs of it. But it doesn't matter where you go, you're going to experience adjustment issues. You're going to fumble around trying to figure out what it is you're doing. That's the catch-22 of studying abroad. It doesn't matter if you're 16 or 60. You will go through this same process of, "If I would have had more time, or if I would have had all the secrets, I wouldn't have wasted so much time doing this and this." In some ways it's part of the natural process, but arming yourself with as much information as possible before you go is a smart move.

Hannah Halder
ETA Fulbright to Romania

I don't know if there is a way for the frustrations of living overseas not to get under your skin. Fulbrighters tend to be high-achieving, ambitious, very capable people and I think it can be a real shock to the system to find yourself feeling completely lost and overwhelmed and isolated. I think it's good to tell yourself, "That is going to happen to me. I'm not going to be a shining exception. And it's going to be part of my learning experience." As opposed to fighting it, feeling inadequate, or feeling like, "This means that I'm doing it wrong. This is not how it should go." Or the flip side of that: blaming your host country, blaming the local culture, blaming the way Fulbright is set up for your experience being less than smooth. I think all you can really do is embrace those moments and know that you're going to emerge out the other end and it's all going to be part of your learning experience.

Deanna Fei
Research Fulbright to China
Creative Writing

Adapting to the realities of your Fulbright work

Many Fulbrighters step off the plane in their host country, look around, and realize how completely infeasible their project proposal was. The shock of this first contact—the moment your plan encounters the realities of implementation—can be intimidating. Every Fulbrighter has a story about early crises: the painter who couldn't find art supplies; the English teacher who suddenly had to develop the school's entire curriculum; the photographer who discovered that the photojournalist he planned to work with died a month before. These have all happened to Fulbright Scholars overseas. Circumstances like these require you to adapt—it is *how* you choose to respond that dictates the quality of your overseas experience.

Most research Fulbrighters find it necessary to change the course of their project in some way. This is normal. It is the nature of fieldwork that it asks us to adapt, which is ultimately why we take our work into the field. What makes this process difficult is that the need for change often looks like adversity or failure, something impeding the success of the project. The trick is to recognize this resistance not as an obstacle, but as growth. It would be wonderful if our projects always grew through inspiring successes and eureka moments, but the reality of fieldwork overseas in an unfamiliar environment is that growth and its lessons are often uncomfortable. Only later do we recognize how important this discomfort was.

When you encounter these challenges, the important thing is to not panic. Fulbright won't take your grant away because you hit a few bumps in the road. After decades of running the program, they know these challenges are par for the course. In fact, if your project isn't encountering challenges, chances are you're not reaching far enough. As long as you try to adapt your work, grow your relationships, and engage your host country responsibly, Fulbright probably won't have any objections to how your project evolves. But do keep your local Fulbright representative apprised of any big shifts so they will know better how to help you. Fulbright wants you to succeed. Your work will grow best not by stubbornly following the original plan, but by realizing there's a better one.

After a week or two in Georgia I realized that my original project was completely based on a false premise. My understanding was that all libraries in Georgia, including children's libraries, had closed stacks, meaning you couldn't go into the shelves. Patrons had to request books specifically. I was going to try and set up temporary open stacks displays and test whether children who were able to look through the stacks and select books were more likely to read and to come back to the library.

But when I got there I discovered that most children's libraries are open stacks. The whole premise was wrong, so the whole library idea had to change. In my case I had absolutely no problems with changing, though it was a little challenging filling out the mid-year and final report because they wanted me to discuss specifically how I had met the goals that I had originally proposed. Those goals were no longer valid. I just explained in the report and they were fine with it.

Fulbrighters should expect change to happen. The Fulbright higher-ups, the powers that be, understand that projects do change. Every Fulbrighter I've known has had their project change in some way.

Heather Wakefield
Research Fulbright to Georgia
Library Science

Flexibility is a very important trait in a Fulbright applicant. It's absolutely necessary for any project, I don't care what the project is. You have to be able to change either the entire project, a portion of it, or the scope of it. Everyone has an idea of what they want to do. Whether or not it's feasible once you arrive is a different story.

Nic Wondra
Research Fulbright to Georgia
Political Science

I proposed doing a study and working with local partners, and also taking classes at one of the local universities. Shortly before I set foot in the country the university went on strike and remained on strike the entire year. Right off the bat about 30 or 40 percent of my project was just unworkable. I wish I had better prepared myself for what to do when carefully laid plans go up in smoke.

It's not like Fulbright should have prepared me and didn't, it just had simply never occurred to me, despite all my experience in the developing world, that everything might just completely go to pot as soon as I got there. And that I would be left scrambling to pick up the pieces. That was one of the really big problems for me, casting about for what to do next and how to salvage this, and I'm afraid I didn't do that terribly effectively.

Tim Slade
Research Fulbright to Benin
Public Health

My project definitely changed from what I had expected to do. I was expecting to focus on how participation in blogs, and this new element of media in general, was influencing the political landscape. But when I got there I realized that topic was too broad to try and tackle, especially for someone like me who didn't have any ties to Armenia or language skills. But I was able to shift gears and look at something more current—social media—and its effect on conflict resolution and how people are engaging in it to communicate with people in other countries in the South Caucasus. Instead of doing a large project, I split it up and wrote individual stories that I was interested in covering for various news outlets. It became more journalistic than academic, and that was actually better for me.

Ashley Killough
Research Fulbright to Armenia
Journalism

I was supposed to write on attitudes towards democracy but I changed the project to focus on attitudes toward political participation. I had no qualms with that because democracy is harder to define than political participation. I decided in my second week in Azerbaijan that I had to change it.

I think some people feel too tied down by their project to change it. It's our responsibility to change it instead of just sitting there. And it's natural for it to change, especially if you don't know anything about the country. I had lived in Azerbaijan previously for two years with the Peace Corps and still didn't realize that writing on democracy would be that difficult.

The important thing is to let your project evolve. I came across some Fulbrighters who realized that their project was less than possible and then they didn't do anything, and I think that's kind of sad. It's better to let it evolve than to let it die.

Joshua Noonan
Research Fulbright to Georgia
**   and Azerbaijan**
Political Science

If you are visiting a developing country, get used to adapting to changing circumstances. I had initially set out to make a documentary film about a large-scale land restitution project. I'd done my research, connected with people on the ground, and confirmed that my story would begin to unfold soon after I landed. I arrived to find that the entire project I wanted to film had stalled due to lack of funds and that the people in charge had gone to great lengths to cover this up.

When my initial plan began to fall through I kept myself busy doing community video projects while I figured out what to do next. I made a point of getting out and exploring South Africa as much as possible. In the process, I met the subject of my next film: an American Fulbright teacher who was stationed in a rural corner of South Africa and was about to launch a remarkable basketball program out there in the middle of nowhere. My new project, "Zuluhoops," provided a lens through which I could examine the phenomenon of international exchange and the challenges that so often accompany it. Truth be told, it's a far more interesting film than the one I'd initially intended to make. And I still managed to shoot the entire film before my Fulbright year ended.

Kristin Pichaske
Research Fulbright to South Africa
Filmmaking

The Slump

After all the excitement of arrival and settling in, the Slump is a challenging time when you don't seem to be making progress in your work. You aren't forming the relationships you wanted. Your life overseas has become uncomfortable on a daily basis. Nearly all Fulbrighters experience this period sometime during the first half of their grant. They feel that their work is sliding backwards. Many start to doubt themselves and their abilities.

The Slump is the result of a combination of culture shock, frustrations with the local language, and project birth pains. It's normal. You are simply adjusting to Fulbright life overseas, and this is an essential growth stage for reaching your goals. For most grantees it lasts a few weeks to a few months, depending how you adapt to new circumstances. It's easy to get discouraged when you feel resistance in all aspects of your life and work, especially early in your project. The following list of symptoms will help you identify whether you are in the Slump:

- You spend more and more time on the Internet
- You are depressed
- You find yourself dwelling on "I should have known" scenarios
- You blame others for your discomfort (locals, Fulbright Program administrators, etc.)
- You find yourself giving up on your Fulbright work
- You retreat into the expat bubble and avoid making friends with locals
- You spend evenings watching movies on your computer, either alone or with other expats who are also in the Slump (a dangerous combination)
- You scale back on language study, telling yourself it's too expensive, too time-consuming, or "doesn't make sense" because you will be in the country such a short time
- You find yourself in daily contact with friends and family back home
- You begin to think that Fulbright made a mistake in selecting you for the program

If any of these look familiar, it's time to take a step back and reassess.

It's not like you wake up every morning and ask, "Am I seizing this opportunity?" A lot of people go through lulls during their Fulbright for all kinds of different reasons. The winter may be horrible. Or maybe everyone wears black. This happens. Most everyone will hit something like that and want to watch 20 hours of The West Wing *on their computer and not leave the apartment. It's important to say, "OK, I did that last week and now this week I'm going to get into the game." Even if you realize your Fulbright plan was stupid, continually revising is important. Everyone stumbles a bit, but you've got to keep going. It's difficult to do. If you have a wasted month, make sure the next month isn't wasted. Even if you only have one month left, you can do a lot in a month. Don't be afraid to say I failed last week, but next week will be a very important week.*

Evan Tachovsky
Research Fulbright to Azerbaijan
Political Science

Tips on pushing through the Slump

_____ **Get out and meet people**

Force yourself out into the world. Schedule meetings in person instead of by phone. Invite people to lunch. Host a dinner party. Organize a group trip to the mountains. Whatever you do, don't retreat into isolation.

_____ **Intensify your language study**

For many Fulbrighters the Slump is made more uncomfortable by inadequate language skills. Keep hammering away at your language proficiency: The moments before breakthroughs are usually the most frustrating. Keep pushing.

_____ **Keep a journal**

Journaling lets you track your progress, even when it doesn't feel like there is any. It's also an opportunity to vent in a safe, diplomatic way that doesn't burn bridges.

_____ **Find a hobby you love**

If you like chess or want to learn, join the local chess club or hang out with the old guys in the park. (Chess and backgammon are two of the most internationally recognized languages.) If you love judo, find a dojo and sign up. Study the traditional dances of your host country. Or a musical instrument. Or wine-making. The possibilities are endless. If you don't find what you're looking for, ask the folks at your country's Fulbright Commission for ideas.

_____ **Get out of town and explore the country**

When in doubt, take a break and get some perspective. Just be sure you change your environment. Don't stop working on your Fulbright just to stay home and surf the Internet.

At first I hit the ground running with my project by meeting people and visiting libraries. But then I hit a slow period where I just sat at home for parts of days looking up policies and things. I think my project would have evolved faster and in a more positive way if I had asked more questions of the people who were there. For example, I didn't find out until January that there were children's libraries in Tbilisi that I hadn't been to. The librarian who had been acting as a translator thought that we had seen them all. I didn't think to ask for a full list of libraries. Once we asked for the full list we learned that there were four more that we hadn't been to. If I hadn't been sitting at home on the Internet I would have had to ask more questions, would have had to deal more with people, and probably would have gotten better information sooner. All the time I was sitting at home on the Internet trying to dig up leads on things, I could have been talking to people.

Heather Wakefield
Research Fulbright to Georgia
Library Science

For Fulbrighters in a slump, definitely talk to whoever your resources are. I was lucky that I was in the Smithsonian Tropical Research Institute, so I had other scientists I knew who I could talk to. I spent a lot of time in Panama City with one scientist who was very helpful. And my affiliate was very helpful. I would also talk to my labmates back home. I know that a lot of people may not have that support system, but research Fulbrighters should at least have some contacts at their university or academic setting. Get feedback as soon as you can on your research. Even if you think it's going well, it's still good to check in with people who you know you can talk to.

My slump of thinking, "Wow, this is not working," lasted a couple months because my project totally changed. I didn't get the data I thought I was going to get at all. So first I had to re-evaluate whether the method I was using to get my data was good. I decided that yes, it was fine. And then I realized that I was actually getting another kind of data, another result that I hadn't expected. Re-evaluating the project and thinking about it in a new way kind of brought me back out of that. And then I actually ended up continuing with what I'd started with, just in a different way.

Maya deVries
Research Fulbright to Panama
Biology

Maybe it's counterintuitive, but if you're having trouble with your project I would say take a vacation. Rather than concentrating on the work that you originally applied to do, I would say take a few days or even a week to travel around the country. Go hitchhiking, or travel around the mountains. Not only will it relax some of the frustrations which inherently develop, but it may stimulate a different kind of thought.

Nic Wondra
Research Fulbright to Georgia
Political Science

Six weeks or two months in, after I got settled in, suddenly I was so incredibly lonely. I had all this time to do my work, and I was doing my work, but I wanted to do something else. I think it can be really difficult sometimes just because you may be in a situation where you're really alone with yourself more than you've ever been before. I think that things like this happen in life. That time will pass and things will change. I just kept working.

Renee Brown
Research Fulbright to Croatia
Political Science

Managing setbacks

Tiffany Joseph
Research Fulbright to Brazil
Sociology

There was definitely a lag in my project in the beginning because I wasn't able to recruit people to participate in my research as quickly as I thought I would based on the timeline that I had established for myself. I had to readjust and think about my expectations of what I would be able to get done. I definitely felt like there were times when my project lagged, and then there were times when I felt like I was able to reach the milestones that I had set for myself. This is something that happens.

You might have a set idea of what you want to do in your Fulbright year that you laid out in your application, but you should also be flexible when you actually get to the field in case things don't work out the way you thought they would. When you're crafting your application you spend so much time on your essays that you feel married to the idea, and by the time you start your Fulbright it can be difficult to say, "I'm going to have to switch gears here a little bit because it's not working out the way I thought it would."

This can create a lot of discomfort, uncertainty, and frustration. It's difficult to deal with. You're dealing with the challenges of being in another country but then your project also starts to unravel, or not unfold the way you thought it would. It comes back to the ability to be resilient, the ability to bounce back, to deal with those types of challenges that can happen when you are doing a Fulbright grant. It definitely requires that you tap into your resources, people you know in the city where you're living. Reach out to the Fulbright Commission in that country. Be resilient, resourceful, and patient. And most importantly, don't give up. Don't get so frustrated that you just want to throw in the towel completely.

You think you know about a different area of the world, you can read books on it, but until you really get off that plane and sit down for your first meal, it doesn't hit you. You have to adapt. I've seen so many of my fellow students go into this mode of, "I brought books." This one guy brought these books and instead of being out in the community he's in his hovel all day reading Lord of the Rings, *thinking he's getting something out of it. Maybe he did, but I'm thinking, "This is not helping you. You're complaining about how you're not picking up even the most basic greetings in the language, but you're sitting in here reading literature all day. What do you expect?"*

Winston Scott
Research Fulbright to Guatemala
Anthropology

Working with your local Fulbright representative

After dealing with all the rules and deadlines of the application process, many grantees are surprised to find how supportive the Fulbright staff in their host country can be. In countries that have no Fulbright Commission, Fulbrighters typically deal directly with an educational or cultural specialist in the Public Affairs Section at the nearest U.S. Embassy.

Get to know your local Fulbright representatives. Their goal is not to police you or your work, but to give you support, advice, and introductions when you need them. They want to hear what you're up to and are usually interested in exploring ways to help you succeed. They can be instrumental in spreading the word about your accomplishments and publicizing events that showcase your work. Fulbright Commission staff have helped grantees organize teaching opportunities and smooth out administrative hurdles with visas and residency permits. They have given leads on potential sources of additional project funding, investigated questionable host organizations, and helped find more appropriate affiliation for grantees as their projects evolve. If you want to continue a professional relationship with your host country after your grant, develop and maintain ties with the Fulbright Commission there. They can be a huge help down the road, and they want you to succeed.

Also let the U.S. Embassy know you'd like to take part in embassy events. These can include Thanksgiving dinners, Fulbright meetings with the U.S. Ambassador, Fourth of July BBQs, and receptions for local Fulbright Scholars returning from the United States. Not all embassies reach out to Fulbrighters with invitations, but those that do should not be ignored.

I had a really good relationship with the directors at the Fulbright Commission in my country. They were wonderful in Romania. During the application process Fulbright basically wants to see that you're a trustworthy, responsible adult, and that's how they treat you if you get the grant. That's how I felt I was treated. If I had things I needed help with, I would talk to them. For example, when I was trying to figure out how I could run classes for kids in the village and I needed to get materials, I sent proposals to non-profits asking for them to donate a few cameras. The Fulbright Commission gave me their non-profit status so I could include that in the letters.

I had no idea where I was going to live. I got there and during orientation the director of the Fulbright Commission introduced me to a woman who had rented an apartment to a Fulbrighter the year before. I would always write them telling them what I was up to and if I needed any help. They were always very supportive and respectful.

That was something that was really nice about the Fulbright Commission in Romania. They gathered us a few times a year. We had a December gathering, then a January gathering, and then there was a Fulbright 50th anniversary gathering. Those were great for getting to know the other Fulbrighters and what they were up to. That was a really nice form of support. That connection was probably the best thing about it.

Lauren Hermele
Research Fulbright to Romania
Photography

The consulate would e-mail me once in a while just to check in on me. They weren't ignoring me, and they weren't invasive at all. It's not like they were bothering me. Whenever there was a consulate function, they would send me an e-mail. They left it at that. The good thing was that they did remember me. I didn't show up to everything, but if there was a consulate luncheon, the consul would remember me and remember what I was doing. So that was a plus.

I got the impression that they felt that they selected us for a reason. They selected us because we can carry out our project and we're mature, responsible adults. And therefore they didn't need to watch us. When you're dealing with someone who's doing a more intellectual kind of project, you need to let them do their own thing and be available if they need you. That's how I felt I was being treated. "You're here because we think you know what you're doing. Do what you want to do, and if you need us we're over here. We're not going anywhere." That's what I really liked.

Jared Sun
Research Fulbright to South Africa
Public Health

The embassy is really there to support you. I had an exhibition of my Fulbright work in Panama during my Fulbright and the woman in charge of PR at the embassy began, on her own accord, to do all the PR work for my exhibition. I got a ton of articles and radio interviews. And the Cultural Affairs officer from the embassy helped find the best space for my exhibition, using the embassy name to try and do that.

Fulbrighters should realize that the U.S. Embassy has a lot of means to make positive things happen with your project in your host country. And not just financial means. It's also the fact that they have been there longer than you have. They gave me a bunch of names of artists in the city when I got there so I could meet with people. But it's also important that you're willing to ask and get yourself out there as much as possible. When the embassy invited me to anything, I would go.

Rose Cromwell
Research Fulbright to Panama
Photography

The Fulbright Commission's biggest interest in my country was with Turks going to the U.S., which is a much larger program. By design, they weren't as much help for American students there. They're great people, but the office wasn't much of a resource, nor should it have been. They helped with logistics in the beginning (registering for classes, finding housing, etc.) but they are not there to help with project execution.

Courtney Doggart
Research Fulbright to Turkey
International Relations

The Fulbright Commission in Poland was small. It's run by a handful of people, but all my interactions with them were very positive. Anything bureaucratic in Poland is kind of a nightmare and you learn to expect that it can take days or weeks to get the simplest certificate. But the Polish Fulbright Commission was really responsive and personable. Every time I got in touch with them they would get back to me with specific answers. They were very helpful. I had a couple questions about healthcare and they put me in touch with people who had had experiences like that before in Lodz. They really went out of their way to try to connect me with other Fulbrighters who had been, and still were, in the area.

Mike Seely
Research Fulbright to Poland
Filmmaking

The embassy is probably the best resource that you'll have. They are 100 percent supportive of Fulbrighters. When I complained about the organization I was working with, they immediately said, "We're going to meet with the head of the organization and hash out a compromise." They were very diplomatic and professional about it, and they really took care of me, especially at the end.

Matt Wesley
Research Fulbright to Nicaragua
Public Health

I sort of knew that on the books Fulbright was a cultural exchange program, but it hadn't occurred to me that anybody actually meant it to be that. I thought, "Surely they meant it to be more than that, because how important can cultural exchange really be?"

So I had a hard time resigning myself to the fact that maybe all I was going to get out of this were relationships, and that maybe the greater purpose I was serving was just being an American face in a place that hadn't seen a lot of Americans. It's so contrary to the American spirit and culture to say, "There's value in simple presence." That's just not something that we acknowledge in most corners of our society and our culture.

But I think Fulbright really is about effective cultural exchange based on this idea of presence. Openness and dialogue are important, but sometimes just being is enough. People who pursue Fulbright Scholarships are usually your high achievers, and I think high achievers are likely to be the ones who will struggle most with the idea that this experience isn't acutally about achieving concrete results in the traditional sense.

Tim Slade
Research Fulbright to Benin
Public Health

The Fulbright experience is bigger than your project. Your project is important and you're going to learn a lot in a year's time, but recognize that the whole thing is supposed to be a learning experience. It's not just supposed to be learning about your project. So embrace the idea that you can learn in other ways in addition to your specialized research. Think critically about everything you encounter and process it, rather than just seeing it as a stop sign on the way to your research goal.

Blake Scott
Research Fulbright to Panama
History

Working with your host organization

Your relationship with your host organization or teaching institution can be one of the biggest influences on your Fulbright work and quality of life. The nature of these relationships can vary widely. Not every collaboration is rosy, and the most productive and satisfied Fulbrighters take initiative to shape them in mutually beneficial ways.

Some Fulbrighters have unrealistic expectations at the outset of their grants about what their host organization, university adviser, research partner, or teaching institution will provide. It is not the responsibility of these organizations to ensure that you have a rewarding Fulbright experience. Some are invested in the grantee's work and contribute positively to their overseas experience, but many are not. And there are always a few organizations that are clearly not a good fit for Fulbrighters.

Fulbrighters pursuing independent research projects have considerable leeway in managing the relationship with their host organization. It is not uncommon for grantees to change the organization they are working with once they are in the field, or even move forward independently. Research grantees are not obligated to continue the affiliation they proposed in their application and should not feel tied to a situation that is not in their interests. Many grantees find it helpful to consult Fulbright Commission staff about making changes. This is particularly important if the host organization also provides visa sponsorship for the grantee.

In contrast to research grantees, ETA Fulbrighters have little influence over the city and institution where they are placed. Changes to ETA assignments are rare but not unheard of. For many ETA grantees the biggest challenge of their Fulbright is making the most of a work situation they have little control over. Difficulties in the classroom and with school administrators don't typically qualify as grounds for changing your placement. For those with challenging placements, it's worth remembering that one's true leadership abilities are tested in adverse circumstances. Try to see such challenges, painful though they can be, as opportunities for growth.

The most important thing to remember is that the Fulbright experience is yours to shape. Every Fulbrighter encounters work challenges; if your host organization, research affiliation, or ETA placement isn't working out, take steps to change the situation.

My host affiliation was an institution that was struggling to stay open. They were not interested in providing very much support. It was a research institution, not a university. They did research on migration and ethnic studies. It was supposed to be a think tank. I figured that they would be a good fit based on having been in contact with a researcher I met at a conference I went to during my previous year there, somebody who worked at the institute.

Many of the people who worked there were academics, but they weren't able to provide much support other than giving me names of people who might be willing to talk to me or who might have information for me. I started e-mailing people: "This is what I'm doing. Do you know anybody who worked on these projects while they were active? Do you know anyone who has any experience with them whatsoever?" Usually, three or four people down the road, I would get to somebody who would have more substantive information for me. I really did feel as though I was on my own in terms of my research.

Renee Brown
Research Fulbright to Croatia
Political Science

The person I was working with was far more interested in the fact that his NGO could now say they had an American working with them than in actually having me contribute in any way. I had to make my peace with this mindset. So here I am going through this experience in Benin where my NGO partner was withholding salaries from all his employees for literally nine or ten months at a time, embezzling funds from his donors, and abusing his position to extract sexual favors. I mean, it was really, really bad stuff. Being young and foolish, I tried to get involved with fixing it, even though I had neither the power nor the standing to really do anything about it. Sometimes the best thing you can do is to be present and have a relationship, rather than be "type A," which is kind of my default setting. It became clear that this NGO really just wanted me as a feather in its cap.

Tim Slade
Research Fulbright to Benin
Public Health

I had established a partnership for the Fulbright application, but hadn't hashed out the details to the extent that I needed to. It could have been an age thing. I might have been too intimidated to say, "This is what I want." I didn't know what to ask for.

Courtney Doggart
Research Fulbright to Turkey
International Relations

My host institution was the Academy of Geography and History of Guatemala, which is a small academic society in Guatemala City. They do very good work and have a small publishing house. Throughout the process of doing a proposal I established some great relationships with them, and once I got the Fulbright they invited me to a couple of seminars and lectures they had going. But they didn't actually have somebody that was working with me all the time. I was eight hours away by car, so getting there was an event, and I didn't leave my research area all that much in the first place. The host institution was there, but once I was a Fulbrighter in-country I didn't have much interaction with them. I talked with other Fulbrighters who worked very closely with their host institution, but the situation was different for me.

Winston Scott
Research Fulbright to Guatemala
Anthropology

My advisor at my host university had never had a Fulbright advisee before, and he didn't know what to do with me. We didn't have a very good working relationship at all. He thought I was going to be a research assistant for him, and I hoped that he would help guide my project.

When applying, find out where previous Fulbrighters have gone. Knowing where there is a concentration of Fulbrighters will be helpful both in establishing a community while you're there, and also for entering institutions where they have experience with Fulbrighters and know what to do with you.

Lilith Dornhuber deBellesiles
Research Fulbright to Germany
Philosophy

When I got to the university nobody seemed to know what the Fulbright was. They were very suspicious of the fact that I wasn't living on campus or enrolled in regular classes, and a lot of trouble stemmed from that. Every time I had to deal with a residency or visa issue I would have to go through the school, but every time I went through the school they would say, "We don't know who you are or why you're here."

There was a situation where I needed to do something with my visa. They were saying, "We can't help you with that unless you get a note from your teacher." Well, how can I get a note from my teacher if I'm not enrolled in a class? They said, "OK, then you have to enroll in a class." So I had to enroll in a class just by the books so I could get a note from my teacher. And of course when I tried to get the note the teacher's response was, "I don't know you. Why should I give you a note?" A few times I had to get in touch directly with IIE in Beijing and eventually things got straightened out. But it took a lot of doing.

Deanna Fei
Research Fulbright to China
Creative Writing

One issue that some Fulbrighters have once they get to their country has to do with how supported they are by their host organization. Some sponsors share their office with the Fulbrighter. They see them every day, they check in, and they write things together. Other sponsors are fledgling NGOs that are barely present in the city to begin with. The applicant might stop in once a month and say, "Hello, I'm still in the country, thanks for supporting my project." It depends on who the applicant is and who made the pledge.

Nic Wondra
Research Fulbright to Georgia
Political Science

The art of living overseas

Being able to live comfortably and productively in a foreign country is a learned skill. Seasoned travelers and natural extroverts can make it look easy, like a gift that a lucky few are born with, but the reality is that each of us learns over time what we need in order to operate outside our comfort zone for prolonged periods. More than anything else, this process requires willingness to engage your environment, take risks, and repeatedly look like a fool in public. Fulbrighters consistently recommend the following strategies:

_____ **Make a conscious effort to push through your fears**

It's normal to be intimidated by new and unfamiliar surroundings, especially when you are operating so far outside your element. But nothing will help you adapt faster than diving in. Forcing yourself to engage in social situations, even when they seem destined for awkwardness, is the fastest path to getting comfortable in your new home.

_____ **Build structure and discipline into your daily life**

The freedom a Fulbright grant provides can be both an asset and a liability. Research grantees in particular need to structure their time to stay productive.

_____ **Reach out**

Living in an unfamiliar environment, we tend to retreat when things aren't going well. But retreat is not productive. It will not help you adapt. Getting out and meeting people might require effort at first, but in the long run it's the best way to have fun and stay relaxed and productive while on your Fulbright.

_____ **Get off the Internet**

It's easy to convince yourself of the value of Internet research when it takes so much effort to maneuver in your host culture. But the Internet can be the kiss of death for developing meaningful relationships with locals. Recognize and avoid this trap.

_____ **Exercise**

Regular exercise is a great way to keep perspective, stay relaxed, and mitigate grumpy episodes. You don't have to be an Olympic bodybuilder; you just need to find the activity that's right for you and build it into your schedule.

Don't be intimidated. I know that sounds a lot like saying "don't panic" to someone who's having a panic attack, but you have to continue to put yourself out there. You can't arrive in your country and immediately curl into a fetal position. Go out. Don't be afraid to ask around. Be audacious. If you've never lived abroad before, the first period will be a period where you just need to learn to float. If you hear someone speaking English, go talk to them. Befriend people on the street and at the airport. Talk to your cab driver, even if you think there is a big language barrier. The more you put yourself out there in the beginning, the more of a network you'll have when things are more stable.

Once you learn that people are not out to get you, that people generally want to help you, then you can begin to swim. Keep reaching out to the people around you. Ultimately that's what you're there to do as a Fulbrighter, and that's what's going to help you get to the next level. Some people take to it very easily and realize, "Hey, this is my lifestyle. This is what I like." For others it takes longer. But it's intimidating for anyone doing it for the first time.

Don't be afraid to take some risks. Set up side projects. The best thing I did was to purchase a car. It opened me up to interact with tons of new people: mechanics, junkyards, auto parts stores—an entire section of society I never would have engaged with otherwise. Make a list of projects. Brewing beer, learning a local instrument, whatever. Even if it's random and crazy, it's going to take you to a new place. Take random leaps that have nothing to do with your project. Don't be afraid to do that stuff.

Evan Tachovsky
Research Fulbright to Azerbaijan
Political Science

_____ **Focus on side projects**

Remember that your Fulbright experience is bigger than your Fulbright work. Spend more time on language study, sports, journaling, or volunteering. Pursue old hobbies in your new environment. Try new ones. Explore an unfamiliar field. Inspiration can strike when you least expect it.

_____ **Cultivate patience and flexibility**

The true mark of a seasoned traveler is patience. Learning to be patient in adverse circumstances is one of the ways that foreign travel makes us better people. Practice taking a deep breath before you respond.

_____ **Don't forget to take a vacation**

Take time to relax and explore your host country. This is a necessary part of your project.

The gossip is always fun. I was a single man in my particular research site. Every time a woman would leave her husband in my community, it was my fault. Especially when I had to leave for two months. Every time a woman left her husband when I wasn't around, people said, "Winston has taken her off to Guatemala City." It was easier for husbands to say that than to admit that she left because they were beating her up all the time. It's easier to say that the white guy has been hexing her and sleeping with her and all that stuff. That's how I got into the community gossip thing. It really angered me at first. Some husband is going to kill me! But wait a minute, they know in their hearts that I'm not sleeping with their wives. But at the same time I was in a community where gossip spread fast and was well-accepted. If it's juicy, they'll take it. So I had to kind of navigate that whole thing. "No, I don't have mistresses here in the community. I'm all alone." I just started making jokes that I'm just an ugly white guy.

Winston Scott
Research Fulbright to Guatemala
Anthropology

Just go with the flow. It's going to be tough and it's going to be great and it's going to be exciting and it's going to be hard. You just sort of have to roll with the punches as they come. Otherwise you're going to be miserable.

Hannah Halder
ETA Fulbright to Romania

Living overseas was always a learning process. I remember thinking at three months, "OK, I feel good. I've got the hang of it. I'm good." And then two months later I would think, "I don't know what I was talking about two months ago. Now I'm feeling good." This would happen every month. You're always adjusting. You see new things just about every day. I remember learning in my eighth or ninth month that it was considered rude to blow your nose in public. I did this all the time because I had allergies. It would be nice to know these things when you start, but I guess I didn't ask those questions.

Ashley Killough
Research Fulbright to Armenia
Journalism

One thing I would emphasize is that it's not all great as far as the experience. Your emotions about your experience are going to fluctuate from extreme excitement and idealism to some sort of pessimism, to some sort of neutrality, to some sort of renewed optimism, and so on and so on. It just keeps repeating itself on a day-to-day or week-to-week basis. Always being willing to try to work on that feeling is really important in moving you forward in a positive way. Try to figure out why you feel that way and how you can readjust. That's where a lot of the self-reflexive stuff comes in. You figure out what makes you feel a little crazy, or what makes you uncomfortable or depressed, and how that relates to where you came from and what's going on there. And at the same time you figure out what makes you feel optimistic and good, and how that relates to where you came from as well. Recognize that this is going to happen. The experience of the Fulbright is almost like a microcosm of the emotions and feelings you might experience over an entire decade. It's very condensed and intense.

Blake Scott
Research Fulbright to Panama
History

I bought a horse, and this horse was my transportation to and from the community, but also I could go and ride wherever I wanted. I would do that a lot actually. I did a lot of hiking. It was a form of exercise, I suppose, especially because it's mountainous. That was helpful.

Matt Wesley
Research Fulbright to Nicaragua
Public Health

When I first got to Panama, if anyone invited me to go anywhere or do anything, I would go, sometimes to the dismay of people who were close to me who thought I needed to have more of a filter. I was doing whatever I could to learn more, to try and immerse myself quickly into Panama, into the community I was in. I met a photographer who connected me to another photographer who I ended up working with in Panama for two more years. I met him at a bar late one night dancing. Even when you think you're not working, you really are. Be yourself and be open-minded to who you might meet and what may happen after that.

Rose Cromwell
Research Fulbright to Panama
Photography

Whenever I'm abroad I always keep a journal. I'm always writing things down. It's a safe space that you can bounce your ideas or thoughts off of without venting, because sometimes it's possible to get really frustrated with society. "Why do Azeri men always demand tea?!" But if you write it down in your journal you can think it through at least. It provides a safe spot to do that. Also, it allows you to evaluate things daily. Is the project moving forward? Is there a language being learned? Are friendships being developed with locals? I think it's useful. The journal is critical. Without that I probably would have offended a lot more people, or broken cultural taboos or something. I can't stress that enough, how important it is just to have a sounding board.

Joshua Noonan
Research Fulbright to Georgia
and Azerbaijan
Political Science

The exchange rate dropped quite a bit while I was there. Our stipend was already fixed in Korean Won, and that became a lot less in dollars. I think it still probably purchased the same amount of stuff in Korea, it was just whenever I exchanged for foreign currency that it didn't give me as much.

Since we lived in a homestay our food was provided for us as long as we were at home, so the stipend was more than adequate. I think it was roughly $1,100 a month in U.S. dollars [in 2008], but before the exchange rate it would have been worth a lot more. I think we lost close to 30 percent of the value. The Fulbright office was worried about us, because for people who were trying to send money home to pay back loans it wouldn't have gone as far. I think they ended up giving us a couple hundred extra dollars a month in the second half of the grant year.

But the stipend was fine for me. I traveled all around Korea and it was enough to do weekend trips where I had to pay for my transportation, food, and hotel. And then I actually traveled quite a bit around Asia and I think it even paid for most of those travels. I probably had to dip into my own savings for about $1,000, but I traveled a lot. I probably had five trips out of the country.

Bethany Glinsmann
ETA Fulbright to Korea

The money was not enough for me. What became expensive for me was actually doing the fieldwork. In this one area where I was getting really good interviews I had to hire two people and they were charging me whatever the daily per diem was in Croatia for translators that year. It just got really expensive. I didn't feel comfortable using my own Croatian, so I needed a translator. But the translator wanted her friend to have a job, so we needed to hire this other person in order to have access to people in certain areas, because she had done work there. My fieldwork got really expensive, and living in Zagreb is not cheap either. I actually borrowed money. It is what it is. I wouldn't have done it differently, but it's too bad. It's one more stress when you get home.

Renee Brown
Research Fulbright to Croatia
Political Science

I thought it was sort of annoying that they didn't give you a lot more information about taxes. I remember trying to file taxes after my Fulbright and thinking, "You don't give us any kind of form or verification? I'm just supposed to report to the U.S. government that I had $25,000 of your money last year?" What I ended up doing was have my parents and their lawyer, who helps with taxes, look into it and figure it out. I'm lucky I had that.

Hannah Halder
ETA Fulbright to Romania

Economically, Brazil changed a lot. This is something that I know the Brazilian Fulbrighters experienced because we were there right as the economy was getting ready to take a downturn. For most of my time in Brazil the Brazilian currency and the U.S. dollar were almost equal. For that reason the Fulbrighters who lived in Rio and São Paulo, cities that were much more expensive, were experiencing the pinch financially. Because of that the usual grant amount wasn't enough for people to find housing in safer areas.

Some of us wrote to the Brazilian Fulbright Commission about it to ask that they increase our grants to make it easier for people to deal with the pinch that was happening. Then when I was getting ready to come back to the U.S., right before the election, when the Lehman Brothers collapse happened, overnight the dollar shot up in Brazil. It was something like three to one with the local currency. And so a lot of the American Fulbrighters said, "Wow. Our money is actually worth something now."

Tiffany Joseph
Research Fulbright to Brazil
Sociology

Teaching English in Korea

Bethany Glinsmann
ETA Fulbright to Korea

I found co-teaching with Korean teachers very challenging, and looking back that's one of the things that I wish I handled differently. We were assigned a co-teacher but that really meant that they were kind of our mentor. Any questions we had we would go to them and they were responsible for making sure we stayed informed. They were supposed to actually co-teach with us and we were both supposed to do the lesson, but I found that some of my co-teachers just didn't even show up to class, and others would show up but they would take a nap in the back or read a book or something. Usually they would try and help me but sometimes they hurt the lesson more than they helped because they would just speak to the students in Korean. When I asked the co-teachers to try to speak in English to the students, I think they were offended.

I finally had a discussion with all my co-teachers but it was in the last couple of months that I was there, so most of my year was over. We had a conversation about how things were going in the classroom and their role as co-teachers. I think there were just some mixed communication signals at some point, so I wish I'd spoken up earlier. Some of them felt that I didn't want them to participate, and I felt they weren't willing to participate. As soon as I started to feel like this was a problem or wasn't right, I should have tried to have a conversation with them, rather than wait until the end of the year when it was too late.

That's definitely one of my recommendations, to communicate any issues early on. I think part of the problem of why I waited longer than I would have otherwise is that I was so young compared to the other teachers and I didn't want to accuse them of not doing their job well. It was a difficult subject for me to bring up with them, but I think I would have been much more successful as a teacher if we had actually partnered in our lessons instead of me trying to tackle it by myself.

If I could go back, I would trust my gut instincts more. I wish I had just kind of stayed more true to myself sometimes. But hindsight is always 20/20.

I was happy with the school I was placed in to teach English. It was a primary school. All the people were really friendly and really nice. They helped me get adjusted to everything. They helped get me a bed and helped me figure out whatever I needed to do in terms of registering in the country.

Lakshmi Eassey
ETA Fulbright to Germany

For ETAs, the educational differences in your host country can be a big challenge. Unless you've taught in that country before, you really have no clue. We come from such a different educational philosophy, educational principles, and educational history that sometimes the differences are shocking. I don't think you can prepare for it. It's something you have to exist in to really understand. That for me was the hardest.

Hannah Halder
ETA Fulbright to Romania

I think one challenge was that while I was older than the students that I was teaching, I wasn't as old as the other teachers, so I was sort of in-between. I didn't want to go out with the students all the time because they were in a different phase of what kept them engaged or entertained. I was lucky that I became friends with a woman who was a teaching assistant at the institute. She had gone on a Fulbright to be a Spanish teacher in the U.S., so she had kind of the reverse experience.

During the orientation we received in Buenos Aires they did a really good job of addressing the money issue. The money we received was above average compared to what teachers make, and even above average for what the average person in Argentina makes. They really tried to make us sensitive to not talking about how much we were getting for our grant. I made about the same amount, working very few hours, as a woman who became a close friend of mine who worked as a teacher in three different schools, who worked definitely more than 40 hours a week. It's not fair, but if Fulbright had paid us less it wouldn't have been fair to us, because it is more expensive to live for a short-term assignment than if you were able to buy an apartment or rent long-term.

Natalia Ksiezyk
ETA Fulbright to Argentina

One of the things that I did—but I don't think I did it soon enough—was to find allies for myself. It wasn't until my second semester that I connected with a couple of professors at the university who were younger and more aligned with a teaching philosophy that I understood. They took education seriously, a little beyond the approach of, "I am the teacher, you are the student, I am right, you're wrong. Listen to me lecture for two hours and write down verbatim everything that I say." So I was able to talk to them a lot about the differences. I knew that I wasn't going to offend them or get into trouble for asking questions like, "Why is this done this way?" That's really important.

Hannah Halder
ETA Fulbright to Romania

Part of getting the most out of the experience was meeting as many people as possible, having as many meaningful interactions as possible, and seeing as much of Nicaragua as I could when I took breaks from my project. Going to the conference and meeting all the other Fulbrighters was great. I couldn't believe how many people didn't go to that conference. It boggled my mind. Even if you don't enjoy the conference itself, the connections you make there are so valuable. Some of the people I met as a Fulbrighter are some of my best friends. For me what really made the experience were the people I met along the way.

Jessie Rubin
Research Fulbright to Nicaragua
Political Science

I highly recommend going to your mid-year Fulbright conference. We had a conference in El Salvador. I was surrounded by people who were so smart and doing such amazing things that I will probably never be in that same position again. Even just the social connections made it worthwhile. One girl I met there ended up coming to visit me in Panama later on, where she met her future husband, one of my friends. I went and worked for another Fulbrighter's non-profit doing an anthropology project in Guatemala. They flew me out there to do a photography project.

These are people who have shared the Fulbright experience and very often have similar interests, concerns, and ideas for what they can do to contribute to a better world. That's a vague and cliché way to put it, but I think that's what all Fulbrighters have in common.

Rose Cromwell
Research Fulbright to Panama
Photography

Learning a foreign language in an immersion environment

Lilith Dornhuber deBellesiles
Research Fulbright to Germany
Philosophy

If Fulbright were a decade-long fellowship, taking just an hour a week of language instruction would work. But it's not. You have 10 months to not only do the project you applied to do, but also to learn the language of your host country. If you're not starting to speak it within the first three months, you're really going to miss out on the remaining six months of solidifying your language skills. And if you don't solidify these skills, you're at risk of losing them when you go back to an English-speaking country. Nothing can replace daily learning, even if it's only a half hour each day. That's easy to hear and often repeated, but I firmly believe it. The following tips will help:

Know your learning style

Not everyone will pick up a foreign language by hearing it spoken. Some people like the framework of grammatical rules to build sentences, while others are distracted by grammar and feel it stifles their expression.

Manage your expectations

Be realistic about your goals and try not to be frustrated if you're not fluent within six weeks. Take joy in the small successes. You don't have to be perfect right away—congratulate yourself for small victories and steps forward.

Prioritize the area of language study most important to you

Do you want to be a fluent social conversationalist, or be able to talk about your research in an academic setting? Is speaking or writing more important?

_____ Make friends beyond the expat community

Get out and meet locals. Dating a native speaker is a great way to learn a language (cliché, but true). Drinking with non-English speakers is also good. Give toasts, haggle at the market, ask him or her out on a date. Remember: The quickest way _not_ to learn a language is to hang out with English-speakers.

_____ Have a sense of humor about the process

Be able to laugh at yourself and your mistakes. Let language learning be fun: Watch films, read novels, sing songs, and write love letters.

_____ Don't get stuck in a rut

There is always room for improvement, so try to have a growth mindset. If you arrive in your host country already able to speak the language well, use that advantage to boost your skills quickly rather than taking it as a license to relax.

_____ Think to the future

Think about how you'll keep studying the language after your Fulbright. Looking forward, make friends with people you'll keep in contact with to practice once you're home.

_____ Put yourself in uncomfortable situations to push your limits

Language is very much a confidence game, and the best language learners find ways to overcome shyness. No amount of exercises at home can compensate for actual conversations.

From what I've seen, Fulbrighters have enough money to hire their own tutors, even without a special language grant. I hired a tutor for my first month in Azerbaijan. It was really great because I was able to hone my academic Azerbaijani, and that was really necessary. After that I just tried to interact with Azerbaijanis and read as much as I could. There are podcasts you can download with news and cultural events, and that's another way to build your vocabulary as well as your listening skills. I really worked on my Russian when I was in Georgia. I sat down for about 30 minutes every day with Rosetta Stone and I just plugged through the program. I probably should have applied for the language grant, but I didn't.

Joshua Noonan
Research Fulbright to Georgia
   and Azerbaijan
Political Science

What was really important for me was that I started taking Spanish lessons from a native speaker right away when I got there. My Spanish was fine when I arrived. I could communicate and have conversations. I think I would have been fine without lessons, but I really learned a whole lot more about the culture, the people, and the language. I had a bunch of grammatical issues I didn't even know about. I think that's really important for people who are going to a country where they speak a different language. Even if they think their language skills are good enough, just to get someone more professional to help you right away is a huge help.

Maya deVries
Research Fulbright to Panama
Biology

The language was a huge challenge. Polish is tough. I could do everything I needed to on the street and get what I wanted in restaurants and markets without any problem. I could communicate to a point, but when it came to conversations about philosophy, politics, or history, it started to get way beyond my skill level. That was way up there in the challenge department.

I took private lessons while I was there, about once every week or two, whenever I could. I paid for this out of my own pocket. But frankly, it was just really hard for me to do the rehearsing and the practicing in addition to completing my research project. It was just a little too much for me in that period of my life. I probably would have tried to study more Polish before I went.

Mike Seely
Research Fulbright to Poland
Filmmaking

Just because the embassy recommends a language school doesn't mean it's going to be good. Be forceful about finding a teacher that works well for you—there can be a lot of floundering if you have a bad teacher. You want a school with a good reputation and curriculum. Maybe a school with connections to the business community, one that has corporate contracts. They'll have a more formal structure. You have to feel it out for yourself whether the school is legitimate or not.

Evan Tachovsky
Research Fulbright to Azerbaijan
Political Science

I didn't know anything about Spanish except some vocabulary and basic grammar structure. The hardest part about learning a language for me was getting over the anxiety of speaking, getting over being embarrassed to speak publicly. I forced myself to do it and eventually became more comfortable. It wasn't that I didn't have the vocabulary, because I understood almost everything people were telling me. It was mostly being nervous and insecure when speaking. It was probably five months into it that I got really good. I don't know what the definition of fluent is, but getting comfortable in a conversation, thinking in Spanish, dreaming in Spanish—that happens.

Matt Wesley
Research Fulbright to Nicaragua
Public Health

I had a really hard time with the language, actually. I was just not progressing as I wanted to progress. And that became really difficult for me. That became something that I struggled with on an ongoing basis. I started to take formal classes. The course was four or five days a week for three or four hours. That sounds great, and when I got there I thought, "This is awesome. I'm going to learn Croatian and this will be it." But unfortunately it really interfered with other things that were important to me, like my fieldwork, volunteering at the International Rescue Committee, and being available when the Minister of Health was able to speak with me. I ended up doing one-on-one tutoring, sometimes with the language school, sometimes with professors who did tutoring on the side. I spent my own money on that. I think it's worth it, but I think that it's more beneficial to have some rudimentary understanding of the language and how it functions before you go.

You really need to delve into it. It's hard when you get to this new place and you're so excited about all these other things. You don't want to sit in a classroom, and you don't want to do the homework. But you have to do the homework and you have to sit in the classroom. That is hard to do when you're on this new adventure, but you don't just acquire a foreign language magically. It's not that easy. And it's so appreciated when you can speak the local language. It's very important to them. It became important to me to learn it because of how important it was to them.

Renee Brown
Research Fulbright to Croatia
Political Science

Fulbrighting with family

Most grantees of Fulbright's U.S. Student Program are young and without families of their own. Married grantees and those with children are certainly welcome, but in the past Fulbright has not provided health insurance or covered transportation costs for dependents. In some cases the program does provide a small "dependent's allowance," but the dependent must accompany the grantee for at least 80 percent of the time to qualify. In the past there have been restrictions on receiving this allowance if the dependent is also receiving separate grant funding.

A big challenge for grantees with family can be the process of adjustment. Often dependents don't have the benefit of project deadlines, a teaching structure, or language proficiency to ease acclimation, and local restrictions may limit their employment possibilities. Having family with you can make it more challenging to immerse yourself in the local culture and more difficult to take advantage of language immersion.

I felt there was a lot of support and understanding from the Polish Fulbright Commission about the fact that we had a baby. They seemed to be very interested in the fact that my wife was Polish and that I wanted to explore her roots a little more. I actually feel that having my family with me was not a negative thing at all. When I asked if there was any way I could start the grant later, because my son was basically born the day I was going to start the project, they were super cool about it. They seemed to be very pro-family, at least in Poland. And I met a Fulbright radio journalist in Warsaw who had the same experience. He had a daughter who is basically the same age as our son, and he and his wife were from Chicago and they had basically exactly the same feeling. They felt very supported.

Mike Seely
Research Fulbright to Poland
Filmmaking

Employment for my wife was a serious concern, mostly because of her psychological health. Not working depresses a person fast. If you're in a foreign culture it's difficult to integrate. She couldn't go to the neighbors and just chat. She was isolated by not working. That was my largest stressor.

We were hopeful that she would find full-time teaching work there. She applied to a number of places and was offered a job, but in neither case was the salary enough to take the job. In hindsight we should have compromised and taken the job, because her emotional health would have been more important than monetary compensation. It's not always about money.

Having my spouse with me increased the stipend by $100 per month. This is negligible in an American setting, but since we were already paying for accommodation, that essentially covered her food. Other Fulbrighters complained that it was too little for their spouse or child.

Nic Wondra
Research Fulbright to Georgia
Political Science

I went with my wife. We touched down in Benin literally nine days after we had gotten married. We'd been dating for three years and she was also raised overseas, in the Dominican Republic. We both kind of assumed that we knew what we were getting into. Tongue in cheek, I'd say that moving to a developing country where neither of you know anything about the way the place actually works does wonders for relationship-building skills in the long-term, because you're either forced to communicate or you'll kill each other.

When she was having a particularly rough time and we were thinking about getting her a ticket to come home early, her folks basically went online and searched for missionaries in Benin, since both of our families were missionary families. We called them up and they invited us over and introduced us to the expat community through a softball game that happened every week at the Sheraton Hotel. And suddenly everything was hunky-dory. Had it not been for my in-laws springing into action in that creative way, the last seven months in Benin would have been brutal. As it was, they were fantastic.

Tim Slade
Research Fulbright to Benin
Public Health

My boyfriend at the time came with me. In retrospect, that wasn't the best thing. It made it harder to integrate. On the other hand, it was nice to have a friend. It makes you feel more at home. Having someone else there definitely helps.

Courtney Doggart
Research Fulbright to Turkey
International Relations

Staying safe overseas

Common sense strategies to stay safe in undeveloped areas

- Make sure the U.S. Embassy knows your phone number, your address, and the organizations you are working with. Always carry the embassy hotline number with you. Or better yet, commit it to memory.

- Remember that desperate times (poverty, conflict, and political instability) often cause good people to do desperate things.

- If there is a threat of evacuation, keep a bag packed with a change of clothes, any medication you take, your glasses or contacts, copies of your passport, and cash.

- Stay away from drugs. They are unsafe.

- Remember: You are not as good at reading people in your host country as you are at reading people back home.

- Listen to your gut. If it's telling you that you're in an unsafe situation, take action immediately.

When it comes to personal safety Fulbrighters are faced with striking a balance. On one hand, creating a rewarding Fulbright experience requires that you take risks and operate outside your comfort zone. But this should never happen at the expense of your personal safety. Living in a foreign culture makes it more difficult to recognize subtle clues that identify danger. The tragic 1993 murder of Amy Biehl, an American Fulbrighter studying in Cape Town, South Africa, is a stark reminder that Fulbright Scholars are not immune to harm. Every country has criminals and none of them care that you're a Fulbright Scholar.

The U.S. State Department encourages Americans overseas to be vigilant about personal safety and constantly aware of their surroundings. Many Fulbrighters are briefed by an embassy official about security issues when they arrive in their host country. This may be part of an in-country orientation or a separate meeting at the embassy. If no one offers you this briefing and you have questions, contact the embassy and ask to schedule a meeting. Briefings are typically given by security experts who know far more than you do about the situation in your host country. Listen to what they say and don't be shy about asking questions. Trust their recommendations over what you read on the Internet.

It seems counterintuitive, but sometimes one of the best ways to stay safe is to engage your local community as much as possible. In some circumstances, the more connected you are to people around you—colleagues, students, your landlord, the corner grocer—the safer you will be. If foreigners are a rare occurrence in your country, don't think you can hide your presence by reducing contact with locals. Chances are everyone already knows you're there, and being a hermit can make you a more vulnerable target. Trust your instincts and trust the instincts of local friends and colleagues even more. If a local acquaintance expresses concern about your safety, take this concern seriously and act immediately. This information could save your life.

If you experience a security incident, whether a threat, petty theft, or something more serious, report it to the U.S. Embassy immediately. Even if the danger has passed, such information helps embassy staff protect you and other Americans, including other Fulbrighters. Don't call the police without also calling the U.S. Embassy.

I had a pretty traumatic first couple of months with my Fulbright. I met the man who was to be my supervisor at my host organization. He had helped me write the letter of affiliation and bounce ideas back and forth when I was doing my grant proposal, to make sure that the research topic I wanted to address would also benefit the organization. Once I was selected for the Fulbright and I was looking for housing, he said I was welcome to live with him and his family. So I signed up for that.

And then about a week before I left for Nicaragua I got an e-mail from a friend of a friend there who said, "I happen to know that the man who is to be your host father and supervisor is a binge alcoholic. You should know that if you're going to be living with them." But it was going to be so convenient. He lived near the project I was going to be working with, and yadda yadda yadda. So I just went for it. It was horrible.

It's really important to set up boundaries and have a safe space for yourself when doing your Fulbright work, especially if you have an emotionally heavy project.

Jessie Rubin
Research Fulbright to Nicaragua
Political Science

For me one of the biggest challenges, other than the language, was dealing with the men there. I just felt very confused and scared and not sure how I was supposed to talk and engage with men, when it's OK and when it's not. That was hard for me. You want to engage with people, but at the same time you have to be careful. Finding that balance was difficult.

I like to interact and make eye contact with people, but you just can't do that sometimes. It actually affected how I deal with people now in the States. I have a hard time looking people in the eye when I pass them on the street. It's very interesting. That's something women should think about and talk to people about when they get there, wherever they go. Fulbright kind of touched on it during orientation, but they made it sound like it wasn't a big deal. But for me it became a big deal. I know my experience was probably a fluke as far as the things that happened, and it doesn't happen to every foreign woman who goes there, but still it's something to prepare for. It's disheartening, because it goes against your nature. But you have to do what you have to do.

Research Fulbright to Eurasia

When you go to the embassy they try to scare you so much: "Don't do this. Don't do that. Don't go to this neighborhood." You've got to be smart about it. Recognize your differences but also be willing to actually try to get to know people and not always have your guard up. It's a balancing act between being smart and protecting yourself—being willing to take a few calculated risks—and not being afraid of occasionally being vulnerable. But you've got to be smart about it.

Blake Scott
Research Fulbright to Panama
History

Tips for women traveling in developing countries

Genevieve Hill-Thomas
Research Fulbright to Burkina Faso
Art & Architectural History

Most countries have different sets of social and economic standards for women and men, and these differences are something that you will not be able to avoid if you are female. As a Fulbrighter in Burkina Faso, which has some of the most progressive laws in Africa concerning women's advancement, I experienced the difficulty of living as a foreign woman firsthand. My advice covers three areas of your fellowship: the practical, the professional, and the personal.

Ask questions and get informed early

Make sure when you first arrive that you set aside time during your orientation to ask questions. What are some problems that American women typically encounter here? Are there any social cues that I should be aware of? Is smiling seen as a sign of interest? Does shaking hands with a man carry additional meaning here?

Get the gear

In rural areas in many developing countries it is impossible to buy a tampon. Although you may be able to find your female necessities in a city, it's best to bring exactly what you need from home. Also make sure that you talk with your doctor about birth control and treatment for common gynecological conditions. Prepare for the worst and make sure you stock up before you leave the States.

Know the dress code

Do your homework and make sure you know what appropriate attire is in your country. Many countries are much more conservative about showing bare legs, shoulders, and even arms. Also be aware that what may be suitable for an urban setting is often not acceptable in a rural environment. It's always best to err on the side of safety so as not to draw attention to yourself. Look at what local women wear and try to abide by what you see.

Respect the customs

Know what is appropriate behavior for a foreign woman in your host country. Remember that your mission as a Fulbrighter is to complete your project and to represent the United States. Don't burn your bra in the streets unless you are ready for a revolution and its consequences.

Prepare for sexism

Many of us have not experienced overt sexism in the workplace. Unfortunately, this may be something that you have to deal with. Sometimes a gentle but direct discussion with a coworker may be the best avenue. Avoid statements such as, "In the United States, women…" You are not in the United States. Concentrate on your professional qualifications and the respect that you deserve as a coworker.

Find female role models

No one knows about being a professional female better than another woman. Find a role model in your host country and ask her how she deals with sexism. This advice can be invaluable.

Married or not, be aware of how you are perceived

If you aren't bringing your other half along, be aware that you are often seen as single until your partner shows up. Know that a wedding ring means nothing to many men. We all know the stereotypical view in the United States that foreigners and their accents are sexy. Prepare to be that foreigner.

Also know that an abundance of sex and violence in our media encourages many foreigners to believe that American women are all promiscuous.

Build friendships and community

Being away from your partner or being single in your host country does not mean that you are alone. Make sure to value the friendships that you form with other women in your host country. The larger your community, the safer you will be. Surround yourself with people you trust and respect. These are the ties that will last beyond your Fulbright fellowship and will ultimately be the most rewarding.

Mentor younger women

Make sure once you understand how to deal with sexism that you pass this information along to other women and girls. Volunteer with a local school to tutor girls or get involved with a women's group.

Think before you date

If you do choose to start a relationship, be aware of the consequences, especially if your sexual preferences do not fit into the norm in your host country. Think about the future and what will happen when you return to the United States. Be prepared for a long-distance relationship if you form a serious attachment.

Trust your gut

If you ever feel uncomfortable in any situation for any reason at all, remove yourself quietly and quickly from the environment and notify someone in your support network.

Know whom to contact if something happens

Is it the local police? Is it definitely *not* the local police? Is it the U.S. Embassy? Be prepared. And most importantly, if something happens, don't be silent.

Expatriate communities

The American expatriate community can be both an asset and a liability for the Fulbrighter overseas. On one hand, spending time with fellow Americans can be a great way to build relationships and manage the stress of living abroad. American expats are often well-traveled, adventurous types with interesting jobs and fascinating stories. Those who have been living in your country for some time can offer advice, introductions, and camaraderie that can make adapting to life there that much easier.

But too much contact with Americans jeopardizes your ability to immerse yourself in the local culture. The answer is not to shun all Americans—they can be a valuable part of your overseas experience—but to find a balance. Be aware of how much time you spend with your compatriots. In the larger arc of your Fulbright experience, hanging out with American expats will make your integration into the local community more difficult. Resisting the temptation to spend time with them can be an uncomfortable decision in the early months of your grant, but it can pay dividends down the road. Often the most life-changing Fulbright experiences are those where grantees succeed in immersing themselves in the local culture most completely.

The American expat community can be supportive, but it can also end up being a crutch. It can prevent you from interacting with your host country, improving your language skills, and really experiencing what it's like to live there. In Berlin, for example, there are over 13,000 Americans. There are special English-speaking bars that have English open-mic nights. There are areas of the city where you can go and you'll hear half the people speaking English. It's very easy to be an American surrounded by Americans. And if that means that you're isolating yourself from the German community, I think you're missing out on an important part of the Fulbright experience.

Lilith Dornhuber deBellesiles
Research Fulbright to Germany
Philosophy

It's really important not to lose yourself in your project, not just for your own mental health but also so that you can make sure to really experience the country. And there is something to be said for figuring out ways to include yourself in activities where it's not just all expats.

Jessie Rubin
Research Fulbright to Nicaragua
Political Science

I tried to stay away from the other gringos as much as possible. Not stay away exactly, because I definitely had a bunch of Fulbright friends, but I didn't live in neighborhoods where all the other foreigners were living. I was really trying to save money, trying to live as cheaply as possible the whole time. I ended up renting a room from a local woman in a part of town that might seem a little bit dangerous to some people, but I wanted to live with someone who spoke Spanish all the time. I really wanted to eat Panamanian food and live in a Panamanian neighborhood. I also tried to understand the public transportation system as fast as possible. Figuring that out was just kind of complicated in Panama. I wanted to be versed in everything local as soon as possible.

Rose Cromwell
Research Fulbright to Panama
Photography

I'm Chinese-American and I think a lot of times there were a lot of questions about my identity. Are you Chinese or are you American? Why don't you speak perfect Chinese? Why don't you look American? All of that questioning can get a little exhausting and sometimes, understandably, you just want to retreat to people who are more familiar with you and who you're more familiar with. I was living in Shanghai, which has a huge expat population. Certainly I did have a circle of American friends and spent some time with them, but I was also careful not to let that overtake my experience.

Deanna Fei
Research Fulbright to China
Creative Writing

I know the expat community can be really tempting, but it can hurt language acquisition if you're only spending time with foreigners who speak English. It's very difficult not to find people who are similar to yourself, but hanging out with foreigners is something you have to regulate. Because the point isn't to find people who think the same way as you, but to engage locals. This was something I dealt with in the Peace Corps, too. I just pushed myself to make local friends. It doesn't always work, but it's better than not trying.

Josh Noonan
Research Fulbright to Georgia
and Azerbaijan
Political Science

There was an interesting expat community in my city that I was hesitant to be a part of. I hate the idea that, "Oh, you're an American? You should meet this other American because you're both Americans and you'll really like each other and want to be friends." I think that happens a lot when you're abroad. But in the end my relations with the expat community helped me get in touch with other Romanians, and that was really helpful for me.

It's really easy to fall into the habit of hanging out with expats. There are some people who need that connection to home, or to something familiar. And so in order for them to stay sane, they need the expat community. If you're trying to break out of that, or not do that in the first place, especially at first when you're trying to adjust to everything, it can be good not to meet other Americans in your community. I think that what you do in the first couple of weeks or months can really set the tone for the rest of your grant.

Hannah Halder
ETA Fulbright to Romania

Life in the Field **223**

Being evacuated from my Fulbright site

Winston Scott
Research Fulbright to Guatemala
Anthropology

About three months into my grant the embassy pulled me out of my research community. I remember it perfectly. I had been planning to come home to visit for the holidays in December. The morning I was at the Guatemala City airport I grabbed a cup of coffee and a newspaper, and on the front page it announced a state siege on drug trafficking in Alta Verapaz, which is the province where I lived. I didn't think much of it. We were dealing with a lot of drug trafficking issues up where I lived.

When I got off the plane in the United States I saw a form e-mail from the embassy representative to everyone in the Peace Corps and Fulbright programs. "Just a reminder that there's a state siege going on in Alta Verapaz, so don't travel up there. Don't go near there because the military is taking control of the situation." So I e-mailed him back: What if I live up there? Within 30 seconds I got an e-mail response: "Where are you right now?" He was worried. We got into an e-mail conversation. He asked, "Where exactly do you live in Alta Verapaz?" I said in Senahú. "How far is that from Cobán?" A half hour on a paved road and about three hours on a dirt road. Cobán was where the military was really cracking down.

He said, "No, you're still in Alta Verapaz. It sounds ridiculous, but we've got to pull you out." You've got to be kidding me! I'm three months in, I'm just hitting my stride!

I got pulled out for a month, and that month turned into two months away from my community. That was a huge challenge. I'm grateful that somebody had my safety in mind, but at the same time it affected what I was able to do. I looked for opportunities to keep my research going via telephone where I could. At one point I actually obeyed the letter of the law and went to a community literally on the border of the province where the state siege was going on. I paid the bus fare for a couple of people to come down so I could continue interviewing. I stayed there for two weeks and did the best I could. Luckily I had friends in Guatemala City where I was able to find a small apartment, wait it out, and concentrate on some of my dissertation writing. I was working on a translation project that took up most of my time. Thank goodness I was able to get back to my area a couple months later.

I think having a closer association with my host institution would have helped. There wasn't much they could do for me other than supply me with books because it wasn't an institution like a research university where they say, "We have this going on, come work with us on this or that topic." They did have a lecture series that I attended and was able to speak at, but that only took up a week. There were a couple of other institutions that I had considered during the application process. Had they been my host affiliation it would have been seamless to just go in and say, "I'm in this city for a month, maybe two. Can I use your space to work, or are there any projects we can do together?" But that didn't happen to be the case this time. I know other Fulbrighters who actually do their projects with professors, but as an anthropology doctoral student I was just on my own doing my research. For anthropologists, you've just got to be there. We observe a lot, we analyze a lot, we interview a lot, and I just had to put all of that on hold until the embassy gave me permission to go back.

Of course I wasn't thrilled at the time that they were pulling me out of my area. I hated it at first and thought, "I'm an adult and I'll make this decision for myself." But when I got to talking with them about it, they said, "This is our reasoning behind it. This is what's going on. There are other things that we aren't privy to discuss." As a Fulbrighter you have a community of people that's looking out for you. They really are. In the case of the embassy in Guatemala, I kind of look back and say, "OK, I really appreciate that somebody was there for me. Otherwise I wouldn't have left." I'm not saying I would have died, I probably wouldn't have. But in an area like mine that is volatile, things can happen and it's good to know that if you need that support and that help, you can get it. They're behind you in making sure you stay healthy, stay safe, and that you have what you need. You don't get that with other grants. On my previous stints with an internal university research grant, I didn't have any of those resources.

The two cultural liaisons at the embassy were fantastic. And I know from speaking with a couple other Fulbright grantees down there in different areas of the country that they were very helpful for them as well. In part it's knowing that you have somewhere to go if you are in trouble. When you're in a foreign country, you're usually alone. But with Fulbright you're not.

Managing your Fulbright work

There will always be external challenges in your Fulbright work: difficult coworkers, bureaucratic hurdles, language barriers, logistical setbacks, and sometimes even cultural mindsets hardwired to resist new ideas. All Fulbrighters encounter these kinds of obstacles. What separates the most productive experiences from the mediocre isn't the number or scale of the challenges, but how well you adapt to them and move forward. Successful Fulbrighters never give up. They either find a way to circumvent these challenges, or they change their goals or methods to accommodate the situation on the ground.

Fulbright alumni stress the importance of setting long-term and short-term goals, devising a schedule for achieving them, and developing a method for self-assessment. Many grantees make a point of setting quantifiable benchmarks in their work: "I will interview five people each week in January and February, and transcribe these interviews by the end of March." Others build action plans for balancing their Fulbright work with outreach activities, as the two often complement each other well.

Whatever the nature of your Fulbright work—whether teaching, research, or study—realizing its full potential will require strategy. The more disciplined you are about implementing your strategy, the more rewarding your Fulbright will be.

One of the biggest challenges was coming to grips with the fact that I wasn't in a fully developed country, and things do move a lot slower. It seemed like I had a full 10 months, but there was actually a lot of down time. I arrived in November. In November, December, and January I really sat around and did absolutely nothing with the project because November is when their summer begins. What I found is that when it's summer in South Africa, a lot of the people mentally check out, especially in academic institutions. Nothing gets done. I turned in my name to get a student ID card at the University of Cape Town in November and I didn't get it until February. I turned in my ethics proposal for research in December and they didn't get back to me until March. I had to get used to the fact that things move a lot slower, and that I needed to prepare for that.

I saw that this was a recurring problem with several of the American students who came to work with me on the project. They were used to doing research in America where their professors are telling them to go faster, faster, faster. If your professor e-mails you in the morning, he or she expects you to reply by that evening. And so they would arrive and want to go really fast and I would have to explain to them that it's good to have high goals, but have a plan B because things move painfully slow sometimes.

Jared Sun
Research Fulbright to South Africa
Public Health

Make a schedule. It's really important to have a schedule when you're abroad, especially if you're not in school. I observed that some Fulbrighters would wake up late and then spend too much time talking with people back home instead of trying to push themselves into the culture. It sounds overbearing to do, to impose yourself on other people, but that's our job, or half of our job at least. To make connections, to understand the place. The schedule is important because it imposes logic on life.

It's really important with Fulbright to have a plan. When you write your project proposal you say, "For the first three months I'll be doing this." And you put action points on it. A schedule gives your day action points. And I think that's important for your Fulbright. Without structure things can deteriorate quickly.

Joshua Noonan
**Research Fulbright to Georgia
    and Azerbaijan
Political Science**

My Fulbright was really productive in bursts, but not the whole way through. I feel like the most productive parts of my grant were right at the beginning and right at the end. Especially the last few months because of the good weather, and because I had gone to a rural village where I was teaching photography to kids and was outside where we were able to go out and take pictures. That was one of the most special experiences I had. That was in April, June, July, and May—at the end of my time there. I always felt like I understood the culture pretty well because they were Latin and I had lived in Spain, but definitely during that last period in the village I felt very prepared. But even though I felt prepared it was still chaos. I loved it.

On a very personal level, it was really hard to be productive during the winter in Romania. I wish I could have done the grant from April through November instead, just because of the way I like to photograph and travel.

Lauren Hermele
**Fulbright to Romania
Photography**

It's really important to manage the time that you have there. I saw it as a challenge to make some deadlines for myself and really try to get better at doing that. I was successful in some ways, and in some ways not. I thought I would have time to edit these pieces while I was there. That didn't happen, so I was a little disappointed in myself for that. I really tried to balance the freedom Fulbright gives with the expectations of myself that I had, and try to take advantage of things while I could.

Mike Seely
**Research Fulbright to Poland
Filmmaking**

One of my biggest challenges was pacing myself. Once I started doing my interviews I just wanted to do more. I just wanted to gather more information. So at some point I just had to sit back and look at where I was, how much more time I had, and what was realistic to expect to accomplish. I had to re-evaluate my situation and really be more targeted in deciding how I would spend the rest of my time there.

What turned out to be difficult were the cultural differences in working with translators. I would say, "This is how I want to do my interviews. This is the process I want to use to find more interviewees." And through e-mail or over the phone they were very compliant with that. But then I ran into trouble when I was actually in the field. My resources were limited, so I wasn't able to do as much as I had wanted to do. I think if I had worked more closely with an academic adviser, someone in the United States, it would have been easier.

Renee Brown
Research Fulbright to Croatia
Political Science

Don't think when you get there that you have all these months and months to do everything and see everything. Because the months fly by. My project really took off in late February and March. I suddenly got very busy. I no longer had time for a lot of the traveling I had wanted to do. Now I had all these research obligations. If you have some downtime early on, go ahead and visit the places that you want to see. Enjoy it. Don't think you'll have time later in your project because you may not. Carpe diem.

Heather Wakefield
Research Fulbright to Georgia
Library Science

Trying to start the research project, trying to identify and connect with the people I needed to participate in my study, that was another exercise in patience, in realizing that I had to develop the concept of "Brazilian time" and stop thinking in terms of U.S. time. I had to readjust my expectations of what I wanted to get done in Brazil that year. It didn't look like I would be able to complete all the interviews because people were so slow to respond. I would schedule an interview and people wouldn't show up, or they would show up an hour or two late. Learning how to adapt to the local norms with regard to time and etiquette—those sorts of things are also part of the process.

Tiffany Joseph
Research Fulbright to Brazil
Sociology

Architectural Painting in Izmir, Turkey

Shadi Khadivi
Research Fulbright to Turkey
Architecture

I went to my research site daily. At first it was a little intimidating because I was going into the squatter districts as a foreigner. People were very curious, and at first there were a lot of assumptions made about me. Somebody thought I worked for the C.I.A. And they were very suspicious about why one would even be interested in the squatter districts. They thought my intentions were a little malicious at first, even though I was just doing drawings. And I think that's just cultural paranoia. If someone didn't want me to sit on their corner they would get a little bit aggressive with me and ask me to leave. They thought I was doing something wrong even though I was just using my paints. But that was in the beginning, and once they got used to my face they accepted it and they were very curious. Because I was there every day for the nine months, we became very close. By the end they would come and talk to me while I was doing my research. To get over that cultural hump was very rewarding for me, to not feel like an outsider in that context and to sort of blend in. It was really a fascinating experience.

The best part about it was not necessarily what I had planned. Through my research I met these young girls that were selling candy on the side of the road instead of going to school. They came and hung out with me once in a while. Finally I said, "Why don't you just paint with me?" I basically negotiated with their parents that essentially they would work for me and I would pay them with food or whatever they needed for the week. So they wouldn't have to stand on the side of the street. We built this mutual friendship and I taught them how to paint a little bit. They taught me a lot of Turkish, these little girls. My Turkish was really poor at the time. So we sort of built a community around this neighborhood while I conducted my research through architectural mappings, paintings, and photography.

Fulbright ambassadorship

Many Fulbrighters at the start of their grants underestimate the importance of their role as a cultural ambassador. The reality is that most people will automatically view you as a representative of the United States, whether you want to be or not. Many will base their opinions of America and Americans largely on their interactions with Fulbrighters like you. This is a tremendous responsibility, and many Fulbrighters discover what an honor it is to serve in this role.

Fulbrighters who explicitly embrace these diplomatic duties often carve out sections of their schedules for outreach activities. This may be volunteering at a local orphanage, speaking at an American cultural event, or teaching English in your spare time. In most Fulbright circumstances, these opportunities are everywhere. Ask yourself what kind of engagement would work best for you, then seek advice and contacts from returning Fulbrighters and the Fulbright Commission or U.S. Embassy in your host country.

Something that I encountered during the Fulbright as a person of color was that people didn't think I was American because I wasn't white. So a lot of times people would ask me where I was from and I would say, "I'm from the U.S." And they would say, "Oh, you're a Brazilian who went to the U.S. and got your papers." I would say no, I was born in the U.S. "Oh, but you're parents are Brazilian and you were born in the U.S."

There was this assumption because of how I looked and because I spoke the language that I wasn't really American, that I was denying that I was Brazilian. This experience contrasted with that of other Fulbright friends who were white Americans who were saying, "We get tired of sticking out here. People assume we have money and assume all these things about us because we're white." I was on the reverse side of that. People didn't associate me with being American because I wasn't white and didn't look white. Navigating racial dynamics in Brazil as a black American woman was a unique experience for me, particularly since I was interviewing people to find out their perceptions of race in the U.S. and in Brazil. Those were some of the biggest challenges.

Tiffany Joseph
Research Fulbright to Brazil
Sociology

I worked as a bartender for the year I was overseas, and that was one of the best decisions I made. If I was just an American at a café, or at a bar, or at the beach, I'd still be viewed as a visitor, as an outsider. A welcome visitor, but a visitor nonetheless. When I was working at a bar, that was a huge signal to people around me, especially the locals, that I was committed to being involved in their community, to being one of them. I found that locals really opened up to me once they saw that I had actually received an official spot in the community as a bartender in one of the local bars on the strip.

Research Fulbright to Africa

One has to be more assertive about accomplishing small tasks. It took ten times longer to get anything done. I think you just have to put yourself out there all the time. I felt a lot of times that people in Turkey didn't believe what I was doing. They thought it was very weird. Explaining not only what you're doing, but also engaging them in the community aspects of it is very important. If I had a gallery opening in Turkey I would invite the community my project focused on so they could interact with people. I didn't want to feel like I was just displaying these people or using them. I wanted them to feel like a part of it. So I would always invite them to all the openings, announcements, and events where I talked about my work. They were already so isolated from the community within Turkey, I had to assert myself to bring them along. And they often resisted. And when they would come they had a lot of opinions about it, but at least they got to be part of the experience and it wasn't all about me displaying them, which felt a little weird sometimes.

Shadi Khadivi
Research Fulbright to Turkey
Architecture

Seek out and take advantage of opportunities to speak publicly, even if it's not about your research topic. Not only will audiences benefit from your knowledge, but any chance you get to practice public speaking, to practice presenting yourself, will benefit you professionally. I can now put on my résumé that I presented at two conferences and a university. I can state that I have experience presenting to an international audience.

Heather Wakefield
Research Fulbright to Georgia
Library Science

There was never any kind of conscious effort to show locals what Americans are "really like." It's just sort of what happens in meeting the people we met there and just being there. I had a great experience with my host affiliate, a professor in Poznań. He had me come out to Poznań twice to present to a few different classes some short films that I had made earlier, and he was also gracious enough to invite me to serve on the jury of a documentary film festival there. And I know there had never been another American on the jury of this film festival. I realized that that's definitely something that Fulbright is trying to do with their mission. I felt like it just sort of happened naturally.

Mike Seely
Research Fulbright to Poland
Filmmaking

I would advise people to get out there and lose yourself. I still see it with undergraduates: Too often they're not out experiencing the new culture, they're just in it. They're not living it, they're just living amidst it. Get out there and put your fears aside. If you don't know the language, go talk to kids and learn how to speak a little bit. They're going to laugh at you, but you're going to pick it up that way. Language is always a big fear for people. People go off to Guatemala and find that in the rural areas there's not a lot of Spanish. They freak out. "What am I going to do?!" Well, learn their language. You're not going to learn it all at once. Pick up a few things. Learn how to say, "What's that called?" Write it down.

Winston Scott
Research Fulbright to Guatemala
Anthropology

Fulbrighter tips on the art of "guesting"

As a Fulbrighter overseas you will be invited to spend time with local friends, colleagues, and acquaintances, often as a guest in their homes. Being a guest carries its own set of responsibilities: Good guests are not passive recipients of their host's hospitality, but active players in a ritual of human exchange dating to the dawn of man. The interaction between host and guest is the original format for cross-cultural exchange, and there's an art to doing it elegantly. Fulbright alumni recommend the following:

____ It is an honor to be invited to dine at someone's home. If you are not familiar with local customs, research guest etiquette ahead of time and be prepared. Dress appropriately.

____ Never show up at someone's home empty-handed. Always bring a gift or something to contribute to a meal.

____ If toasts are given, ask for permission to give your own, then do it with confidence and poise. Practice beforehand if necessary. Be poetic and articulate, and engage your listeners. Don't mumble and don't meander in your speech—everyone is listening. If toasting is part of the culture, commit to learn at least one good toast in the local language.

____ Manage your alcohol intake. Always assume that whoever is refilling your glass is a better drinker than you are.

____ Never complain about your experience in the host country, no matter how challenging it has been. There is a time and a place for that, but it's not when you are someone's guest.

____ Find ways to reciprocate invitations.

I made it a point to take every Azerbaijani I met in Georgia out for coffee or lunch. That allows for a time that you can build the relationship. If you budget well, the stipend gives you enough money to be able to do that. It wasn't every day, but at least once a week I would take Azerbaijanis out for tea or coffee or lunch and I think that allowed me to build a better relationship with them, to establish some credibility. I could talk about my work, I could talk about what I've done with different communities, and I think Fulbrighters should not discount the impact that they can have, just paying for someone's lunch. It's not buying friends— it's using resources wisely.

Joshua Noonan
Research Fulbright to Georgia and Azerbaijan
Political Science

Reporting to Fulbright

On a personal level, the most rewarding part of the Fulbright was putting myself out there in the South African community and getting involved. I lived in an international suburb of Cape Town, so I was constantly exposed to people of so many different nationalities. I purposely lived in a house that could house 10 people. People came and went, but it was always people from interesting places. Switzerland, Holland, Namibia, whatever. Learning from and conversing with people who are different than me not only gave me many friendships that I still keep to this day, but also taught me so much about myself. I feel like it definitely led to a lot of personal growth in terms of being able to converse with people from all sorts of different nationalities.

Jared Sun
Research Fulbright to South Africa
Public Health

Fulbright requires little official accountability from its grantees. There are no mandatory expense reports, no requirement to submit drafts of your Fulbright work, and no third-party evaluations. This freedom and the trust it confers are a big part of what makes the Fulbright Program so successful.

Fulbright does however need two important bits of administrative housekeeping from all grantees in the field: the mid-year and end-of-year grant reports. Fulbright asks that you complete the online report by responding to written questions and rating various aspects of your Fulbright experience to date. Answers can be short and sweet or long and detailed—it's up to you.

Don't blow off these reports. Your answers are one of the best sources of data for program administrators about what the Fulbright grant experience is like on the ground. Your help keeps the Fulbright program running smoothly and responsive to grantees' needs. If your Fulbright experience could be improved on an institutional level, use these reports to let Fulbright know how.

Perhaps more importantly, these grant reports give you a valuable opportunity to step back and assess your progress. Past reports have directly asked what your goals were at the outset of your grant and how much progress you've made toward achieving them. It's easy to hedge when you ask yourself these questions, but much more difficult to do so with a third party. The mid-year report can give you the perspective needed to course-correct your Fulbright. The end-of-year report can help situate your Fulbright grant in the larger context of your project and your career.

Fulbrighters who received a Critical Language Enhancement Award are required to take part in a language evaluation at the end of their grant. This is typically done over the phone with a language expert, often a contractor for the State Department. Don't be nervous: You will not be penalized for poor progress in learning the target language. These evaluations help program administrators track what works and what doesn't so that they can make adjustments to the program.

Grant extensions

Grant extensions for research Fulbrighters are rare, but they do happen. To explore options for extending your grant period, start by asking your local Fulbright Commission for more details, but bear in mind that decisions about extensions are often made by Fulbright administrators in the States and are contingent on program funding. You will be asked to make the case why an extension is necessary, and it never hurts to have the support of the local Fulbright Commission staff. (This is yet another reason to take the time to get to know them and to keep them informed about your work.) What new opportunity justifies a few extra months in your host country? How will an extra few months further the Fulbright mission of exchange?

Many grantees elect to stay on in their host countries beyond the end of their grants. In the past Fulbright has discouraged this decision by releasing the final stipend payment only after grantees show proof of their return itinerary. The program views your return to the States as an important part of cultural ambassadorship. Fulbrighters who choose to stay on should consult the local Fulbright Commission about their visa and residence permits and should not expect support from Fulbright in this regard. Regardless of immediate post-Fulbright plans, most grantees maintain close ties to their host country, often returning later with bigger and better projects.

I ended up getting an extension on my Fulbright, which was really helpful. I went from August to May, then got a three-month extension, then did my exhibition in October. Officially I was not a Fulbrighter any more, but I guess you're always a Fulbrighter. One thing I was really surprised at was that only two out of 225 people at the mid-year Fulbright conference applied for an extension. You write a one-page proposal about why you need the extra three months of funding. Obviously you want to make sure that it makes sense for your work. I definitely needed it. I definitely had a lot of work I still wanted to do. I think it's a great way to keep doing whatever work you're doing.

Rose Cromwell
Research Fulbright to Panama
Photography

How to say goodbye

How can Fulbrighters say goodbye and leave on a good note?

You need to celebrate the accomplishments that you've had. In my case I was proud of the professional communication course that I developed and taught. I had spoken at a couple of conferences. I helped students with their normal daily classes. I think that it's hard to say goodbye to friends that you make, but I also knew from the beginning that it was going to end at some point. It's a natural part of the process.

In terms of effecting more systemic change at the university, I didn't have aspirations to do that even though I'd love to make things better. But it wasn't really my place to do that. It wasn't my role. I don't think anyone expected it to be my role. I didn't go in with that mentality.

I still keep in touch with quite a few of the people I got to know. I've gotten to see a couple of them. One of my former students from that program actually got a Fulbright and just spent a year in New York. I got to see her for a weekend and that was really fun. I'm proud to say that she was in my professional communication class and I hope some of the things that we worked on helped her when she was writing her essays.

Natalia Ksiezyk
ETA Fulbright to Argentina

Three months before the end of your grant is a good time to start thinking about your departure and what you want your continued relationship with your host country to look like. Don't just pack and leave. Take time to bring proper closure to your experience. Consider taking these steps:

____ **Leave with a completed body of work**

Come home with something tangible that represents your Fulbright work. It doesn't have to be a magnum opus, just something concrete to hang your experience on. This can be written research conclusions, an article for publication, a new series of paintings, or journal entries formatted for posterity.

____ **Remember that last impressions matter**

Many people will remember you most by how well you play your last hand. Be sure to say your goodbyes and personally thank everyone who helped you during your time there. Take a picture with colleagues and give them a copy. Send flowers, a card, or a small gift to people who had a significant impact on your experience.

____ **Host a goodbye event**

With a goodbye event you not only mark the end of your time in that country, but you celebrate your experience there. It lets everyone know what your plans are and how they can be involved. Go out with a bang, not a fizzle.

____ **Organize your contact list**

It's amazing how quickly we forget names, dates, and professional details. Organize your contacts in one document, with notes. The day will likely come when you need to contact someone on the list who you've lost touch with.

It's very important to do something at the end of your grant that puts your work out into the world. I had the opportunity to publish my final statement with some photographs in an academic journal, and it just felt really nice to do that. I definitely tore myself up over this project for a year. I obsessed over it and fully invested in it. It was nice to put a cap on the project. It was nice to be able to say, "OK, this is what came out of my time there." If you can get an idea of how you'd like to present this to the community you've been working in, or to the greater world, try to visualize that sooner rather than later.

A lot of people who apply to Fulbright are very ambitious people. We like to finish things. I also showed my work at a gallery in Panama City. Getting everyone I had met, everyone who had supported me, in one place at the same time was a really meaningful event for me. A large part of it for me was to give back to the people that helped me in my work. A lot of the people who I photographed or had given me interviews or had put me in touch with other people, I got to show them the final outcome of the project.

Try and get your work out there right after you're done. Don't put it off. A lot of people I know wanted to publish papers and waited too long. You'll regret it later if you don't do it.

Rose Cromwell
Research Fulbright to Panama
Photography

I feel like I reached pretty good closure with my organization. My own personal goals were to seek publication, but I presented all of my results in a 40-page report in Spanish for the organization. I presented it to the staff and the director, distributed copies, and gave them the file to print out if they wanted to share it. I happen to know that they did share it because I continued to be in contact with them. That was really gratifying. Making sure that there was some kind of tangible end result for the organization, some sort of benefit for them, that was my goal all along. That put a good conclusive point on the project for me.

Jessie Rubin
Research Fulbright to Nicaragua
Political Science

I probably should have gotten the word out about my work a bit more. It would have been useful to lay the groundwork for a job hunt. In the end I gave an interview on Azadliq Radio, Radio Free Liberty. I talked about the results of the project. It was good. After that I felt that my obligation to Fulbright was fulfilled: I had produced a product and had talked about it. If it's going to benefit anyone it will benefit Azeris, and anyone who listened to that radio program knows about it now.

It would be good for Fulbrighters to consider not just how to promote their research, but how to keep in contact with people back home about what they're doing. It's hard sometimes to target the right audience.

Joshua Noonan
Research Fulbright to Georgia
    and Azerbaijan
Political Science

Chapter 7

Life After Fulbright

Coming back to the States was like coming up slowly from the depths of the sea and trying not to get the bends.

Mallory Powell
ETA Fulbright to Vietnam

F or many Fulbright Scholars, coming home is the most challenging part of the grant experience. The bottom line is that it is extremely difficult to replicate the level of daily adventure, stimulation, and growth that most grantees experience while living overseas as Fulbrighters. But what Fulbright alumni are able to see that current grantees often cannot is that the Fulbright Scholarship is only the first chapter of your Fulbright experience.

Fulbright alumni are members of an international community of highly successful scholars and professionals who are often fiercely loyal to the Fulbright mission and hungry for collaboration and further exchange. How you choose to engage this community will define your future as a Fulbrighter. Some alumni view their Fulbright experience as a chapter in their career that ended with the plane ride home. Others see it as the beginning of a much deeper and rewarding lifelong pursuit.

As an alumnus of the Fulbright Program you will have opportunities to continue the program's commitments to leadership, community engagement, and international exchange. But doing so requires taking initiative. There are many opportunities for you as a program alumnus to continue your Fulbright experience, but you must be prepared to seize them.

Why is returning home so difficult?

There is an interesting trend in how Fulbrighters deal with returning home: Often those who had the most transformative experiences are the Fulbrighters who struggle most with re-entry. Regardless of what kind of experience you had overseas, it's easy to underestimate how challenging this transition can be.

There are two main aspects of reacclimation. The first, commonly known as reverse culture shock, is caused by a dramatic change in your environment. You might experience a wash of emotions and confusion much as you did when you arrived in your host country. But this experience is more surreal because none of it is actually new. Many Fulbrighters describe being able to see their own culture through the eyes of a foreigner for the first few days back in the States. Enjoy this rare perspective while you can, because it will disappear quickly as you fall into familiar rhythms.

The second source of difficulty in reacclimating to life back home stems from the fact that you aren't the same person you were before you left. The Fulbright experience changes people in important ways. Many of these changes don't surface until you're back home, and sometimes not until years later.

How do you make a smooth transition to life back in the United States? Unfortunately, there is no easy answer. Everyone seems to have their own recipe for adapting. Many Fulbright alumni wish they had allowed more time to decompress and process their Fulbright experience, to come to terms with how it changed their perspective and their goals. Others see value in jumping directly into the next chapter of their lives. Whatever your approach to re-entry, remember that your obligation as an ambassador has not ended, but rather entered a new phase in which you will share your Fulbright experience with your own culture. Most grantees feel that the Fulbright Program gave them an invaluable gift, and once home they start to search for ways to pay this gift forward.

Tips for managing the transition to life back in the States

- Prepare for your transition: Seek closure before leaving your host country. Make an effort to complete a body of work.

- As much as possible, return to a structured environment in the States, whether it's school, work, continuing your Fulbright research, or a volunteer position. Staying busy and focused is one of the best ways to smooth out the bumps of reacclimation.

- Seek ways to connect your Fulbright experience with your life back home.

- Connect with the Fulbright community in the States, either online or through a local chapter of the Fulbright Association.

- Recognize that re-entry will involve episodes of feeling down. Don't dwell on hypothetical scenarios of what you could have done on your Fulbright. Ask yourself the important question: *What's next?*

Coming home was rough. It was nice having a closet and a toilet and water and electricity, but I felt that I couldn't do anything that I wanted to do anymore. I felt constrained, actually. Where I was living in Nicaragua, I could get anywhere by horse or by foot. But in the U.S. I couldn't get anywhere. If I wanted to go to the grocery store I couldn't just walk down the road, I had to take a car. I felt very confined.

Matt Wesley
Research Fulbright to Nicaragua
Public Health

Going home, that was hard. During my Fulbright my mom had sent me the book, "Eat, Pray, Love." I never got around to reading it until I was on my flight home. I remember crying the whole way. I had a layover in Miami and I'm reading this book and crying in Miami. And on the flight passengers are seeing tears streaming down my face. It was a mode of catharsis, that book.

Having my family there to greet me was great. I remember I stayed with my mom for a month or so before I got a job. But in that interim, that month of being surrounded by family and by my home community, that was really nice. If people can make that happen for themselves, I recommend it.

I also didn't go directly back to the States after I finished my grant. I used some of the money that I had saved and traveled in Central America and met up with other Fulbrighters. I included Panama in my travel plans and met up with Fulbrighters there. One of them introduced me to my husband, who is Panamanian. When you put it that way, I guess Fulbright really changed my life.

Jessie Rubin
Research Fulbright to Nicaragua
Political Science

I felt bored when I came back to the U.S., and part of that was because everything was so easy. Everything was just so familiar. I had come to feel very at home in the town where I lived in Vietnam. I didn't travel away from my town as much as other Fulbrighters did because I had such a great community. Even at the end of the year there was something that still amazed me there every single day. It must be how a child feels when they're learning something totally new every day. And when I came back to the U.S. I felt like there was nothing to learn, like there was no sense of awe or amazement. Ultimately I had to relearn how to be inspired in America.

Mallory Powell
ETA Fulbright to Vietnam

I remember I flew into Dallas. All these big, noisy, crazy Americans! Texas is larger than life, and coming from meek little Asia it was like, "Whoa. What are these people doing?" I remember bowing to flight stewardesses and thinking, "What am I doing? I'm back in America!" I had two or three weeks between when I got home and when I moved to Madison for graduate school. I stayed with my parents and just let myself adjust in a safe zone. I even felt that going to Walmart in my hometown was overwhelming. So I'm glad that I wasn't forced to move to a new city right away where I didn't know anyone, on top of having the culture shock. I think having a few weeks of not being isolated, but being somewhere that you're comfortable and can adjust to life in America, is good. I probably would have taken more time if I could have. I would have been happy to have another month, or even longer.

Bethany Glinsmann
ETA Fulbright to Korea

*Coming home is a little rough, especially
if you had a great time. I remember when
I came back I was really, really depressed.
It was such a strange feeling because in
Cape Town I was having so much fun. I
was in a powerful position and a lot of
people there knew what Fulbright was. I
felt like I was self-actualized, like I was
approaching my potential at that moment.
To go straight from that sense that you're
reaching your potential, that you're doing
everything you can, that you're giving
back to society, to coming back to the U.S.
where suddenly you're just another person,
that was really hard for me to handle. I felt
ineffectual. It was difficult.*

    *Luckily I moved back to my home
town and not to a random city, so I was
surrounded by close friends and family
members. That was pretty much what
got me through. The void that was now
in me from leaving the Fulbright project
was being filled by all the close connections
I had with the people around me. It not
only helped fill the void but in some ways
improved me. Now that I had come back
and was a changed person—much more
mature and much more enlightened—the
relationships I had with friends and
family back home seemed a lot more
substantial, a lot more meaningful.*

Jared Sun
Research Fulbright to South Africa
Public Health

*When you leave to go overseas you expect
culture shock, but you're not expecting it
when you come back. And especially for
Germany, having been abroad other places
that on the surface seem so much more
different, I was not expecting to have any
trouble. But I did have trouble adjusting. I
kept saying things like, "Well in Germany
the public education is so great." Little
things like that. I don't know what I
would have done differently. It takes time.
You almost need to expect that you will
have trouble transitioning back, so that
you can be prepared for it. But I don't
know what you can do about that.*

Lakshmi Eassey
ETA Fulbright to Germany

*I've definitely continued to emphasize
people-to-people diplomacy and getting
to know other cultures, because the job
that I got when I came back was with the
Institute of International Education! I
worked on a contract for a university in
Saudi Arabia that was trying to recruit
students from all over the world. I got to
do a lot of student advising and pre-
departure orientations for students coming
on short-term assignments to the U.S.
and for students going for their graduate
studies at this new institution in Saudi
Arabia. So I got to put into practice a lot
of the experiences that I had while in the
Fulbright Program.*

Natalia Ksiezyk
ETA Fulbright to Argentina

Returning home

Shadi Khadivi
Research Fulbright to Turkey
Architecture

I stayed in Turkey one extra month on my own dime to sort of wrap things up. I needed some extra time. In that month I started applying for jobs via the Internet and then when I got back I had interviews lined up. But while the Fulbright is prestigious and a good thing to have, I suffered a year's worth of experience. Although I gained this wonderful Fulbright experience, architecture firms were thinking, "We can't depend on you to draw details all day long any more." That was a bit of a blow in the face for me. I couldn't believe that was happening.

I started working three weeks after I got back. It was pretty difficult. I came to realize that my whole experience in Turkey had changed my perspective on what I wanted to do in the States. When I was in Turkey I realized that I only wanted to work on buildings that affected the public environment, such as low-income housing or institutional projects such as universities. I didn't want to do single-family residential projects any more. So I quit my job after five months.

I started teaching, and this is where the Fulbright helped me. I networked via my Fulbright research. I basically cold-called universities. I was living in Boston and called four universities and said that I was interested in teaching part-time. While I didn't have very much teaching experience, I had given a couple seminars in Turkey on the research that I was doing. I told them about the project I did as a Fulbrighter, and they were really interested in it. And so they hired me to teach drawing courses, and then it built up from there. It was a lot of calling and talking and describing my research.

If you are stuck with the financial obligation of having to pay back an immense amount of school loans, you're sort of forced to go back to work immediately. If you have more flexibility, I recommend perhaps transitioning back more slowly, taking a little break and looking at the big picture. To digest what you have done, either through publication, or research, or however one pushes forward. When I got back I met with a lot of the Turkish community and it was very exciting for me.

What if I'm not ready to leave my host country?

Many Fulbrighters reach the end of their grants and realize they aren't ready to leave. Some want more time to complete their work; others want to travel around the country. A small group always puts down deeper roots for a much longer stay.

But Fulbright wants you to return to the United States at the end of your grant to share your experience with other Americans. It considers this an important phase of Fulbright ambassadorship. In the past the program has encouraged Fulbrighters to come home by releasing the final stipend payment after the grantee submits a copy of their return itinerary. Plenty of Fulbrighters make the trek home only to travel right back to their host country.

If you want to stay overseas, talk to the Fulbright Commission and your host institution to see what they recommend. If you know ahead of time that you want to stay longer, ask about getting an extension on your grant. These are rare, but not unheard of. Be aware, however, that countries with stricter visa rules might require sponsorship for you to stay in the country.

What will happen to my Fulbright work after I return home?

Many Fulbrighters return home, put their Fulbright project results on the shelf, and begin their life's next chapter. Without any requirements by the Fulbright Program to submit one's work, and after such an intense experience overseas, it's natural to want a break. Those interested in realizing the full impact of their Fulbright work, however, should make an effort to situate the results of their year in a larger professional context. If you produced a series of photographs, find a way to have them exhibited publicly in the United States. If you produced a scholarly paper, find a way to present it at a conference or have it published. If you taught English to schoolchildren, find ways to contribute your experience to the discourse on international education. Keep Fulbright updated about how your work has grown and contributed to your career. If nothing else, find ways to share your Fulbright experience with future grantees.

Basically, I came to the conclusion that eight months isn't long enough. With Fulbright I was only teaching at the university level and I wanted a different experience. I did not apply for an extension, but I could have. After my Fulbright grant ended I moved to Bucharest, the capital city, to start teaching at a state school. I wanted to get that aspect of the experience, to see the beginning stage of the students that the system produces, so I could compare it to the end stage, which I saw on my Fulbright. So I became an employee of the state of Romania. It was interesting. It was a challenge, to say the least.

I'm still pretty closely connected to the Fulbright Commission in Bucharest. I hosted a Fulbright application essay workshop for Romanian applicants. I usually attend the orientations to speak about the education differences that exist and what Fulbrighters can expect.

Hannah Halder
ETA Fulbright to Romania

I've been meaning to publish my work, but all of my research was done in Spanish. Right after my Fulbright I got a job that I really loved, so the data kept getting older and older and I just couldn't find time to dedicate to it. So it never got published, unfortunately. But it's still there. Hopefully I'll figure out something to do with it.

Jessie Rubin
Research Fulbright to Nicaragua
Political Science

Continuing your Fulbright work in your host country

Rose Cromwell
Research Fulbright to Panama
Photography

One thing that was important about my Fulbright experience was that I stayed in Panama after it was done. I founded a not-for-profit with a Panamanian friend that facilitated educational workshops for a specific community. I got a big grant from the U.S. Embassy in Panama, mostly through being a Fulbrighter and having that connection to the embassy. And we have had a lot of other Fulbrighters in Panama over the years who have done workshops with the kids. We even had one Fulbrighter who was going to make a documentary in Panama but decided to dedicate her time to working with the kids in the community.

That's been the most important thing to come out of my Fulbright experience: creating this organization and having the support of so many other Fulbrighters around me to do that. It's an organization that was created around Fulbright and supported by Fulbrighters. I think a lot of Fulbrighters are inspired to do post-Fulbright work in the place they've been living, and supporting these projects is important.

I always had a good relationship with the Cultural Affairs Officer at the U.S. Embassy when I was a Fulbrighter. I went to all the embassy events and tried to play an active part in that space. There was a small museum in Panama, the Afro-Antillean Museum, and they got a grant from the U.S. Embassy to put on a show of my Fulbright work. The woman who got the grant had received grants from the U.S. Embassy before and knew that it would be attractive to support the work of a Fulbrighter.

The Cultural Affairs Officer saw that we had a ton of Fulbrighters involved in our project. They funded one small event where we had a family day in the community we focus on. They gave us a grant of about $2,000 for that. We also applied to the Alumni Innovation Fund, a grant that the State Department puts out every year for people who are exchange program alumni. You can apply to do a project anywhere in the world with 10 other alumni who sign on to your project and support it. We applied for $30,000. We wrote to the embassy in Panama, asked for their support, and they gave it to us. They were very enthusiastic, but unfortunately we didn't get the grant. But then the embassy came to us and said, "We'd still really like to support your project," and decided to give us the grant directly. For us it was a big deal. The embassy's been really nice to work with and very supportive.

If you're looking to have projects funded in the future, see what the embassy has done in the past and get a sense of what kind of projects they are funding in your country. Be creative about it. I know one Fulbrighter in Panama who organized a conference where she brought theater artists from the U.S. to Panama. She got funding while she was on her Fulbright to host an artist residency. The embassy wants to support projects that involve Americans doing positive things in the host country. Because she was bringing Americans down to Panama, it was very beneficial to the mission of the embassy. After seeing her example, I realized that option is there.

I think the big challenges were really post-Fulbright, when I felt like I didn't have the same purpose that I had during the grant. Even though Fulbright doesn't really have any official expectations, I think that I was kind of on this high the whole time, and living in Panama post-Fulbright I didn't really know what to do next. Even though I had a job, I still had a lot of free time. I was grappling with not knowing what to do with that. I just felt like I didn't know my place in the country if I wasn't doing what I had been doing on my Fulbright.

I think that trying to keep yourself busy is really important. Try not to view the Fulbright grant as the end of a major project in your life—try to keep doing it, or keep doing a different project in the same capacity. For me, it was stopping that energy that was problematic.

Rose Cromwell
Research Fulbright to Panama
Photography

It was a strange experience. Coming back to the States was a bit hard because suddenly you're back on someone else's time. I had a couple gallery openings, which were really successful, and the Rhode Island School of Design wanted to do this whole presentation on the work that I had done. So they invited me to present the work and talk about it. I think I even talked to the next group that was applying to Fulbright.

Shadi Khadivi
Research Fulbright to Turkey
Architecture

Don't expect to be employed right away. The Fulbright is a boon to one's ego. I'm guilty of it. Other people I've met are guilty of it, of thinking, "I'm a Fulbrighter. I shouldn't be treated this way. This is something huge. This is special. This is prestigious." In some cases people do say, "Wow, that's really prestigious." But we have to be careful and think to ourselves, "So what?"

In my case the Fulbright did not turn into instant employment. Not letting it go to your head is important. Not only had people back home not heard of the Republic of Georgia, some of them had never heard of the Fulbright Program. Half of what I do is education.

Nic Wondra
Research Fulbright to Georgia
Political Science

I wanted to do more on my project after coming home but it never went anywhere. That was a letdown. I didn't have the resources around and wasn't able to see the project through to another conclusion. If I had been more formally integrated into some sort of institution, or working with someone, it would have been easier.

Courtney Doggart
Research Fulbright to Turkey
International Relations

Your career after Fulbright

Evan Tachovsky
Research Fulbright to Azerbaijan
Political Science

Whatever you're going to do after your Fulbright, plug into that. An unpaid internship, a paid internship, a part-time job, whatever. Nobody is going to hand you anything just because you had a Fulbright. And your peer group will be a little out in front of you. They've been at it for a year while you were on your Fulbright. There are a lot of people who went to college, then came to D.C., then interned for a congressman for six months, and now they have a job. Fulbright doesn't allow you to skip ahead. It allows you to develop personally and allows you specific knowledge, but for entry-level positions it all comes down to the people you know.

You're going to have to fight to get into the field you want. Or fight to get back in, because people forget you. Make your Fulbright look relevant to your career goals. Play up your independence and ability to dive into large problems, wrestle them to the ground, and get a firm understanding of them. If somebody is interested in your country, or your field in that country, you are the expert, you are the person they want to talk to. This is important in a job search. Be confident in your abilities, but know that nobody is going to give you anything just because you were abroad for a year. Be prepared to work hard.

Going to graduate school is a great idea if you time it right, so that you come back in the summer and start a program in the fall. Coming back into the workforce can be a more difficult transition. Don't be afraid to say, "I had a Fulbright and now I'm an unpaid intern." You need to embrace that.

How can I stay connected to the Fulbright community?

Since I've been home I've checked out some of the different Fulbright community networks online. Like the alumni.state. gov website, where you have a whole community out there that can offer you opportunities, support, or collaboration, if that's what you're looking for. You have such a wide array of people. Being a part of a community that I could discuss issues with was really helpful for me.

Winston Scott
Research Fulbright to Guatemala
Anthropology

It's your choice whether you want to have a continued relationship with Fulbright after your grant, whether you feel committed to what Fulbright is about. Personally, every time someone asks me if I want to talk about Fulbright or help out with an orientation or a seminar, or even read people's proposals, I feel a commitment to what Fulbright is about. Because we were offered this opportunity, I feel that we should pay that forward. Find ways to take what you've learned and share it with other people. Fulbright will give you those opportunities—it's your choice whether or not you embrace them.

Blake Scott
Research Fulbright to Panama
History

Most returning Fulbrighters hunger for contact with fellow program alumni. The excitement and ideas that flow when Fulbrighters meet can be truly inspiring. If no events in your area bring together program alumni, do what Fulbrighters do best: take initiative. Organize a monthly brunch meeting for alumni and Fulbright Scholars visiting from other countries. Plan a volunteer service event. Schedule a Fulbright lecture series at your local university. But before you set to work, make sure a local chapter of the Fulbright Association isn't already active in your community. The Fulbright Association exists to make these sorts of networking and exchange opportunities happen. If there is a chapter active in your city, get involved with its leadership.

If you want to develop new ties with Fulbrighters from other countries, there are a number of ways to pursue this. The Department of State manages a website—*alumni.state. gov*—where alumni of U.S. government exchange programs, Fulbright and others, can connect, collaborate, and exchange ideas. It offers online research tools to help you find funding opportunities and share news about what other Fulbrighters from around the world are up to.

The Institute of International Education (IIE), one of the Fulbright Program's main partners, often hosts weekend-long enrichment seminars for visiting Fulbright Scholars. In the past they have looked for recent U.S. Fulbright alumni as volunteers to help with these events. Typically these events offer a mix of workshops, guest speakers, and networking functions. U.S. alumni volunteers have reported very inspiring experiences at these seminars (see *Volunteering at a Visiting Fulbright Enrichment Seminar*).

Alumni who want to engage Fulbrighters on a more individual basis need only to remember that thousands of visiting Fulbright Scholars arrive every year in cities across the U.S. They come from countries all over the globe for a year or more of Fulbright study, teaching, and exchange. For many this is their first experience in the United States. Who better to help them transition to their new home than a fellow Fulbrighter? Show them their new city. Help them locate housing. Organize a Thanksgiving dinner with a local American family. The Fulbright experience can be a powerful unifying force.

The Fulbright Association is a private non-profit organization whose members are Fulbright alumni and friends of the Fulbright Program. Managed by a national office and governed by a board of directors, the Fulbright Association exists to continue the Fulbright experience by promoting opportunities for international exchange, networking, collaboration, community engagement, and service at home and abroad.

The Fulbright Association's national office guides and supports local chapters in cities and regions across the United States. The chapters organize events for local Fulbrighters, from lectures and educational events, to wine-tasting excursions, networking functions, and Fulbright film festivals. Events offer a welcome venue for visiting Fulbright Scholars and American Fulbright alumni to interact. Each chapter is run by a volunteer board of directors committed to strengthening the Fulbright community and furthering Fulbright's mission of exchange. Joining the leadership of your local chapter is a great way to give back to and stay connected with the Fulbright community.

The Fulbright Association also hosts an annual international conference where Fulbrighters are encouraged to present their research, network with colleagues, and hear speakers on topics of international interest. The organization also awards a Fulbright Prize that recognizes outstanding contributions to the mission of fostering understanding among peoples, cultures, and nations. The inaugural Fulbright Prize was awarded to former South African President Nelson Mandela in 1993.

Volunteering at a Visiting Fulbright Enrichment Seminar

Thomas Burns
Research Fulbright to Armenia,
      Azerbaijan, and Georgia
Photography

Each year the Institute of International Education, one of the Fulbright Program's main administrative partners, hosts seminars for visiting Fulbright Scholars studying at graduate institutions in the United States. IIE often invites American Fulbright alumni as volunteers to help coordinate these seminars. The following is a Fulbrighter's blog entry written after volunteering at one of these events.

I just returned from a three-day Fulbright Enrichment Seminar in Sacramento, California, that brought together 140 foreign Fulbright Scholars from all corners of the globe to network, exchange ideas, and study the U.S. electoral process. I was a U.S. Fulbright Fellow to Azerbaijan, Armenia, and Georgia in 2009 – 2010, where I produced a collection of large-scale portrait photographs exploring the post-Soviet condition in the South Caucasus. I also taught photography and cinematography to university students throughout the region. It was a life-changing experience, a rare professional gift that allowed me to develop my leadership skills, build relationships with colleagues overseas, serve my country, and focus on an aspect of photography that is central to my practice.

The Sacramento seminar was a fantastically successful event. As one of six U.S. Fulbright alumni who were chosen to help facilitate the seminar, I was excited about the chance to give back to the program, but I never expected to be quite so inspired. The visiting Fulbrighters who participated, all of whom are studying in graduate programs in the United States, are some of the brightest young minds from around the world. When put together in one room they constitute tremendous potential for progress, innovation, and international leadership. They were law students from Austria, engineers from Iraq and Nigeria, an architect from Hungary, public health specialists from Norway and New Zealand, psychologists from Russia—the list goes on and on. After hearing them debate American electoral politics, I am certain that there were multiple future heads of state among us.

One of the most salient features of the event for me was the unspoken understanding that breakthroughs happen at the intersection of disciplines, and there was a tremendous willingness among participants to think outside the box. At the seminar's closing dinner, for example, I sat next to a cellist and a chemist, both from Germany, and the topic of conversation flowed freely across our collective areas of specialty: From the third dimension of the periodic table, to syncopation in Bach's fugues, to the role of portraiture in cinema, to the promise and limitations of organic photovoltaic cells. What I found so exciting was that the conversation didn't *shift* from topic to topic, but evolved naturally through explorations of their common ground. It would have been enough if the seminar had provided the opportunity for just one conversation of this caliber, but exchanges like these were the norm, and with that level of stimulation ideas flow at an incredible rate, building on each other with striking speed.

When you have that many nationalities in attendance, there are inevitably times where nations with historically less than ideal relations are placed in contact with one other. In a small group discussion that I facilitated, for example, there were Fulbrighters from both Israel and the West Bank, and from both India and Pakistan.

Their differences didn't fade away, of course, but they were contextualized, for a few short days, within a calling that we all felt to a greater international cause. Here they could at least have a conversation, something that in many venues would be totally unfeasible. On the dance floor on the final evening the DJ played songs from each country. "And now Turkey!" she announced. Everybody cheered. Halfway through the song she corrected herself, "Whoops. Sorry, that's actually Greece!" Everyone kept dancing.

One of the biggest challenges for me working in the film industry in Los Angeles has been finding a community that I feel I belong to, a professional family that shares my commitment to leadership, international education, and giving back. I have many strong individual relationships, but the model of connection often feels more like a wagon wheel than a cloud, and this has been an ongoing and serious challenge to my work and training as a cinematographer. A few hours into the seminar I walked into the main room filled with all of the participants and felt a warm realization wash over me: These are my people. The shared Fulbright experience is a powerful unifying force.

On the plane ride back to Los Angeles I experienced something I hadn't felt since I returned home after my own Fulbright overseas, a strange state where ideas were firing faster than I could write them down, but at the same time were cloaked in a kind of sadness, a feeling of loss that the intense intellectual experience of the seminar was over. The three days of the event were some of the most inspiring I have experienced in the United States. In many ways it felt like a three-day Fulbright Scholarship.

I am humbled by my Fulbright colleagues and honored to be part of their community. The question now is how to deepen these relationships, how to continue to pay forward the opportunities and community the Fulbright Program has provided. I look forward to what lies ahead.

February 2012

How can I give back to Fulbright?

There are so many ways to give back to the Fulbright Program and the Fulbright community. Consider one of the following:

_____ Join the Fulbright Association and get involved with your local chapter

_____ Volunteer to attend pre-departure orientation for American Fulbrighters preparing to leave on their grants

_____ Volunteer at your college or university to help mentor Fulbright applicants, talk about your Fulbright experience, or write a short article for the school newspaper or alumni magazine

_____ Become an IIE Fulbright Ambassador

_____ Volunteer for IIE Fulbright events like Visiting Fulbright Enrichment Seminars

_____ Mention the opportunities the Fulbright Program has given you when speaking or writing about your work

_____ Write letters to your members of Congress about the value of the Fulbright Program

_____ Encourage promising young leaders to explore what the Fulbright Program offers

_____ Contact recently arrived Visiting Fulbright Scholars and help with their transition. How can you help them make the most of their Fulbright experience in the U.S.?

_____ Help promising candidates from your host country apply to the Fulbright Program

_____ Blog about your Fulbright experience

_____ If you work at an institution of higher education that doesn't have a campus Fulbright Program Adviser, volunteer for the role

_____ Publish, exhibit, or publicize your Fulbright work

_____ Stay connected to your host country

The Fulbright Program needs your help!

As successful as it is, the Fulbright Program is not safe from budget cuts. Most of the program's funding comes from an annual appropriation from the U.S. Congress, and the amount of this appropriation can change from year to year.

One of the most effective ways you can give back to the program as a Fulbright alumnus is to write a letter to representatives in Congress. Your letters *do* make a difference. Politicians and policymakers need to understand the program's impact on international relations, and its contribution in the development of America's next generation of leaders.

More funding could mean more Fulbright Scholarships, larger Fulbright stipends, more Fulbright partner countries, and more support for the Fulbright alumni community and their projects. Take the time to write a letter by hand—it shows more effort and commitment than an e-mail or online petition. The Fulbright Program needs your help.

The thing that we as Fulbright alumni can do is better inform the grantees that come after us. I knew the person who was in the same location I was the year before and I talked with him a couple of times, but I didn't know what questions to ask. Before I left Argentina I wrote a "Fulbrighter's guide" to the city I was in. I listed a lot of logistical things like recommendations for places to go and locations for the post office. I left that with the Fulbright Commission in Argentina and sent it in as part of my program evaluation that goes to IIE. I hope that the next person that got placed in that city was able to use that information.

Natalia Ksiezyk
ETA Fulbright to Argentina

I've been doing medical school interviews since I've been back and interviewers often ask me what I noticed were the big differences between American culture and that of South Africa. I tell them what I saw was different. But more importantly, I always also mention that after several weeks and months of always picking out what is different, you stop seeing the differences and you start seeing the similarities. Across the entire world, people value friendships. Guys enjoy going out to get a drink with one another. People have family values no matter what culture you're from. Seeing this common thread of similarities—these common threads of humanity in all these different cultures—that was much more rewarding than learning that "we do this and the French do that." That was what was important.

Jared Sun
Research Fulbright to South Africa
Public Health

Paying your Fulbright forward

Many Fulbright Scholars begin their grant with a view of the Fulbright Program as a way to pursue their overseas teaching and research goals. Most know that Fulbright's mission of exchange exists on paper, but many don't fully realize how central the exchange mission will be to their Fulbright experience. What is truly impressive about the Fulbright Program's impact is how many of its grantees come to embrace this idea, either while overseas or after they return home, and how deeply transformative this awakening can be.

In researching this book I noticed an interesting pattern among Fulbright alumni. Those Fulbrighters who had the most transformative experiences overseas, and often those who have gone on to make the most pronounced impact in their communities, often speak about their Fulbright experience in terms of the relationships they built. Many feel that these relationships, and the program's success in encouraging them, enabled them to achieve their true potential at that moment in their lives. Few people can say they have experienced this kind of self-actualization. The fact that the Fulbright Program facilitates this level of growth for its grantees testifies to its profound success as an international exchange program.

The Fulbright experience gives many grantees a new perspective on the value of relationships and the potential they hold for understanding, collaboration, and positive social change. This perspective opens new vistas of opportunity in our work and partnerships. Honoring this commitment to the Fulbright mission—to forge new relationships across cultural lines—is one small but potent way that we alumni can pay forward the incredible gifts that the Fulbright Program has given us.

Sample Application Essays

The following pages contain essays from successful applications to the Fulbright U.S. Student Program. These essays should not be used as templates for your own writing. The Fulbright Program is constantly evolving, and the requirements and formats of today's application essays are most likely different than when these were written. These examples can, however, provide a general sense of the kind of research and thoroughness that go into crafting a successful Fulbright application. Check with the Fulbright Program Adviser at your college or university for more recent samples.

STATEMENT OF GRANT PURPOSE

Thomas Burns
Multi-country research Fulbright to Armenia, Azerbaijan,
**   and Georgia**
Photography, 2009 – 2010

Memory and Moment in the South Caucasus

The countries of the South Caucasus—Armenia, Azerbaijan and Georgia—are emerging from a challenging period of post-Soviet transition into an era of independent and democratic statehood. I intend to document this moment in the region's history by photographing residents of each country as they incorporate this transformation into their daily lives. Unscripted and intimate, these photographs will explore this evolution not through coverage of political events, but rather through candid portraits of the ordinary men and women who experience their effects on an everyday basis. With logistical support from local media organizations and academic institutions in all three countries, this year-long assignment will produce a constellation of images celebrating national rebirth and the legacy of a shared past.

Shadowed by more than fifteen years of economic instability, political upheaval, and ethnic conflict, Armenia, Azerbaijan and Georgia have shared in a common struggle to reinvent themselves in the wake of the Soviet Union's collapse. This process, which has often thrown ethnic and cultural distinctions into stark relief, has also underscored a need for regional solidarity. Located on the peripheries of powerful neighbors at a key point on the Eurasian transcontinent, these countries today stand at a historic juncture, a moment in which they have begun to finally leave behind the instability and chaos of transition for the strength and optimism of democratic statehood. Examining this moment from a regional perspective helps us understand the challenges that lie ahead for each country. At their core, these photographs will investigate how the peoples of the South Caucasus today view themselves and their place in the world around them.

Western images of the South Caucasus have traditionally focused on the icons of yesterday: faded busts of Lenin, ethnic costumes, and sweeping mountain vistas, to name a few. Rejecting the clichéd grandeur that characterizes such "tourism" photography, this project eschews the picturesque, instead pursuing the quiet meaning found in scenes of the prosaic. Inspired in part by Richard Avedon's *In the American West* and the Magnum Photos collection *East of Magnum*, this project consists principally of black and white portraits captured in a documentary fashion. A shoemaker in Vanadzor, a chess student in

Baku, a displaced family in Kutaisi—all of these faces bear the indelible traces of hope, fear, love, hardship, promise, and nostalgia that are often the true metric for social change.

Documentary photography is a medium uniquely suited to the goals of this project. Unlike many journalistic formats, the documentary photograph provides the viewer a visceral, personal connection to the experience of its subject. Distilled from larger narratives, the photograph functions as a meeting place for the past and the present, and is by nature infused with a sense of time and loss: Its structure causes stories to be longed for. The images produced by this project will educate western viewers about this important moment in the region's history. For audiences in Armenia, Azerbaijan and Georgia, the collection will recognize where they've been, how far they've come, and where they're headed.

The shooting platform of this project will be black and white 35mm and medium format film. I own all the necessary shooting equipment (cameras, lenses, tripod, and accessories). To offset the cost of film stock and other research-related expenses, I am seeking additional material support from several academic and photographic organizations, though I am prepared to bear these expenses personally. Film processing and proofing will take place on an ongoing basis at facilities in Baku, Tbilisi, and Yerevan, access to which will be organized through supporting organizations in each country. Over the course of the project I plan to seek out opportunities for exhibition of the completed collection in all three host countries, as well as in the United States.

I will undertake this project over a ten-month period beginning in January 2010. The schedule consists of approximately 14 weeks of principal photography in each of the three countries. The Russian language remains a lingua franca in the region and is the most valuable language to the success of this project. I speak Russian and plan to use a Critical Language Enhancement Award, starting in September 2009, to improve my language skills further by studying in Yerevan, Armenia, for four months prior to the project's initiation. I also have a strong interest in undertaking an introductory study of each country's local language, as such an effort can only bring me closer to local residents.

Interacting with communities in the South Caucasus is the primary method by which I will pursue these images—their very nature demands that I form relationships with my subjects. The project will be structured into smaller assignments, each focused on distinct sub-narratives within the larger story of the region's transformation. Supporting organizations in each country have agreed to facilitate introductions, site visits, and homestays with potential subjects in both urban and rural areas. I look forward to partnering with local groups to initiate dialogue with colleagues in the region, host photography and cinematography workshops, and provide apprenticeship opportunities to local students interested in the photographic arts.

This is a project that I am qualified to execute successfully. I hold a Bachelor's degree in Soviet history from Reed College and a Master's degree in documentary film from Stanford University, where I produced, among other documentary projects, a historical film about jazz in the Soviet Union. In 1998, prior to attending graduate school, I worked for a development organization in the South Caucasus, where I collected interviews, in Russian, from successful foundation grantees. I continued my professional training as a photographer following graduate school by apprenticing for motion picture photographers in Los Angeles while continuing to develop my still photo portfolio. Committed to the strength of image as a narrative instrument, I now work as a cinematographer shooting both fiction and non-fiction films. Documentary photography—in my opinion the purest form of visual storytelling—has always remained at the core of my photographic work.

The collection of images produced by this project will provide exposure critical to the growth of my career by opening new doors for exhibition and publication. More importantly, this project will introduce me to new modes of thinking about image and narrative, hone techniques needed for prolonged fieldwork, and forge lasting relationships with colleagues in the South Caucasus. Upon returning to the United States I plan to prepare my Fulbright work for exhibition, begin researching future documentary photo projects, and seek out college-level teaching positions in the fields of still and motion picture photography.

STATEMENT OF GRANT PURPOSE

Hannah Halder
Fulbright English Teaching Assistantship to Romania
2009 – 2010

I seek an English Teaching Assistantship in Romania to deepen my understanding of higher education in a transitioning country. With this improved knowledge and experience, I plan to pursue graduate school in the U.S. in international education and development. Dialogues with local scholars, professors, and students about the trials of an educational system in a fledgling democracy will help me better understand the challenges facing Romania today and how these might relate to those in other countries.

      The transition of education in Romania is a compelling case study, as the country works with the European Union and raises demands for basic competencies in the private, public, and social sectors of society. The EU looked at Romania as a recent member that could be a stimulating partner in the implementation of reform in education across all member states. The Bologna Declaration (1999) calls for a common network of education qualifications across Europe. Through this process a project, called EQF by NQFs (European Qualifications Framework by National Qualifications Framework), sought Romania as an obvious choice in joining the states mandated with the project to reform higher education. Romania's Ministry of Education and Research was already working to update the national framework for higher education and could help administer the project. Additionally, through the implementation of a law in 2004 to institute a new higher education structure providing for the framework of the three cycles of higher education (bachelor, master, and doctoral), Romania was on its way to more cohesively match the education system of the rest of Europe.

      To further the goals of this common European network, ACPART (National Agency for Qualifications in Higher Education and Partnership with the Economic and Social Environment) was established in Romania to administer the EQF by NQFs project across Europe. The agency, a subsidiary of the Ministry of Education, sought to partner with social institutions within the economic sector in Romania, who will directly benefit from the construction of a more cohesive education system. In the end, the project hopes to promote sustainable development through education for all member countries. This project is one of the many compelling transitions taking place in Romania today, and I wish to observe it firsthand by working in Romania's higher education system.

Working as an English Teaching Assistant in the Romanian university system and interning at the regional Fulbright advising center will allow me to gain an understanding of the social development of higher education. Following my graduation from Beloit College, I spent 11 months at the college as an international education intern. As an intern I worked with international students and came to a greater understanding of the cultural challenges they face when confronted by an educational environment completely different from their own. Conversely, my current job as a study abroad advisor to American students provides a perspective on the reverse direction. Similar questions and concerns arise as both sets of students embark into the unknown educational system of a foreign country.

As a teaching assistant, I would also draw on my past experiences teaching English. I tutored Hispanic youth in the Beloit College community, served as a teacher's aide in a Hungarian ESL class, and volunteered with an organization in Chicago as a tutoring assistant in an ESL course. The latter led to an invitation to help develop an ESL program for senior citizens. Planning and working to start this program, developing curriculum, and leading sessions has been an invaluable opportunity to grow and challenge myself. I look forward to further developing these same skills in a university setting in Romania. In addition to my interest in teaching the English language, I also will employ the talents I developed in leading several classes in American Studies during college, in which I focused on the growth of the American jazz movement in the U.S. and its permeation of society, culture, and art from the early 1900s onward. Using visual art media was particularly helpful in understanding pieces of jazz music, and I plan to adapt this knowledge and experience as a classroom teaching tool.

I look forward to participating in the intellectual life of higher education in Romania both inside and outside the classroom. Assisting working scholars and professors in the classroom will allow me to see day to day how they operate as new educational policies are realized. I see teaching English as a way for people to effectively communicate and to learn from one another, to synthesize and approach problems so that we can all become contributing members of society. In teaching it is important to use real world examples and to facilitate an effective and collaborative environment for discussion and analysis. It is through commonality that we can begin to learn from each other, and I see teaching English as a forum for doing so.

Additionally, I will gain firsthand opinions and take part in discussions of the implementation of EU educational policies in Romanian higher education. I hope to further my understanding of educational transitions by volunteering and participating in groups that promote social change, art, and education in youth. Using these experiences, I plan on conducting research into the informal sector of education in Romania outside of the classroom setting. Student experiences in Romania will be one of the best windows into their vision for the future of education and consequently, of their country.

Teaching English, advising, and researching will give me the practical and scholarly experience to attend graduate school in international education and development when I return to the U.S. The combination of the three is crucial to understanding the transitions in education today. I am interested in graduate programs such as those at George Washington University and American University that allow for the study of education systems and development with the goal of advancing equality through learning opportunities. Following completion of graduate school, I plan to use my practical experience in Romania and my education to work for a development agency that believes in promoting sustainable development through education, such as USAID, AED, or even the Fulbright Commission. All of these organizations work in education internationally and seek to further dialogue across nations and states with the goal of using education to improve quality of life.

The work and research I undertake in Romania will contribute to a growing dialogue on the importance of education to encourage the sustainability of democratic principles. The country sits poised as an intriguing example of the changing nature of higher education in Eastern Europe, the EU, and beyond. I strongly believe that higher education is a means for fostering democratic principles that encourage social cohesion, limit inequalities, and raise competencies within a society, and the Fulbright English Teaching Assistantship will allow me to become involved in that invigorating process.

STATEMENT OF GRANT PURPOSE

Blake Scott
Research Fulbright to Panama
History, 2008 – 2009

The Development of Ecotourism in Panama: A Historical Perspective

How, in less than one hundred years, did Western perceptions of Panama's tropical environment shift from viewing the region as a malevolent and diseased backwater to an attractive, tropical paradise? With my research project I plan to explain how such ideological and cultural shifts have evolved and subsequently shaped nature-based tourism (i.e., ecotourism) in Panama.

Over the last thirty years, ecotourism has developed into the fastest-growing sector of the tourist economy worldwide. Many of our neighbors to the south have been at the center of this economic boom. Ecotourism is now Central America's number one industry. For many U.S. tourists, Costa Rica's rainforests and beaches epitomize nature-tourism—the U.S. Adventure Travel Society dubbed Costa Rica the "number one ecotourism destination in the world." As a result, Costa Rican ecotourism has become a model for sustainable development in the region. Panama, traditionally known as a transoceanic stopover, has adopted a similar ecotourism model and quickly turned into one of the more popular eco-destinations in Latin America. In the last ten years the number of visitors to Panama has increased over fifty percent.

Yet few scholars have attempted to contextualize these developments. Most of the extant literature tends to be journalistic or policy-oriented, rarely focusing on historical roots. Thus critical questions remain to be answered. Nature-tourism reflects an important historical shift in human-environmental relations. William Cronon explains that in the early twentieth-century, upper-class U.S. citizens began to form a "wilderness ideology" that encouraged the preservation of natural environments for recreation and spiritual renewal. In the following decades, ideals of nature protection came to influence environmental discourses internationally. The adoption of such ideologies among a broader audience, combined with improvements in public health, transportation, and technology, extended the boundaries of nature-tourism. In the second half of the twentieth century, local communities in Panama and other tropical locales, as a result, received an increase in foreign visitors seeking pristine nature.

Many local residents of ecotourism destinations, however, have not held the same environmental beliefs as affluent Western tourists. The conflicts and cultural interactions created by the mixing of these contrasting philosophies will, therefore, be a major focal point of my research. The intermingling of tourists and locals can have both positive and negative effects on a country's culture, economy, and natural environment. Sorting out exactly what those pros and cons are and how they have shaped Panama's environmental and socio-economic history requires archival research and in-country fieldwork.

Although I intend to conduct this research independently, I will maintain an academic support network in the U.S. and Panama. At the University of Georgia I have studied under Professor Paul Sutter, one of the leading U.S environmental historians of Panama. The graduate course I took with Professor Sutter in Spring 2007 helped me develop a background in environmental history and theory. Moreover, Professor Sutter has graciously agreed to advise me with this project. While in Panama, I will also work with some of the foremost Panamanian environmental scholars. Professor Guillermo Castro Herrera, the Academic Program Director at the Ciudad del Saber (City of Knowledge), has taught and published extensively on social-environmental relations in Latin America. Professor Castro has offered to be my in-country mentor and has invited me to collaborate with the International Center of Sustainable Development (CIDES) at the Ciudad del Saber, which is located in the Panama Canal Zone.

With the help of these academic mentors, I will establish the necessary contacts to complete this project. The Ciudad del Saber will provide me with access to the National Library of Panama and resources at the Smithsonian Tropical Research Institute. As a foundation for fieldwork, I will collect land-use records, publications from local organizations, newspaper articles, and tourism statistics from governmental organizations, such as the Panama Tourism Bureau (IPAT). My research will also rely on semi-structured interviews. By interviewing government officials, local townspeople, tourist entrepreneurs, and ecotourists, I will be able to identify the various perspectives surrounding nature-tourism. Human and archival sources will allow me to track how ecotourism has affected everyday Panamanians. The use of a variety of sources will also help pinpoint whose vision of nature-tourism has been implemented and for whose benefit. Is it the vision of certain government officials? Local farmers? Foreign tourists? Or is it something more complex?

Archival research and fieldwork will be carried out over a nine-month period between August 2008 and April 2009. From May to August 2009, I will then share my research findings with the Ciudad del Saber and other local organizations. During those last three months, I will also turn my research into a scholarly paper, which I will submit for publication in both Spanish and English.

Over the course of my stay in Panama, I will complete a research project that addresses all of the objectives mentioned above. Considering the relative size of the country and the good quality of the roads, I will be able to focus my research on several distinct locales: the Panama Canal Zone, the mountain resort town of El Valle, and the coastal town of Santa Catalina. All three sites have experienced ecotourism development, yet all are geographically and culturally distinct. Such variations will allow me to comprehend how particular local conditions have impacted ecotourism's historical development. Local and foreign environmental perceptions and/or development projects, for instance, might differ between a coastal and mountainous site.

This project can provide an important contribution to both local and international communities. Within the context of increased globalization, cross-border cultural and environmental concerns are becoming ever more important to U.S.–Latin American relations. In post-Cold War Latin America new questions of tourism, environmental protection, and cultural exchange are replacing traditional concerns, such as Marxist revolutionaries and strong-armed dictators. With this proposed project, the Fulbright Program has the opportunity to support a needed and timely investigation.

My year in Panama, of course, will also abet my own academic objectives. By conducting research abroad in between graduation at the University of Georgia and my future work in a PhD program, I will have laid the groundwork for a future dissertation project. More broadly, my studies in Panama will further increase my knowledge of the region, making me a more qualified and dynamic student and eventual professor of Latin American history.

STATEMENT OF GRANT PURPOSE

Jared Sun
Research Fulbright to South Africa
Public Health, 2009 – 2010

Empowering South African Township Communities
with Emergency Medical Skills

For cities in America and across the world, growing populations, industrialization, and urbanization will result in more crowded cities with higher risks of violence and accidents. Because of this, emergency medicine will play an increasingly critical role in growing cities and must aid developing nations as they progress in the near future. I propose to implement an Emergency First Aid and First Response (EFAFR) training course, and to assess it as a model to address life-threatening emergencies and alleviate overstressed emergency medical systems.

The Problem: Inadequate Emergency Healthcare in South Africa
In the past century, socio-historic factors have caused South African townships to dramatically increase in both population and concentration. In addition to population growth and widespread modernization, the apartheid government's Group Areas Act of 1950 forced much of the nation's citizens to relocate to overcrowded and impoverished slums. These informal settlements have the highest rates of crime, accidents and violence in South Africa, and the inhabitants face a heavy cost from traumatic injury and emergency incidents.

However, the townships' desperate needs overwhelm the Cape Town Emergency Medical System. According to township members, ambulances often arrive hours after patients die. Other times, language barriers between the caller and the dispatcher delay life-saving help. As a result, crime, gangs and catastrophes overrun Cape Town townships such as Manenberg, and the victims have inadequate emergency medical care.

The Solution: Training Community Members with Emergency Medical Skills
In addition to advanced care from medical professionals and government health policies, public health workers can teach ordinary citizens to care for themselves in some capacity, thereby lightening the burden on limited medical officers and exhausted healthcare systems. This type of intervention builds upon a community's existing strengths and abilities, and capitalizes on these resources through specialized

instruction.

In response to Cape Town's emergency medical need, I spent eleven weeks of Spring 2008 setting up the EFAFR training course, which prepared the EFAFR students to keep a critically injured patient alive long enough for professional medical care to arrive. I taught the course with the support of the University of Cape Town, the Manenberg Health Committee, and Stanford University.

Project Details

For the Fulbright Scholarship, I propose to examine the effects of this EFAFR training course as a model to empower urban citizens with the skills to keep near-death patients alive after traumatic injury or acute illness. The objectives of the project and its evaluation are as follows:

1. To identify a sustainable model that alleviates the heavy burden on the South African emergency medical system and can be brought to other townships in and outside South Africa.

2. To evaluate the effectiveness of teaching by determining how much the students learn.

3. To evaluate the EFAFR course's impact on township mortality rates due to traumatic injuries and immediate life-threatening illnesses.

4. To identify a method for sustainable funding for the EFAFR course.

I will spend my first five months in Cape Town implementing the EFAFR training course in Manenberg. During each course, I will give EFAFR students a pre-course exam and a post-course exam to test for changes in managing life-threatening injuries.

I am qualified to run this course. I have been certified as an Emergency Medical Technician (EMT) for over two years and have been part of the teaching staff for the Stanford University EMT training program for a year. Also, I have already set up the foundation for the course in Manenberg, and taught it successfully twice. Christine Jansen, head of the Manenberg Health Committee (MHC), produced the EFAFR students and teaching space and she has agreed to do so again for my project. The Manenberg community members determined the course curriculum based on what they identified as the most prevalent traumatic injuries and immediate life-threatening illnesses. As for my security, MHC members belong to the Manenberg community, are familiar with the area, and can be entrusted for ensuring my safety in the township.

After I implement EFAFR, I will devote my second five months to evaluating the impact of the course on Manenberg's mortality rates due to traumatic injuries. I will measure this impact through a ratio of the traumatic patients from Manenberg who were admitted to a hospital and survived over the total number of Manenberg patients with traumatic injuries.

Dr. Lee Wallis, head of the emergency departments of the medical schools at Stellenbosch University and the University of Cape Town (UCT) and head of Emergency Medicine for the Provincial Government of the Western Cape, has invited me to study under him at UCT, where I will have access to university resources, medical records from Cape Town emergency rooms, and Manenberg's mortality statistics.

For the course's sustainability, I will recruit competent EFAFR alumni and train them to teach future courses so that the program will continue after I depart from South Africa. I will collaborate with UCT and the MHC to identify sustainable compensation for these new instructors. I will serve as the teacher until we can obtain sufficient funding. The MHC will generously provide a long-term class space, free of charge, at the Manenberg People's Centre.

With the support of the UCT Emergency Department, the MHC, and the Western Cape provincial government, I am fully able to carry out this project. The EFAFR course has worked before, and so I can plausibly implement and evaluate it within ten months. All parties involved have agreed to do their part, and the project presents a great opportunity for everyone.

Outcomes

Researching methods to alleviate the emergency medical systems in Cape Town has critical implications for developing nations worldwide and for growing cities in America and abroad. Cape Town sits at a convenient crossroads to study emergency public health because there the townships grow at an exponentially faster rate than the emergency medical system can handle. UCT, the MHC and I have already identified empowering the community with medical skills as a possible solution, and we have the EFAFR course ready to execute. For the final step, I will develop this course further and test its viability for mitigating death in urban communities.

The Fulbright Scholarship will help me prepare for a future in medicine and health administration. When I return to America, I plan to attend medical school, and my experience in South Africa will allow me to more effectively consider how to render the health interventions I learn to the public and underserved populations. Within the next century many developing nations will urbanize further, and many established cities will continue to grow larger, and I want to be available and prepared to help keep their citizens safe and healthy during this imminent transition.

STATEMENT OF GRANT PURPOSE

Laila Plamondon
Research Fulbright to Canada
Psychology, 2008 – 2009

Study of Second-generation South Asian Immigrants in Toronto

In 2008 – 2009, I propose to conduct a survey study on the ethnic and religious identity development of South Asian immigrants in Toronto, Ontario, with a particular focus on how the arduous acculturation process affects psychological well-being in second-generation citizens. The study will focus on Bangladeshi and Pakistani Muslims, as personality psychologists have largely ignored this population and Islam holds particular relevance in the world today. I will analyze how demographic information (e.g., current age, socio-economic status, and community composition) affects national, ethnic, and religious identity and acculturation style—factors that greatly influence psychological well-being in immigrants.

Despite the potential for physical conflict among immigrant groups in any country they may inhabit, progressively more immigrants find the discord to be an internal clash between cultural values, attitudes, and expectations within themselves as they attempt to acculturate (Phinney, 2001). Canada, whose population includes about 5.4 million foreign-born citizens (2001 Census), seems to be the prototype for successfully integrating immigrants. Nationwide research suggests that most Canadian immigrants, among the psychologically healthiest in the world, undergo particularly healthy integration into Canadian culture. They adopt identities that correlate with high levels of adjustment, self-assertiveness, social competence and overall psychological well-being (Farver et al., 2002). Despite high levels of support for multicultural policy and tolerance, a nationwide survey found Canadians, especially those from Quebec, are least comfortable with immigrants of Muslim, Indo-Pakistani, and Sikh origins (Berry and Kalin, 1995).

This particular demographic has recently caught the world's attention. The news reveals South Asian immigrants in Europe participate in Al Qaeda's extremist activities, while novels and movies, such as *Monsoon Wedding* and *Bend it like Beckham*, display the joys of South Asian culture. Unfortunately even in positive accounts, stories of the detrimental acculturation styles of second-generation South Asians filter through North American popular culture. For instance, in *The Namesake*, Jhumpa Lahiri uses a Bengali immigrant family to reflect the ways South Asian immigrants form identities in America. The parents acculturate superficially, decorating Christmas trees and Easter eggs, while expecting their children to uphold Indian traditions and values. Although their son, Gogol, eventually recognizes his Asian heritage as an integral part of his American identity, initially he distances himself from his Indian roots by changing his name and casting himself as solely American.

This period of denial, evoked by the daunting task of developing both personality and ethnic identity simultaneously, can be harmless or have dire consequences. The two processes represent related, yet distinct, aspects of one's identity. Early psychologists, such as Erik Erikson, established models of personality development, focusing on childhood expressions of autonomy and industry as important precursors to adolescent identity development. Although Erikson's theory may be useful for understanding normative adolescent development in the ethnic majority, his ideas are less informative on special issues faced by minority group members. The emerging field of ethnic identity development attempts to fill this gap.

John Berry, a key figure in ethnic identity development, created a framework for the acculturation process which includes four types of ethnic identities: marginalized, separated, integrated, and assimilated. These identities vary in degrees of acceptance and rejection of the parents' birth culture and the host culture. The integrated individual, who becomes "bicultural" and preserves both the host culture and his or her parents' culture, maintains the psychologically healthiest identity. Although most individuals eventually find a healthy balance, the complicated process can lead an adolescent to feel a lack of belonging, as seen in Gogol in *The Namesake*. "Belongingness" (a positive attitude and commitment to one's heritage) and positive group identification correlate strongly with well-being (Phinney et al., 2001).

Young adults lacking a sense of belonging sometimes turn to "self-selected cultures," a local culture, such as strict religious groups, that are often in opposition to the overriding culture of the greater community. Such groups may provide more meaning and structure to the individual than the global culture; however, enclaves like extremist groups can provide a harmfully strong sense of membership (Arnett, 2002). Although most second-generation South Asian individuals turn to less offensive "self-selected groups," the lack of identification and belonging to the host country leaves some more susceptible to recruitment into extremism.

Examples of these phenomena can be seen around the world, in countries like England (2005 London underground suicide bombings by second-generation South Asians), the Netherlands (murder of Theo van Gogh by second-generation Dutch Islamist) and the U.S., which acknowledges risks of fostering "homegrown terrorists – even among second- and third-generation citizens" (National Strategy for Combating Terrorism, 2006) who do not feel a sense of belonging to the country or community and turn to self-selected cultures. Although American immigrants adopt proportionally more healthy styles of acculturation than immigrants in the Netherlands, Finland and Israel (Phinney et al., 2001), new statistics show the need for improvement. For instance, the Pew Research Group found that compared to older Muslim Americans, Muslim citizens under 30 are more religious and accepting of Muslim extremism (2007). With the odds against South Asian immigrants, psychologists must strive to understand the acculturation process in order to foster psychological health and prevent the search for destructive, self-selected cultures. Despite the differences between the U.S., deeply affected by 9-11, and Canada, observing these events from across the border, the U.S. can learn from successful Canadian strategies that aid healthy acculturation among South Asian immigrants.

Toronto, possibly the only city whose population consists of 49 percent foreign-born citizens, will be my main resource (2001 Census). The University of Toronto and the city, both composed of recent immigrants and ethnocultural communities, have all the necessary ingredients for a large yet specific sample of participants. For instance, the University of Toronto alone has Bangladeshi, Muslim, and Hindu students' associations. The city also has several Islamic organizations, including the Muslim Services for new immigrants, where I plan to volunteer. I received written notice from University of Toronto Professor Romin Tafarodi, whom I met personally in Toronto, that the institution would sponsor my activities. (See enclosed email.) With his support, I will create an online survey using scales, established by research psychologists, to measure acculturation style, importance of identities (religious, ethnic and Canadian) and involvement and "belongingness" in associated communities. The interaction between these factors, interpreted by computer-based statistical analysis, may create a clearer picture of the Canadian "integrated" identity.

My study should shed light on the ethnic identity development of second-generation South Asians. I also hope that it will fulfill a larger goal of helping Western countries adopt services that will aid South Asians in retaining their ethnic identity while also acquiring a strong national identity. In the U.S., these small steps have the potential to lead a healthier American-immigrant population to a strong sense of identification, belonging, and investment.

STATEMENT OF GRANT PURPOSE

Matthew Wesley
Research Fulbright to Nicaragua
Public Health, 2010 – 2011

Collaborative Solutions to Rural Water Contamination in Nicaragua

As a project leader in Nicaragua for Engineers Without Borders (EWB), I have had the privilege to work side-by-side with residents of rural villages in achieving access to basic health care, water, and energy. These trips have provided me with the opportunity not only to share my knowledge and resources, but also to learn about the culture, values, and daily challenges of native Nicaraguans. These trips, however, have been restricted to a period of one to two weeks during university holiday. I have been seeking an opportunity to work and study in Nicaragua for an extended period of time in order to immerse myself in the rural communities and study in depth the hardships related to water, health, and sanitation. Only by doing so will I be able to truly understand the needs, and the barriers that prevent alleviation of those needs. Through the Fulbright program, I hope to achieve these goals.

San Jose de Cusmapa is a rural municipality in northern Nicaragua comprised mostly of subsistence farmers. The district contains twenty-six separate communities: an urban capital of roughly 1500 people and a dispersed rural area of more than 5500. Although residents of the capital utilize an intermittent water and electric supply, the vast majority of rural residents lacks these amenities, as well as access to basic health care. I recently visited Cusmapa as a guest of a well-established, non-profit organization called Fabretto Children's Foundation to conduct a preliminary assessment of the needs in the area. I was unsurprised to find that the communities within Cusmapa, like most rural villages in Nicaragua, have severe problems related to water, sanitation, and health. In one community I visited, I found that nearly every family drank water directly from the nearby river and no family filtered their water. This is cause for concern, primarily because rivers are downstream of many sources of contamination. These include nearby latrines and farms in which animals reside. Especially during heavy rains, runoff will carry fecal contamination, namely *E. coli*, into rivers and unprotected wells. The World Health Organization (WHO) names *E. coli* as a significant danger to the health of residents in rural communities. Furthermore, the WHO has cited *E. coli* as causing infections leading to "infants presenting with malnutrition, weight loss and growth retardation."[1]

I propose a study of child health with respect to water

contamination in rural Cusmapa. The goal is to investigate the effects of a locally available ceramic water filter on the health of residents in the rural communities of Cusmapa, with a specific focus on children under five years of age. This filter is an appropriate, sustainable technology for removing microbial contamination. There are two mechanisms built into the filter: a mechanical barrier that forces water to travel through micron-sized pores, preventing passage of bacteria and parasites; and a colloidal silver lining that has both antibacterial and antiviral properties. This filter is manufactured in the capital city of Managua and can be directly distributed from the factory to rural communities. The communities in Cusmapa are already familiar with these filters because they are in each of the schools.

This research project is part of an ongoing investigation conducted by Fabretto. Fabretto has invited me to join their project, which currently focuses on infant and child nutrition. A recent study conducted by Fabretto has shown that 43 percent of surveyed children under five in Cusmapa are malnourished. They also found that a large number fall below the WHO's height and weight standards. Fabretto addresses the problem of malnutrition with its meal program that aims to provide children with sufficient caloric and vitamin intake. They supplement this program with a large educational facility featuring a full-time physician and Internet access. Until now, Fabretto has focused its research and resources on child nutrition as a critical factor in overall health. My proposal aims to expand this research to understand the effects of poor water quality on infant and child health.

From August to October 2010 I will visit each community in Cusmapa and meet with both the leader and members of the community to introduce my project. I plan to hold an educational workshop to discuss the ceramic water filter, which will be purchased from Potters for Peace, a local non-profit organization. Potters for Peace has offered to supplement this workshop with educational materials tailored for this water filter. The workshop will include information on how the filter operates and how to maintain the filter. The filters will be provided at a subsidized cost to the community as part of Fabretto's research project. I will also take baseline data that will consist of the following: quantitative analysis of all drinking water sources in each community for *E. coli* and total bacterial coliforms; a health survey aimed at measuring incidence of diarrheal rates specifically for children under five years of age; and mapping of all available water resources (wells, streams, and springs). Diarrheal rates have been used in the past as an indicator of contaminated water and should reflect the effect of water filtration on health in the community. Such a metric is recommended in the WHO's *Guidelines for Drinking-water Quality*.[1] The water testing will be conducted immediately before and after filtration through the ceramic filter. The water testing and health surveys will be repeated after six months. I will periodically evaluate the maintenance of the filters and if necessary conduct follow-up community education sessions on use and care of the ceramic filter. These sets of data will serve as metrics by which to evaluate the effect of the filters on water quality and health.

During my stay I plan to lay the foundations for a supply network that will allow the communities of Cusmapa sustainable access to water filter resources. This is the most important and ultimate goal of my Fulbright proposal. It involves the cooperation of each community, Fabretto, Potters for Peace, and the municipal government. It is critical to emphasize that Fabretto and Potters for Peace have formally agreed to collaborate and support this project. The Mayor of Cusmapa also formally supports this project and has supplied documentation that states the lack of potable water in nearly every community. Together we will develop a sustainable, permanent supply network. Each community will have a representative managing the distribution, education, maintenance, and funds of the filters. There will be a district representative overseeing the community representatives and managing orders for the materials from the filter factory. Both Potters for Peace and Fabretto will help with communication between the factories and communities with their extensive local networks and infrastructure. The success and long term viability of this project is not limited to my ten-month grant. By properly fostering relationships amongst the groups mentioned earlier, we can create a permanent and expandable collaboration. These are the people and organizations that live in Nicaragua, and thus will be most invested in the development of this project. My hope is that after the Fulbright grant is finished, the collaborations toward solving the problems of health, water, and sanitation will continue to flourish and set an example for others to follow.

Potters for Peace and Fabretto are well-established organizations, each serving more than ten years in Nicaragua. In the past, these groups have successfully implemented and maintained projects such as the one I propose here. A large part of the success of these organizations is due to the grass-roots nature of their research and volunteerism. I greatly admire this approach to sustainable development, and I intend to employ this method in my work as a Fulbright Scholar. Of most importance in developing a relationship with the communities will be my daily involvement with them. As I conduct my investigation, I will take advantage of the opportunity to visit, share, and learn from the families in the communities. By doing so, I hope to connect with and further understand the culture of rural Nicaragua.

During my tenure with EWB, I have developed contacts in government that will aid me in my project, including Jorge Sanchez, Mayor of San Juan del Sur, and former Nicaraguan President Enrique Bolaños; in aid organizations, including Connie Johnson, Chief of USAID Health and Education Office; and in municipalities, including Dr. Lea Jennys, Director of San Juan del Sur Hospital, and the Government of San Francisco Libre. These contacts can help me streamline logistics within my project and smooth out any complications that may arise.

As a Fulbright Scholar, I intend to engage on an individual basis with members of these communities. The only way for me to truly understand the challenges people face is to dive right in, to live and learn alongside of the people I am trying to help. I hope this study will provide insight into the issue of child health related to water quality in rural Cusmapa. This research and volunteer project will also hopefully lay the foundations for future collaborations between the community, local government, and non-profit groups. Working together, we can foster relationships that will continue effecting change for those in most need.

[1] *Guidelines for Drinking-water Quality.* Geneva: The World Health Organization, 2008.

STATEMENT OF GRANT PURPOSE

Maya deVries
Research Fulbright to Panama
Biology, 2010 – 2011

Food web interactions in a changing coral reef: one step to forming a baseline ecosystem

It is no secret that the world's coral reefs are declining at astronomical rates. Volumes of literature on overfishing in coral reefs, habitat destruction, and agricultural run-off all support the hypothesis that coral reef loss is due to human impact. Yet for many indigenous people of tropical coastal and island regions, survival depends on accessing resources from coral reef ecosystems. The Kuna people in the Kuna Yala Province of Panama provide an excellent example of the fine line between sustainable living and living beyond an ecosystem's limited resources. The Kuna migrated to the San Blas Islands on Panama's Caribbean coast during the early 1800s. Since then, almost all of their nutrition has come from fish. However, unsustainable fishing practices and habitat degradation have ultimately led to a 70 percent decrease in live coral cover since 1970. As a result, the Kuna are losing sight of their unaltered, or "baseline," coral reef ecosystem. For example, Kuna youth are unaware that only one generation ago the coral reefs surrounding their islands were healthy, well developed, and teeming with life.

Despite documented coral loss, San Blas is actually considered to be one of the least disturbed coral reef systems in the Caribbean. Thus, establishing a measure of San Blas' baseline ecosystem has become a high priority for marine conservation in Panama. Galeta Point Marine Reserve (GPMR) is a marine protected area to the east of San Blas. Given its protection under federal law, GPMR can serve as an excellent long-term comparison for the reef health of San Blas. GPMR is surveyed monthly under the Panama Coral Reef Monitoring Network run by the Smithsonian Tropical Research Institute. This long-term, large-scale survey of biodiversity provides infrastructure and basic data required for understanding an undisturbed ecosystem.

The essential next step is to determine how organisms are linked to one another so that when a group of organisms is in decline, researchers will know how the decline affects other coral reef organisms and overall reef health. One approach is to determine food web links between predators and their prey. The main goal of this project is to quantify food web interactions between a ubiquitous coral reef predator, the stomatopod crustacean, and its prey. Stomatopods and their environs provide an excellent system with which to study coral reef food web interactions, because these creatures are thought to be a major predator of many small coral reef invertebrates. Some species crush snails and hermit crabs with predatory appendages that produce among the fastest and most forceful strikes ever reported in the animal kingdom. My preliminary research at GPMR tested the full range of prey that stomatopods can consume through behavioral experiments and isotopic diet analyses. My results indicate that stomatopods consume many different prey types, including fish, snapping shrimp, and brittle stars. Thus, stomatopods are connected to a wide diversity of coral reef species through their predatory links. To determine the strength of predator/prey interactions in healthy reefs, I will conduct a two-part, comparative study in both GPMR and El Porvenir in the San Blas archipelago.

First, I will determine the percent of each prey type that contributes to the diet using novel methods in the stable isotope ecology. Stable isotopes of carbon and nitrogen can be used to track all food items in a predator's diet, because different prey types have distinct nitrogen and carbon isotopic compositions that assimilate into a predator's tissue when prey are consumed and metabolized. Methods in Bayesian statistics can then be used to parse the percent contribution of each prey type to the diet. I have already conducted the background experimentation required for implementing these methods. This project will begin with a large-scale collecting effort in August, 2010. I will collect stomatopods and all potential prey items by breaking the coral rubble in which the animals live. I will then dissect muscle tissue from all stomatopods and their prey items. Samples will be analyzed at the UC Berkeley's Center for Stable Isotope Biogeochemistry. This study will reveal the major prey items in stomatopod diet at both sites.

The second phase of the study will be conducted from September, 2010, to June, 2011. This field experiment will test whether the presence or absence of stomatopods alters prey density following Caldwell, et al., 1989. Specifically, I will define three replicate pairs of plots in the inner reef flat at both sites. Each plot in each pair will be assigned either an experimental or control treatment. Before the experiment, all coral rubble will be removed from the plots. Same-sized artificial cavities that I have constructed will be placed in all plots. The control plots will have closed cavities, while the experimental plots will have openings into which stomatopods will recruit. Once the burrows are placed, I will record the number of cavities with stomatopod occupants every week. I will also sample all prey items in 10 randomly selected 0.25 m^2 quadrates from all plots. I will then compare prey densities between treatments and between sites using analysis of variance statistics. I predict stomatopods to significantly alter the density of all prey items at both sites. This result would suggest that the interactions between stomatopods and their prey are strong. In addition, because GPMR is a healthy reef system, if the prey densities at both sites are equal, then GPMR should be an accurate representation of the baseline ecosystem at El Porvenir.

The Fulbright objective to promote cross-cultural interactions and mutual understanding is fully integrated into this project. Learning about stomatopod food web dynamics is one part of a very large-scale study that requires cooperation from Panamanian scientists and local people. My research will be guided by Dr. Gloria Batista at the University of Panama. Dr. Batista has researched intertidal algae for over 20 years and is an expert in their ecology. We will combine our expertise to make significant contributions to the Panama Coral Reef Monitoring Network and to achieve our common goal of establishing a baseline ecosystem at GPMR. My connection to local villagers will be fostered through GPMR's education program, which has become a cornerstone of science education in Panama. On average, one school group per day visits GPMR, where a team of students from the University of Panama teaches students about coral reef biology. During the 2008 field season, I gave a series of lectures and field demonstrations in Spanish about my behavior experiments. I will continue to contribute to this program when I return to Panama to complete the proposed research. Dr. Stanley Heckadon, the director of GPMR and a member of Panama's National Council on Education, has become my close collaborator. Together, we will work to establish an onsite education program in Kuna Yala that focuses on teaching youth about the baseline ecosystem approach to conserving their natural resources. We hope to inspire the development of sustainable fisheries in Kuna Yala.

While I have already conducted research in Panama for brief periods, an extended stay will ultimately allow me to make a significant contribution to our knowledge of coral reef food web dynamics. I also value the opportunity to transform my locally learned, colloquial Spanish into fluent speech. In the future, I plan to continue my work at GPMR, with the intention of taking a postdoctoral or teaching position in Panama. Through the Fulbright Scholars Program, I will gain invaluable in-country field and language experience that will facilitate personal contacts and help me to establish a long-term research program in Panama which is based on cross-cultural understanding between the science community and local Panamanians alike.

STATEMENT OF GRANT PURPOSE

Natalia Ksiezyk
Fulbright English Teaching Assistantship to Argentina
2006 – 2007

I often worry about our global society. Will we overcome problems like poverty, AIDS, and environmental degradation before it's too late? Despite this grim picture, I believe a transformative shift will happen in my lifetime that will lead to collaborative solutions to the most pressing issues worldwide. Specifically, I find hope in the rapid development of the nonprofit sector (Salamon, Anheier, et al. "Civil Society in Comparative Perspective," 1999) and the growing impact of social entrepreneurs within that sector (www.ashoka.org). The Teaching Assistantship program in Argentina is an ideal opportunity to contribute my knowledge and skills, learn about civic participation in another part of the world, and build relationships for the future.

I believe that I would be an asset to an Argentinean university as a Teaching Assistant. First of all, the ESL teaching certificate program at Rice gave me a solid foundation of second-language acquisition theory, pedagogy, and a structural understanding of the English language. More importantly, teaching in a variety of settings—serving as an ESL tutor, volunteer teaching an adult group at a community center in Washington, D.C., and two years of teaching upper-level English to adolescents in Poland—has put my theoretical knowledge into practice. I have proven to be an engaging, creative, and nurturing teacher. Furthermore, having learned English as a second language allows me to relate personally to the challenges that my students face. I also cherish the greatest gift of teaching: learning and growing along with my students.

My current position with the Leadership Rice program has honed my interpersonal skills, including the ability to listen to and understand how people make decisions in a variety of ways. I also believe that my cross-cultural background and my various international travel and study experiences will contribute to my ability to represent the United States well in Argentina.

The most exciting aspect of the Teaching Assistantship program is the opportunity for immersion in Argentinean culture and society. Ever since I learned about the tango in eighth-grade Spanish, I have dreamed of going to Argentina. I cannot imagine a better way of experiencing the country than engaging fully in a university town. By interacting with my students, attending local events and lectures, and volunteering at a career or community involvement center, where my leadership development experience can be an asset, I hope to learn about the impact of the tumultuous economic and political history, and people's motivations and aspirations. What are students passionate about? What extracurricular opportunities exist at the university? What perceptions of the U.S. are most prevalent?

I want to dig deeper into the social fabric of Argentina by conducting a qualitative study of the factors that influence civic participation among Argentinean youth. The project builds on my master's thesis and is rooted in the concept of civil society. I am adopting a broad definition from Ruben Cesar Fernandez: civil society is the domain of voluntary private initiatives carried out for the public good. This definition includes both the system of specific social groups characterized by independence from the state and the market, i.e., the non-profit sector, and the collective awareness, which mobilizes people to act for the common good of society. It is also important to add that civil society requires the rule of law and the guarantee—in theory and in practice—of civil liberties (Ralph Dahrendorf) and, thus, correlates with the success of democracy.

Civic participation is the activity that creates civil society. When civil society is well developed, as in stable democracies, the feeling of collective responsibility and awareness of others' needs stimulates action. Civic participation can be measured by attitudes, participation in the democratic process, and volunteerism.

Research conducted by the Johns Hopkins Comparative Nonprofit Sector Project, 1999, points out the tremendous growth of non-profit organizations worldwide and the increasing social and economic impact of civil society organizations in addressing needs not met by the public and private sectors. Compared to other world regions, the non-profit sector in Latin America is smaller and less significant economically. Only 2.2 percent of non-agricultural workers are employed by the non-profit sector in Latin America (3.8 percent in Argentina), as opposed to seven percent in developed countries. Similarly, Western Europe, the U.S., Australia, and Japan have significantly higher volunteerism rates than Latin America. Furthermore, the Johns Hopkins project highlights the existence of "dual" nonprofit sectors in Latin America: traditional charitable organizations and agencies linked to the social and economic elite vs. relatively newer forms of grassroots movements and NGOs.

My interest lies in the latter. Using the questionnaire method, I will assess the degree to which the feeling of collective responsibility that characterizes stable democracies exists, and examine the correlation of factors such as socio-economic status, the presence of involvement opportunities, reward systems, beliefs and values about civic duty, and encouragement from school, parents, or church, with the level of civic participation in grassroots movements and NGOs reported by young Argentineans.

I will devote my first semester to deepening my understanding of the current state of civil society in Argentina, including NGO statistics, trends, barriers and facilitating factors, and youth involvement. As part of my literature review, I will seek recent data from CEDES (Centro de Estudios de Estado y Sociedad), the Argentinean leader in the Johns Hopkins Project, and academic journals. At the university where I am placed, I hope to take a class on contemporary social issues. I will also hold interviews with civil society leaders: Ashoka Fellows, who are recognized experts-in-the-field on civic participation. Finally, by interacting with students and volunteering at a community involvement office, I will supplement my academic understanding of Argentinean civil society with firsthand experience and observations. Based on the initial research I will write a questionnaire to assess civic participation and the factors that influence it, which will be distributed to students at the university, as well as non-university peers from the same age group. Data collection and analysis will occur during my second semester. I am proficient in the statistical software SPSS.

My intention is to contribute to the growing body of civil society research by submitting a report of my findings to both CEDES and the Johns Hopkins Center for Civil Society Studies. I hope that a better understanding of the factors that influence civic participation in Argentina will lead to further studies and, eventually, to more effective engagement of young people in addressing social issues in their communities and globally. Upon return to the U.S., I plan to enroll in the Stanford MBA program, with a focus on Social Entrepreneurship. The program will give me the credibility and network of like-minded people needed to put my multi-national understanding of civic participation into practice. I want to collaborate with leaders worldwide to tackle our most pressing social problems.

STATEMENT OF GRANT PURPOSE

Tiffany D. Joseph
Research Fulbright to Brazil
Sociology, 2007 – 2008

Effects of Immigration to the U.S. on Brazilians' Racial Conceptions

In recent years, there has been significant comparative research conducted on racial classification and inequality in Brazil and the U.S. (Telles 2004, *Race in Another America*; Marx 1998, *Making Race and Nation*). Given Brazil's myth of racial democracy, a society where Brazilians of mixed racial origins co-existed in peace, Brazil was considered a racial utopia when compared to the U.S., a country where legally sanctioned racism oppressed non-whites for centuries. However, Brazil's racial democracy is now considered obsolete, as many racial disparities have been documented in various studies. Due to a history of more socially accepted miscegenation and the prevalence of racial democracy ideology, racial classification and race-based group identities have been difficult to ascertain. Brazilians of all phenotypes acknowledge having African ancestry, and almost half of Brazilians self-identify as racially mixed, not as solely white or black. The elusiveness of Brazilian racial classification creates special challenges for Brazilians who immigrate to the U.S., where, by contrast, rigid racial categories are the social reality. This is particularly true for Brazilians who cannot phenotypically pass for white. The U.S. "hypo-descent rule," although not formal, still categorizes individuals with one drop of black blood as black. This rule directly contradicts Brazil's history of miscegenation where one drop of white blood makes an individual less black. These differences can have a profound effect on Brazilian immigrants in U.S. society, especially since recent immigration literature suggests that immigrants with "blacker" physical features are more likely to exhibit negative social outcomes (i.e., education, income).

While there has been some attention paid to certain Latino groups in the U.S., only a few studies have investigated the effects of the U.S. racial system on Brazilian émigrés who: 1) remain in the U.S.* or 2) return to Brazil. Through in-depth interviews with returned immigrants and Brazilians who have never immigrated, my project will examine how Brazilian immigrant experiences with the U.S. racial system change their conceptions of race and racism upon their return to Brazil. This work will fill a significant gap in immigration and race literature in both countries.

I will conduct my study in Governador Valadares, the largest immigrant-sending city in Brazil. In a population of 246,000, 15 percent, or 35,000, are estimated to be living in the U.S. (Margolis 1998, *Brazilians in New York City*). The predominant motivation for emigrating is to work and earn money to improve their quality of life in Brazil upon returning. Existing U.S. immigration literature suggests that although some immigrants leave for the U.S. with the intent to return to their home country, very few actually do. Governador Valadares provides a different case since a number of its inhabitants do return (Goza 2005, "Immigrant Social Networks: The Brazilian Case"). It is important to be in Governador Valadares for this project since the city has such a high concentration of individuals who immigrate to the U.S. This is a select group of individuals whose experience has not been well documented in sociological literature. To properly examine how U.S. migration influences return migrants' racial conceptions, a comparison group of Brazilians who have never immigrated is needed. Therefore, interviews will be conducted in Belo Horizonte, a city (also located in the state of Minas Gerais) with less emigration.

To ensure a sufficient sample size, I will conduct thirty in-depth semi-structured interviews with recently returned migrants (1996-2006) in Governador Valadares to explore their experiences before, during, and after the U.S. migration. These individuals will be able to more easily recollect the effects of their U.S. experiences on their current perceptions of race in Brazil. Thirty semi-structured interviews will also be conducted in Belo Horizonte for non-migrants. The interviews will focus on: 1) self-ascribed racial classification; 2) defining race in Brazil and/or the U.S., and 3) experiences of racism in Brazil and/or the U.S. Each interviewee's education, income, occupation, and motivations for immigration (if applicable) will also be ascertained. Fifteen men and women from ages 25 to 50 in each city will be interviewed to incorporate gender effects and examine the age group that is more likely to have emigrated. This research design allows for similar demographics among both groups of interviewees.

While this project will be conducted using primarily qualitative methodology, I will add quantitative data analysis. Brazilian Census data will be used to give demographic information (i.e., income, race, education, sex) about Governador Valadares and Belo Horizonte. U.S. Census data will also be used for similar demographic measures of the Brazilian immigrant population in the U.S. Regression models will be used to examine the association between racial classification and education, income, and occupational outcomes in Governador Valadares, Belo Horizonte, and the U.S.

As a sociology doctoral student, I have made extensive use of quantitative and qualitative methodologies. Although matriculation at a local university will not be necessary for this research, an institutional affiliation with the Federal University of Minas Gerais (UFMG) in Belo Horizonte will provide valuable assistance (see attached letters). Sociology professors Dr. Neuma Aguiar, Dr. Otavio Dulci, and Dr.

Antonio Augusto Prates can serve as resources and provide access to social networks that will ease social entry into the field. Dr. Dulci has also offered to acquaint me with Dr. Sueli Siqueira (a former student) who has conducted immigration research in Governador Valadares. Her familiarity with both cities and research experience will be very helpful.

This research should take nine months to complete and will be conducted from March – December 2008. I will spend four and one half months in Governador Valadares and Belo Horizonte, respectively. I will use the first two months in each city to begin quantitative data analysis and become acquainted with citizens through participant observation. I plan to get involved in each city's cultural, social, and civic activities (e.g., tutoring students, community meetings) so I can establish relationships with citizens. Such relationships are essential for interviews because a certain amount of trust is needed for individuals to share their personal stories with an interviewer, especially one from the U.S. As a proficient speaker of Portuguese and an African American woman who has been mistaken for Brazilian in both the U.S. and Brazil, these attributes should grant me the insider status helpful for a project of this nature. The final two and one half months in each city will consist of interviewing, interview transcription and translation, and qualitative and quantitative data analysis. The knowledge and skills gained from this experience will help me become a U.S.-Brazil ambassador, the primary mission of the Fulbright Program.

* Ines Fritz, Helen Marrow (2003), and Teresa Sales (1999) have conducted studies on this population.

STATEMENT OF GRANT PURPOSE

Tim Slade
Research Fulbright to Benin
Public Health, 2004 – 2005

My project will address the potential for community-based health care to improve the health of the rural population of Benin. Despite rapid advances in medical research, more people than ever lack access to basic primary care. The rural populations of developing countries throughout Africa continue to be underserved by their governments, even as the incidence of AIDS, diarrhea, and malnutrition continues to increase. The World Bank recognizes the need for decentralization of primary health care in Africa, with a greater burden of responsibility to be placed on local village and community systems of health care, and an emphasis on the effective use of monetary, pharmacological, and human resources. The most cost-effective model of health care places hygiene-related education, the treatment of certain basic diseases, and community health promotion in the hands of trained community members, with an external oversight body providing training, specialized medical care, and low-cost medication. Provadenic, a grass-roots public health care organization in Nicaragua, has developed a model of public health care based on those principles. Despite working with uneducated and semi-literate community members, Provadenic has reduced infant mortality by as much as 75 percent while almost completely eliminating maternal mortality and malnutrition in many of its partner communities. This project will investigate the relevance of Provadenic's experience to providing community-based health care in the areas of maternal and child survival and malnutrition to remote and isolated communities in Benin.

While health indicators in many developing countries have improved, Benin's gains in critical areas such as under-five mortality (U5MR), infant mortality (IMR), and maternal mortality rates (MMR) have been modest. From 1961 to 2001, Benin's U5MR and IMR have dropped from 296 and 176 to 158 and 94, respectively, with a life expectancy at birth (LE) of 54 years. To attain the benchmarks for success outlined in the 1976 Alma Ata Declaration's "Health for All" campaign (U5MR <70, IMR <50, LE >60), Benin must still improve its mortality rates by approximately 50 percent.

As a member of the UN's list of 49 least-developed nations, it is unlikely that Benin will make significant progress without radically restructuring its methods of health care delivery and dissemination of health education. The public sector contributed only 1.7 percent of its 1999 GDP to health services; evidently, either the financial resources for a major overhaul of the health system simply do not exist, or the government is unwilling to devote a greater portion of its income to improving health care for the Beninese population. Efforts to improve the situation will therefore require making more effective use of what limited financial resources currently exist. This is where implementation of the principles of community-based primary public health care could make a substantial contribution to the provision of health services to rural populations.

Under the Provadenic model, communities are encouraged to elect a health promoter and a five-person health committee; the only guideline regarding election to the committee is that the nominee must be able to read. The health promoters attend a three-month training session, at the end of which they are equipped to address the community's primary care needs and help it develop its own yearly plans for further communal development, health education, and sanitation, based on its own local priorities. This allows communities to take ownership of their own health care while placing the burden of manpower on them, thus allowing Provadenic to provide continuing supervisory care for a large population while employing a small staff.

This method has allowed a single group of health workers to serve over 30,000 individuals in 32 communities with great success. The U5MR and IMR in Provadenic communities are 24 and 16 respectively, with less than one maternal death per 100,000 live births. What is more, all this has been carried out at a per capita yearly cost of $7.30, or $6,837 per clinic per year.

This project cannot be carried out without substantial direct communication both with the population receiving the care and with the organizations providing the training, guidance, and support. My firsthand experience working with Provadenic will serve as the background for evaluating the feasibility of applying the World Bank's principles of community-based health care to the issues of maternal and child survival and malnutrition in Benin. It will require identifying which aspects of Provadenic's success in implementing these principles have universal applicability and which are culture-specific, as well as those obstacles which might frustrate efforts to establish a similar system of primary health care elsewhere. Universal obstacles might include resistance by national physicians, who may be unwilling to relinquish control of health care to less-trained individuals; a lack of literacy in rural areas; inadequate transport and communication infrastructure, which may hinder communications between the group's headquarters and local communities; and insufficient funds to pay for transport or to procure medication. Culturally rooted difficulties may include a tendency to rely on traditional forms of health care, gender bias, and a devaluation of women or children, whose health is often the key to achieving community-wide prosperity. Working closely with the local health outreach programs is critical to identifying those obstacles which are potentially significant in Benin.

My internship with Provadenic demonstrated the value of working within an organization, interviewing its members, and interacting closely with those individuals in leadership positions in identifying and evaluating the obstacles to achieving desired objectives. I can accomplish this with the aid of Mr. Théophile Hounhouedo, the Director of the ROBS (the Beninese Health Services Network), who has pledged his full support to this project. Through his efforts, I will have access to several groups whose work addresses these health care issues, which will permit me to evaluate those methods and target populations most compatible with the principles of community health. These groups may include the Benin branches of Catholic Relief Services (literacy programs, nutrition) and John Snow Inc. (BASICS II - child health interventions), as well as several national groups. I will work with each organization for one month, in the process becoming directly acquainted with its structure and methodology. This experience will help to identify the cultural and location-specific challenges confronting national health care providers.

My first step in working at the local level will be to perform a pilot study of a representative rural community, conducting a thorough assessment of social and health needs as perceived by the community members. Combining this with a community needs assessment from the perspective of the health professionals or organizations engaged in serving them will allow me to evaluate the receptivity of the community to the principles of community health. I will perform this study in conjunction with staff from one of the ROBS groups, evaluating my results and methods with experienced local professionals upon completion of the pilot study. This will help me refine my approach to interviewing the populations of subsequent communities.

At the Université d'Abomey-Calavi, I will work within the Faculté des Sciences de la Santé (FSS). Coursework such as *Santé Communautaire*, *Médicine Préventive*, and *Santé Publique* will provide me with a background on Benin's methods of public health care. With the contacts I have established at the ROBS, the Ministry of Health, and the university, I will have the opportunity to work within the national system of primary healthcare. This will permit me to evaluate the relevance of Provadenic's methods of improving child survival and nutrition to Benin, as well as to outline the steps required to make similar assessments in other African nations. As the academic year commences September 1st, I would like to arrive in Benin by August 15th to get settled in and have some time to work directly with the ROBS before starting my coursework.

STATEMENT OF GRANT PURPOSE

Winston K. Scott
Research Fulbright to Guatemala
Anthropology, 2010 – 2011

Coffee and Conflict: Maya Responses to Economic Uncertainty
in Senahú, Guatemala.

Statement of Problem

On March 12, 2001, a mob numbering greater than one thousand men gathered at the central park in Senahú, a rural Guatemalan community, and lynched the local judge. As a witness to this event, I was able to observe direct reaction of the causality of this violent occurrence. Numerous inhabitants of Senahú linked the anger of the mob to recent economic hardships associated with coffee production in the region. Many rural Maya communities have expressed concern about their economic prospects due to emergent labor and trade policies since the end of the country's civil war in 1996. This investigation will examine various aspects of economic and social pressures associated with coffee-based economies in Guatemala and global market impacts on Q'eqchi' Maya laborers in Senahú and social deterioration in the municipality since coffee production began to decline at the turn of the 21st century. In particular, the investigation is concerned with the impact of a steady decline in coffee value in the international market on Maya laborers living and working on large-scale coffee plantations in Senahú, Guatemala, and the causal effect that decreased coffee production has on increased acts of violence in the community. Steady decline in coffee value in the global market forced local and regional economies to examine the economic viability of large-scale coffee production. The goal of this research is to analyze how global market fluctuations impact emerging social and economic responses by Q'eqchi' Maya laborers on coffee plantations in Senahú who are involved in large-estate coffee production.

Research Plan

In order to analyze how plantation laborers respond to economic uncertainty, I will conduct the proposed research in two separate phases. During the first phase (July 2010–October 2010), I will select a comparative sampling pool of 60 households located on coffee plantations to participate as consultants in the proposed research. I will select key consultants and will distribute questionnaires, attitudinal surveys, crime victimization surveys, and gather free list data. The attitudinal surveys and free list data will allow me to identify different types of violent acts that people experience in Senahú and their reactions to social deterioration. During the second phase (November 2010– June 2011), I will conduct in-depth semi-structured interviews with key consultants and household interviews within my sample pool to investigate how issues concerning economic uncertainty and violent acts are addressed in the community. This involves observing and analyzing social mobilization efforts engaged in social and economic development at the local level. I will also examine municipal archives to collect data on the number of violent occurrences in Senahú over a span of the last 16 years (1992–2008). Having honed my language skills in Q'eqchi' Mayan over the past nine years, and as a fluent Q'eqchi' Mayan speaker, I am able to enter the field with the tools to execute the research plan and conduct the tasks that are necessary to produce the results of this study. My language abilities give me credibility within the community as a researcher and as a scholar who will take the time to learn all aspects of the local culture.

Methodology

Structured and Semi-Structured Interviews — Structured interviews, including questionnaires, attitudinal surveys, crime victimization surveys, and free list exercises allow me to collect data in an informal and less intrusive setting. Because most occurrences of violent acts are not reported to police, anonymous crime victimization and attitudinal surveys allow consultants to relate their experiences that otherwise are ignored in community discussion. Free list and pile-sort data will supplement surveys to examine various forms of violence and social deterioration that individuals internalize through their everyday experiences.

Information gathered in the structured interview process provides a base for subsequent in-depth semi-structured interviews that will address consultant responses. The core of these interviews will elicit consultant views regarding community security and the role of government and police in combating crime and violence; community access to abandoned plantation land and agrarian reform; relations between the local government and plantation owners; future economic development in Senahú.

Temporal Measurement of Violent Crimes in Senahú — In order to examine occurrences of violence in Senahú, I will review archival records in the municipal offices and police records to determine levels of community violence. I will analyze records in intervals of eight years before and eight years after coffee production began to decrease in Senahú (1992–2000 and 2001–2008). In doing this, I am able to examine reported major violent occurrences chronologically and by geographic region. This is important because I will be able to compare violence and economic responses in communities of coffee laborers through time and place.

Interpretation of Language Use — Language use links social and economic production as groups sanction and legitimize cultural norms by authorizing language practices in communities dependent on time, place, and context and appropriate sanctioned practices through various community discourses. Language interpretation is a valuable resource in examining how language affects economic and social deterioration. I will examine speech events and narratives to examine language ideologies in Senahú and to determine how different forms of language use, including bilingualism, contribute to inclusion or exclusion of various social and economic networks and how consultants express their understanding of violence.

Importance of Proposed Funding and its Broader Impacts

This research contributes to scholarly exchange in a various fields of social science, including anthropology, history, sociology, economics, and agrarian studies by investigating large-scale plantations and how global markets impact the socio-economic realities of laborers at the local level. Examining how laborers and their families react to economic uncertainty and its impact, such as social deterioration, contributes to the body of research concerning ethnic and class divisions and historical and political processes on marginalized laborers. This is a timely project that contributes to ongoing debates concerning laborers and social and economic uncertainty to global capitalism's effects on rural economic and political processes. The study engages sociolinguistics and shifting language practices in a world in which language use can either help or hinder one's chances at advancing both in social and economic arenas, and engages economic decline and how laborers strategize to restructure legacies of post-colonial hierarchies and mobilize community social and economic development efforts. My time in Senahú will allow me to direct a series of seminars dedicated to cultural exchange between Mayan language groups. I have prepared a schedule for monthly seminars that will provide opportunities for economic, social, linguistic, educational, and political exchanges between Q'eqchi' residents in Senahú and K'iche' and Kaqchikel Mayan speakers from various regions in Guatemala. These seminars will support ongoing efforts that promote cultural unity in the years following the 1996 Guatemalan Peace Accords. Finally, I will provide the research data and dissertation to the municipality of Senahú so that the information may be accessible to all who are interested in the history of the community.